MW00443576

CALM
WITHIN

Transform Anxiety Naturally with the 3 Step AIM Program

Nafisa Sekandari, Psy.D.

transforminganxiety.com

Avagana Publishing
Phoenix, AZ

Calm Within: Transform Anxiety Naturally with the 3 Step AIM Program

Calm Within: Transform Anxiety Naturally with the 3 Step AIM Program by Nafisa Sekandari, Psy.D.

Copyright© 2023 Nafisa Sekandari (Avagana Publishing)

All rights reserved. No part of this book may be produced or transmitted in any form or by any means, electronic or mechanical, including photocopying, recording, or by any information storage and retrieval system, without prior written permission from the author, except for the inclusion of brief quotations in a review.

Edition ISBNs

ISBN: 9780990901624

Library of Congress Control Number: TXu2-391-659

Cover Photo: Nafisa Sekandari
Cover Design: rebecacovers via Fiverr

DISCLAIMER: Information in this book is provided for informational purposes only. This information is not intended as a substitute for the advice provided by your physician or other mental health care professional. Do not use the information in this book for diagnosing or treating a health problem or disease, or prescribing medication or other treatment. Always speak with your physician or other health care professional before taking any medication or nutritional, or herbal supplement, or using any treatment for a health problem. If you have or suspect that you have a medical problem, contact your health care provider promptly. Do not disregard professional medical advice or delay in seeking professional advice because of something you have read in this book. Information provided in this book does not create a doctor-patient relationship between you and Dr. Sekandari. information and statements regarding dietary supplements have not been evaluated by the Food and Drug administration and are not intended to diagnose, treat, cure, or prevent any disease.

Acknowledgements

This book is dedicated to Malia. Thank you for helping me not only recognize my anxiety but also teaching me patience and understanding. Thank you for teaching me to share and love unconditionally. You have helped me grow tremendously as an individual and for that I'm eternally grateful.

I would like to express my thanks to my younger sister, Nelofer, for her unwavering support, invaluable assistance in editing, and valuable feedback throughout the creation of this book. I am also deeply thankful to my father for his enduring support and understanding throughout the years.

A special thanks goes out to my patients and online students. You've taught me how to be a better therapist, teacher, and guide. Often, I learn just as much from you as you do from me. I hope the information in this book contributes to your knowledge and understanding of long-term anxiety management.

Also by Nafisa Sekandari

Afghan Cuisine: A Collection of Family Recipes

Steps Towards Gratitude: A Journal

Love Is Hidden In Small Places

Books available on amazon.com

Visit transforminganxiety.com for more information

Learn More About Online and **On Demand Courses** and join the online membership community by visiting transforminganxiety.com

Listen to the **Mental Health Break Podcast** on your favorite podcast platform or visit transforminganxiety.com/podcast

Table Of Contents

INTRODUCTION

Oh, how different my life would have been if I had known earlier what I now understand about anxiety. As a licensed clinical psychologist specializing in anxiety based disorders, I find myself reflecting on how valuable it would have been to possess my current training and experience back when I struggled with debilitating anxiety during my teenage and early adult years.

Many people go through life without fully understanding how much anxiety can hold them back in all aspects of their lives, and make it harder to build strong, healthy relationships. I didn't realize just how much anxiety was affecting me until I turned 35.

The constant worries, my irrational thoughts and fears, my overwhelming shyness, my reluctance to explore anything that was uncertain or unknown, my fractured relationships, and the overwhelming stressors were elements I hadn't directly connected to anxiety. Despite being constantly on edge, I attributed my experiences to *everything but anxiety*. Once I realized what I was struggling with was in fact anxiety and Obsessive Compulsive Disorder (OCD), I began searching for ways to regain control of my life again.

At the time of my awareness, I was a new mother, navigating the challenges of raising a baby while still pursuing my doctorate in clinical psychology. Despite my education and textbook familiarity with the clinical diagnosis of anxiety and OCD, it never occurred to me that the diagnosis of anxiety could be relevant to my own life.

During my studies and years of working as a psychologist, I learned that experts diagnose anxiety or OCD based on observing extreme behaviors that *seriously disrupt* people's daily lives. But in my 15 plus years of experience, I've observed that anxiety doesn't always have to be *extreme* in order to cause distress and hold you back. Even if you're someone who succeeds and aims for achievements, you can still be affected by anxiety's negative impact. In reality, many successful individuals achieve their goals partly because they're driven by anxiety.

This holds true for members of my family as well, where anxiety and OCD are very common, but even with these challenges, some have used their anxiety to their advantage to fuel their drive and become very successful. These individuals are super organized, efficient, and they work really hard. Like many ambitious people, anxiety pushes them to succeed, and society often admires and rewards their accomplishments.

I've always been someone who's motivated and focused, but I worked hard to hide my anxious feelings. Because I was afraid of being judged and criticized, I wanted to avoid drawing any unnecessary attention to myself. Over time, I realized that my desire to succeed was closely tied to my anxiety. I noticed that my anxiety pushed me to accomplish more, even though it also made me feel stressed and overwhelmed. Since I wasn't aware that I was struggling with anxiety back then, I didn't direct my efforts toward uncovering the root cause of my anxiety. Instead, I tried out quick fixes and different methods to manage the stress related to my excessively anxious thoughts.

One of the main reasons for my failure to connect my symptoms to anxiety stemmed from the fact that I didn't used to be a nervous or overwhelmingly shy person.

The course of my life took a dramatic turn in the summer of 1979 - over a year after the Russians had invaded Afghanistan. Prior to the Russian invasion, my life was stable.

I thrived in school and had many friends. Living in Herat, we found safety and security within our tight-knit circle of family and friends. I was also a very confident child who wasn't shy about leading games and activities with the kids in my neighborhood. They would often come to me for ideas, and I'd keep them entertained with the stories I heard on the radio. I also really enjoyed reading and sharing what I learned with others.

The feeling of safety and security was stripped away from each one of us when the coup d'etat unfolded in April 1978. The Afghan communist party ousted the first sitting president of Afghanistan, and within the following year, the Russian army entered the country. The initial signs emerged as propaganda leaflets rained down from airplanes into our neighborhoods. There was a lot of uncertainty after the initial invasion. As a young child, I didn't understand much of what the new changes meant, but the memories remain vivid.

I can still remember stories shared by others, detailing the chilling scenes of soldiers' lifeless bodies scattered on the streets, tanks rolling into cities, and the surrender of these cities to the control of the communist forces. Initially, I didn't attach much significance to these stories, but that changed when the war reached our doorstep – quite literally.

I have a vivid memory of a day, right after my bath, peering out of my upstairs window to witness distant explosions as bombs descended. A few days later, my father abruptly woke us up and gathered us all outside. Hearing the bombs falling closer, we joined our neighbors to huddle in ditches that were dug up for grapevines, hoping to escape the bombing. I squeezed my eyes shut and silently prayed to myself that our house be spared, and thankfully it was.

The next morning during class, my teacher was noticeably absent. Despite the quiet whispers circulating among us, the class had to go on, and as the top student in my class, I was expected to lead the others. After class, all students were led to a mandatory assembly where we were expected to sing what I thought was the Russian national anthem. I was paralyzed with fear, worried that the song's lyrics might somehow convert me.

We were also supposed to attend school the next day to receive tape recorders for a dubious "project" where we were to record our families' conversations. Intuitively, I skipped school that day to avoid getting a recorder. It turned out later that those tape recorders were used to incriminate many families, leading to their abduction by soldiers, never to be seen or heard from again. My family found this particularly frightening because my father is a direct descendant of the first ruler of Afghanistan. This connection to the Afghan Royal Family and the old government was seen as dangerous by the communist government and there was a chance he could get arrested because of it.

Within days, my family decided to leave our home and take refuge at my grandfather's house in Kandahar. From there, we met up with my uncle and his family, rented a jeep and driver, and began our difficult journey to flee our country. Donning layers of clothes and sneaking out in the middle of the night, my family escaped out of Afghanistan and crossed into neighboring Pakistan, leaving my happy childhood home behind.

The next day, I woke up in a stranger's house, far away from our home country, with a family that couldn't understand my language. Everything had happened so suddenly and without any prior explanation. It was only after we safely crossed the border that my parents revealed the truth—we were fleeing Afghanistan due to the war. Years later I learned that this plan had been in the works for months. This abrupt migration felt devastating because I hadn't been given the chance to say goodbye to my friends or bring along my favorite belongings.

We sought refuge in Pakistan, staying with my dad's aunt for several months while we anxiously awaited acceptance and visas to either the United States or Saudi Arabia. It was a challenging period of uncertainty and longing for a stable future.

After months of waiting, we were finally granted political asylum by the United States, and our journey to a new home began. Coming to America was a daunting experience. It was my first exposure to the English language and American cuisine. The smell of coffee on the plane made me nauseous, and enduring the cigarette smoke in the airplane cabin during the long journey was difficult in the confined space without fresh air.

Upon our arrival in the United States, my maternal aunt warmly greeted us. Her support played a crucial role in our successful immigration. We all stayed in a tiny two-bedroom apartment, sharing it with three other adults. Incredibly, there were 16 people in the apartment, including nine children aged ten and under. The crowded living situation and constant hunger made life challenging, but having my siblings and cousins together was a source of comfort and solace during those difficult months. However, amidst the hardships, I fell seriously ill for several weeks after arriving. The transition to a new country and lifestyle was overwhelming, but we persevered through these trials, holding on to the hope of a better life ahead.

The next two decades of my life were filled with uncertainty as we embarked on the journey of adapting to a new language, culture, and way of life. We faced an immense learning curve without any role models to guide us through the process. In those early years, we encountered challenges like being bullied for wearing different clothing and shoes. Our thick and heavy accents also made us the target of teasing, and we found it difficult to assimilate into the mainstream American culture, which was vastly different from our cultural norms back in Afghanistan.

As a result of these experiences, I became overwhelmingly shy and found it tough to make friends or express myself in the classroom. Initially living in Virginia, and attending a mostly White school, our struggles to connect with classmates were compounded by being among only a few minority students in the school. This brought us unwanted negative attention, making it even harder to find our place.

However, four years later, we moved to the East Bay in California, and this change was a much-welcomed one. Enrolling in an ethnically diverse high school, we found it easier to make friends and feel less exposed. The newfound sense of belonging and inclusivity played a significant role in helping us overcome some of the challenges we had faced earlier in Virginia. Despite the ongoing uncertainties, this new environment provided us with opportunities to grow and thrive, gradually shaping a brighter future for ourselves.

By the time I reached the 11th grade, I found a sense of belonging within my social circle. However, I still struggled immensely with classroom presentations, constantly haunted by the fear of being judged or ridiculed. Determined to break free from this fear, I made a bold decision at the age of 19. I challenged myself to overcome all of my fears by the time I turned 20.

With this newfound determination, I embraced opportunities that pushed me out of my comfort zone. Additionally, I took a significant step and moved five hours away from home, choosing to live on campus with complete strangers. Embracing my newfound courage, I also ran for a student government position despite feeling terrified. In an intense debate with my opponent, I emerged victorious in the election. I continued to push myself, expanding my comfort zone and seeking challenges.

However, despite these brave endeavors, my twenties remained a period filled with fear, uncertainty, and overwhelming anxiety.

During my early college years, I discovered the practice of meditation and mindfulness. One particular day, while engaged in a deep meditation session, I experienced something truly profound. As I opened my eyes, tears were streaming down my face and I found myself uttering the words, "I don't want to die." This moment was incredibly powerful, especially considering the struggles I had faced with suicidal thoughts during my teenage years. However, it was during this moment of awakening that I came to realize that it wasn't death that I longed for, but rather a sense of peace and relief from the overwhelming anxiety and stress that had burdened me for so long. Meditation helped calm me in moments of high stress and anxiety on numerous occasions.

Even though I had managed to conquer some challenges, the struggle with anxiety didn't go away. I had to keep looking inside myself and stay determined as I continued trying to find peace and calmness.

During this period, anxiety had a negative effect on various aspects of my life, including my friendships, finances, academic performance, and overall well-being. Additionally, I was diagnosed with endometriosis, which brought about physical pain, weight gain, and the challenge of dealing with painful cystic acne. The physical discomfort caused by endometriosis further intensified my anxiety regarding my health.

Little did I know at the time, my lack of self-care, emotional suppression, and perpetual stress significantly contributed to the worsening of my anxiety and its overall impact on my health. When I received the diagnosis of endometriosis, things became even more challenging. The doctor informed me that I required surgery to remove a 10 cm cyst from my ovary. However, as a student without health insurance and limited financial resources, I couldn't afford the procedure for another year. The urgency of the situation was overwhelming, as I was warned that delaying the surgery could result in the cyst rupturing, potentially leading to infertility and damage to my reproductive organs.

Feeling desperate, I decided to look for another way out and began exploring acupuncture and herbal remedies. As I learned more about alternative medicine, I made important changes to my lifestyle to help with my symptoms. Surprisingly, as I made these changes, I started feeling much better. My sleep improved, I had more energy, and I could manage my emotions better.

These positive changes that included meditation along with alternative medicine really helped my overall health. They prevented the cyst from getting worse during that year of waiting. When I finally had the chance for surgery, I was relieved to see that everything went well. The procedure was successful, and my ovaries and other reproductive organs were not harmed.

Exploring alternative medicine and mindfulness turned out to be a great way for me to take care of my health. It made me realize how important it is to consider my mind *and* body when it comes to staying well. Because I've seen positive results from meditation and alternative medicine in my own life, I make sure to talk to my patients about it and use a well-rounded holistic approach to treat them. I truly think that this approach is a big part of why my practice is successful.

Way before I found out I had endometriosis, I began to realize that anxiety was taking over my life. It was affecting every choice I made and I felt stuck in a life that wasn't satisfying. Even though I didn't know for sure that anxiety was behind my problems, I felt like something, maybe fear and being really shy, was stopping me from moving forward.

I became concerned when I realized I was opting for career opportunities that kept me in the background. I would pick jobs where I didn't have to be in charge, which was very different from the confident and in-control 8-year-old me back in Afghanistan. I stayed away from jobs that required me to lead or manage people. I also avoided speaking in public and teaching. And because I was scared of job interviews, I ended up stuck in jobs that didn't make me happy.

After I came to the United States, I soon noticed that something changed inside me. It felt like I had lost my connection to who I really was, and anxiety started making me feel powerless. Wanting to get back to my true self, I started reading self-help books and took psychology classes to help me grow as a person. Even though therapy and psychology were new to me, I became really interested in the science behind it. Psychology helped me understand my life better and see my problems in a different way. I became more and more interested in training my mind and getting mentally stronger. As I started feeling better, I also began helping the people around me.

This strong interest pushed me to get a Bachelor's degree in psychology, and later I went into a Master's program in Counseling and Education. Working as a school psychologist was fulfilling, as I could help families and students with their learning challenges. But I felt a deep need for more advanced training in handling mental health issues.

After six years of practice as a school psychologist, I made the decision to return to school and focus on earning my doctorate in clinical psychology. My own journey of learning about myself and getting better professionally motivated me to explore clinical psychology further. I wanted to use my knowledge to help others deal with their mental health issues in a caring and knowledgeable way. Because of my own experiences, I really wanted to make a positive difference for people who are dealing with anxiety and OCD. This strong drive led me to start a program that could empower people all around the world. And so, my 3-step AIM Program was born.

With this book, I want to give you a well-rounded and comprehensive way to handle your anxiety. My goal is to make you feel strong, confident, and help you gain lasting control over these difficulties without relying on medication or long therapy sessions. As you read this book, you'll go on a deep journey of healing. You will look at your anxiety from different angles and find ways to manage it.

If you're tired of anxiety controlling your life and want to take back control, you now have the tools to reach your goals right at your fingertips!

Introducing the AIM Program

One of the main reasons for writing this book and creating the AIM program is for the numerous patients who came to me and talked about their battles with anxiety. They would share that the so-called "quick fixes" offered to them weren't really making them feel better in a steady way. They had tried so many interventions like breathing exercises, taking various medications, numbing themselves with drugs or alcohol, and even using marijuana, but their anxiety was still a problem. When I introduced my holistic approach to treating anxiety, it made a noticeable difference right away. After the first session, they would return and tell me how much better they felt. They were surprised that their previous doctors hadn't looked at the root causes of their symptoms before.

In this book, I strive to provide you with another way to manage anxiety, free from a lifetime dependency on medication or therapy. I will introduce you to a simple but effective approach that considers both your mind and body.

Welcome to the AIM Program, a transformative journey that can lead you to lasting results.

The first important step on this journey is becoming **Aware**. By being more in tune with yourself, you'll deeply understand how your anxiety shows up and recognize the specific type of anxiety you're dealing with. This newfound knowledge sets the foundation for lasting change. This *awareness* marked the beginning of my healing journey. It wasn't until my 30s that I realized I had been struggling with anxiety and OCD all along. Before this realization, I had been in a constant struggle, trying various approaches blindly to regain control over my life. Once I identified and acknowledged what I was truly dealing with, it became significantly easier to target and implement effective interventions.

The second phase of the AIM program is the **Intervention** phase—a crucial step where you'll put into practice proven and effective strategies that lead to lasting transformation. These well-thought-out plans are designed to bring you genuine and lasting results in your battle against anxiety.

With over 15 years of professional experience and a lifetime of dealing with anxiety myself, I've seen how effective this comprehensive approach can be. The strategies that I share with you in this book are the same strategies that I used to not only regain control of anxiety in my life, but I've used them to help my daughter, as well as the hundreds of patients that I've worked with over the past 15 plus years. These strategies will also empower you to handle your anxiety and feel confident.

The ultimate goal is **Mastery**—a place where you can confidently maintain the progress you've made throughout the program, gaining lasting control over your anxiety. Mastery involves feeling empowered in the face of anxiety, a force that once seemed like it would forever dominate your life. Achieving mastery doesn't guarantee you'll never encounter anxiety again in the future, but it does mean that you can quickly redirect anxiety when it does come up. It means harnessing anxiety as a source of motivation to accomplish tasks more efficiently and effectively, without allowing it to take over your thoughts, actions, and emotions.

In this book, you'll discover a complete guide for using the AIM Program. I know that finding time for therapy or finding good mental health experts can be tough, so I offer this book as a source of hope and a self-contained guide for taking control of your anxiety. The AIM Program is adaptable and designed to fit what you need. You don't have to use every strategy in the book. Instead, you'll find many ways to treat your anxiety, and you can choose the ones that fit your situation the best.

Anxiety is different for everyone, so there's no single solution that fits everyone. But with the AIM Program, you'll have what you need to start a journey that can make a big change. This journey will provide you with the tools to effectively manage anxiety in the long run, allowing you to live a life free from the limitations imposed by fear or anxiety.

CHAPTER 1: AWARENESS

Let us not look back in anger, nor forward in fear,
but around in awareness
~James Thurber

In this modern world, despite the over abundance of anti-anxiety pills available, anxiety continues to reign as the number one disorder worldwide.

In the United States alone, approximately 42 million adults, or 19% of the population, struggle with anxiety each year, while the global count surpasses 264 million. Interestingly, anxiety affects more women than men across all age groups, with a ratio of 2 to 1. An estimated 31.9% of adolescents in the US have some type of anxiety disorder. Of the adolescents with an anxiety disorder, an estimated 8.3% had severe impairment.

The persistence of anxiety in our lives raises a critical question: If pills were the ultimate solution, why hasn't anxiety been eradicated? The answer lies in the fact that anxiety demands more than a simple pill to be effectively managed. Although medication has been heavily relied on to help with anxiety, it's not effective for long-term control. If medication was enough for managing anxiety, we wouldn't need mental health professionals. Sadly, only relying on medication, without addressing the root cause of anxiety, can lead to severe long-term consequences, like getting addicted.

The existing standard treatments for anxiety are outdated and no longer universally effective. As technology and treatments evolve, we must adapt and explore new avenues to effectively address anxiety. Unlike the past, where psychotropic medications were prevalent, there now exist numerous non-medication approaches to treat anxiety and OCD effectively. As our understanding of mental health advances, we have learned that some previously common medications are now considered too risky for regular use.

Another reason for the global rise in anxiety is due to what some believe to be the AGE of ANXIETY—a time where the world's relentless barrage of media, politics, and ecological challenges take a toll on our mental health, inducing a pervasive sense of anxiety. Just think about the constant stream of news we see, talking about the major political and environmental problems around the world. Each headline can make us worry about what's coming next.

With so much information coming at us, it's not surprising that anxiety is on the rise. Our lives are fast-paced, too. We're trying to handle work, family, friends, and our own goals all at once. There's a lot of pressure to do well, but that can mix with the fear of not being good enough, which can worsen our anxiety. Even though technology has its good sides, it's also made anxiety worse. Social media shows us people's perfectly edited lives and impossible standards, which can make us feel like we're not good enough. This keeps us comparing ourselves to others all the time. In this world, anxiety becomes a natural reaction to the difference between what we see online and what's real.

The digital age has also introduced us to an abundance of social media influencers and life coaches who share their advice on handling anxiety with quick fixes that don't provide real and lasting help. Modern society has trained us to look for quick fixes for our problems, but just like your anxiety didn't develop overnight, it will not be managed and controlled overnight. We also can't just put a band-aid on it and be done with it. The truth is that addressing anxiety requires a deeper effort. To overcome anxiety, we must confront the underlying emotions and lifestyle patterns associated with it.

Long term control over anxiety lies not in quick fixes but in addressing its root causes through a more holistic and integrative healing process.

A process that takes into consideration your whole self rather than focusing on isolated symptoms. A holistic process will help you feel better mentally and physically. That's because this approach considers various factors, such as lifestyle, hormonal imbalances, stress management, spirituality and overall chemical balance. Getting better involves looking at many different aspects, like finding out what's causing the issues and understanding all the ways your symptoms show up.

In this world of endless information online, it's really important to be careful about what we believe. Trusting trained mental health experts is the best way to understand and manage anxiety. Our training and guidance is anchored in scientific research and clinical experience, offering the best chance for long term control over anxiety.

Anxiety Has A Purpose

I want to emphasize that getting long-term control over anxiety does not mean eliminating it completely. Anxiety actually has a purpose – it's like a built-in alarm that's supposed to keep us safe. While unmanaged and out of control anxiety can be debilitating and harmful to our mental health, a certain level of anxiety can be adaptive and beneficial. Anxiety is a natural response that alerts us to potential threats and challenges, helping us stay vigilant and prepared for the unknown. It can motivate us to take necessary actions, enhance our performance under pressure, and improve our problem-solving skills.

Anxiety, along with other ailments in the body, often show up as a way for the body to communicate with us. If we're PAYING ATTENTION, we can recognize the NEED to change or course correct when we're headed in the wrong direction.

"Anxiety has a purpose. Originally the purpose was to protect the existence of the caveman from wild beasts, and savage neighbors. Nowadays the occasions for anxiety are very different. We are afraid of losing out in the competition, feeling unwanted, isolated, and ostracized. But the purpose of anxiety is still to protect us from dangers that threaten the same things, our existence... or values that we identify with our existence. This normal anxiety of life cannot be avoided except at the price of apathy or the numbing of one's sensibilities and imagination.
We must avoid the numbing of our sensibilities and imagination by actively working on understanding anxiety, and then control it so it doesn't control us."

~Rollo May, author of
"The Meaning of Anxiety"

Quoting the insightful words of Rollo May, in "The Meaning Of Anxiety," we are reminded that anxiety, in its essence, serves to protect us. Understanding this purpose empowers us to work on understanding and controlling anxiety so that it no longer controls our lives. But when we don't understand anxiety and allow it to overpower our rational thinking, anxiety can turn into a *disorder*. When we believe the lies that anxiety tells us and let those lies control how we act, anxiety takes control.

Instead of trying to totally erase anxiety from your life, *the goal is to train your brain and become really good at managing it*. This way, you're in charge and anxiety is no longer calling the shots in your life. Instead of trying to totally rid your life of anxiety, you should focus on handling and changing how you see it. By training your mind and finding ways to use anxiety in a positive way, you can take its energy and use it for good.

Practices like mindfulness, ways to change your thinking, and exercises to lower stress can help you control how you react to anxiety and have a healthier relationship with it. Instead of pushing anxiety away, you can acknowledge it, understand why it's there, and use it to help you. When you do this, you can actually use anxiety to help you grow and make positive changes in your life. By turning anxiety into something useful, you become better at facing life's uncertainties and feeling more balanced.

In this book, you'll not only gain a deeper understanding of your brain and the source of your emotions, but you'll also discover how to harness anxiety to work for you instead of letting it control your life. The tools and strategies you'll learn here will empower you to redirect anxiety, granting you the confidence and control to pursue your dreams and face uncertainty with courage.

Embracing anxiety as part of the human experience allows you to grow stronger, more resilient, and adaptable in the face of challenges. When you're dealing with a brain that tends to get too anxious and reacts too strongly, it's really important to train your brain and keep a close watch on it. This helps you take care of your brain health and stop it from going out of control again.

When you make mental health a priority and work on healing your brain and calming down your overactive mind, you'll experience a greater sense of empowerment and control. Several of my patients and online students have done really well with the techniques in this book. They've felt so much better that they sometimes think they're totally "cured" and don't need to keep using the methods that helped them in the first place. However, they often find themselves taken aback when anxiety returns after they revert back to their unhealthy lifestyle and habits, which lead them to neglect their mind and body.

Prioritizing your mental health will ultimately lead you to feel more in control of your anxiety.

As best selling author Elizabeth Gilbert wisely said, "My actual job in life is managing my mental health." Just as we prioritize physical health, we must equally focus on mental well-being because they are interconnected.

Build Your Invisible Toolbelt

Throughout this book, I will present you with numerous effective options to choose from. Feel free to explore and adopt the strategies that resonate with you best. Some may be effortless to incorporate, while others might require more effort and discipline, such as dietary changes. I encourage you to try each option for at least a week to discover what works well for you and what may not fit seamlessly into your daily routine. Having various approaches to choose from is essential because it prevents you from feeling overwhelmed by anxiety.

Having this invisible toolbelt filled with effective tools and strategies to manage anxiety is a powerful and invaluable asset for navigating life's challenges. Anxiety is a natural response, but when left unchecked, it can become overwhelming and disruptive. Having a range of coping strategies readily available empowers you to take control of your emotional well-being when anxiety strikes. Similar to a skilled craftsman with a toolbelt, having effective and proven coping tools ready empowers you to handle anxious moments with confidence and calmness.

Mindfulness techniques, deep breathing exercises, grounding practices, positive affirmations, and journaling are some of the valuable tools that can be part of your invisible toolbelt. These methods will help you regulate your emotions, bring you back to the present moment, and challenge your negative thought patterns.

The wonderful thing about having this invisible toolbelt is that you can customize it to match your unique needs and likes. As you gather different coping methods, you can try them out and figure out what's most effective for you in different situations. With regular practice during calm times, you will become familiar and skilled, so you can use these techniques when anxiety shows up.

Beyond that, the invisible toolbelt will empower you. Instead of feeling powerless against anxiety, you will become active in looking after your emotional health. This level of self control will boost your confidence and resilience, helping you handle tough moments with more ease.

Life is full of surprises, and anxiety can show up when you least expect it. Having an invisible toolbelt stocked with effective coping strategies empowers you to face anxiety directly, without letting it overwhelm you. These tools and strategies have the potential to transform anxiety from a paralyzing force into an opportunity for growth and personal development. Ultimately, this invisible toolbelt symbolizes your preparedness to tackle any obstacle, making you more resilient and skilled at handling anxiety while enjoying a more balanced and satisfying life. With a range of strategies in your toolkit, you can navigate tough situations with greater confidence and less difficulty.

A great example of how to effectively use your invisible toolkit is demonstrated by Monica Lewinsky.

Monica Lewinsky, who gained notoriety as Bill Clinton's intern at the White House, shared the process she underwent and the tools she used before her famous TED talk. She used several techniques from her invisible toolbelt, such as bio-resonance sound work, breathing exercises, Emotional Freedom Technique (commonly known as Tapping), chanting, warm-up exercises with her public speaking coach, grounding visualization, and power posing. This arsenal of tools helped her transform her fear into a calm, confident, and captivating stage presence despite being initially paralyzed by fear.

We all need our toolbelt full of options to navigate through tough situations. As you read this book, you'll find an array of strategies to equip yourself with, enabling you to face anxiety with strength and poise, just like Monica Lewinsky.

How Anxiety Impacts Your Brain

Truly, we can not have great physical health without great mental health, as they are intricately linked. When one aspect is affected, it inevitably impacts the other.

Anxiety is a natural response to stress and perceived threats, but when it becomes chronic or overwhelming, it can have a significant impact on your brain and overall well-being. Long-lasting anxiety can actually change how your brain works, impacting how you think, how you manage your emotions, and even impact your physical health. However, your brain's remarkable neuroplasticity allows it to heal and rewire itself, making it possible to regain control over your anxiety.

A healthy brain and an anxiety-affected brain can exhibit distinct characteristics and functions.

Here's a comparison of both:

Healthy Brain	Anxiety-Affected Brain
Balanced Emotions:	*Heightened Anxiety:*
A healthy brain can regulate emotions effectively, experiencing a full range of feelings without being overwhelmed or overly reactive.	An anxiety-affected brain experiences exaggerated and persistent worry, fear, or nervousness, often disproportionate to the actual threat.
Optimal Cognitive Functioning:	*Impaired Cognitive Functioning:*
It maintains sharp cognitive abilities, including memory, attention, learning, and problem-solving skills.	Anxiety can negatively impact cognitive abilities, leading to difficulties in concentration, memory, decision-making, and problem-solving.

Adaptive Stress Response:	Dysregulated Stress Response:
The brain can appropriately respond to stressors, releasing stress hormones like cortisol in a controlled manner, which aids in coping with challenges.	The brain may trigger an excessive release of stress hormones, leading to a constant state of arousal and a fight-or-flight response even in non-threatening situations.
Positive Outlook:	Negative Thought Patterns:
Generally, a healthy brain tends to have a more positive outlook on life and is resilient in the face of difficulties.	Individuals with anxiety may tend to have negative thought patterns, **overestimating** risks and *underestimating* their ability to cope.
Restful Sleep:	Sleep Disturbances:
It is capable of maintaining a regular sleep pattern, ensuring proper rest and rejuvenation for optimal brain functioning.	Anxiety can disrupt sleep patterns, leading to difficulty falling asleep, staying asleep, or experiencing restful sleep.

Effective Communication Between Brain Regions:	Disrupted Brain Communication:
The different regions of the brain communicate efficiently with each other, allowing for smooth information processing and integration.	The communication between brain regions may become less efficient, leading to difficulties in processing information and emotional regulation.
Healthy Neural Plasticity:	*Altered Neural Plasticity:*
The brain can adapt and reorganize its neural connections when needed, facilitating learning and adapting to new experiences.	Chronic anxiety may lead to maladaptive changes in neural plasticity, potentially reinforcing anxiety-related neural pathways.

Here's a brief look into the impact of anxiety on specific regions of your brain:

- **Amygdala and Fear Response:** The amygdala, a part of the brain responsible for processing emotions, particularly fear, becomes hyperactive in individuals with anxiety disorders. This heightened reactivity can lead to a constant state of perceived threat, making it challenging to regulate emotions and maintain a sense of calm.
- **Hippocampus and Memory:** Chronic anxiety can impact the hippocampus, which plays a vital role in memory and learning. Prolonged exposure to stress

hormones, such as cortisol, can lead to a reduction in hippocampal volume, affecting memory consolidation and recall.

- **Prefrontal Cortex and Executive Function:** The prefrontal cortex, responsible for executive functions like decision-making and impulse control, can be negatively affected by anxiety. Over time, excessive worrying and rumination may weaken this region, leading to difficulties in making clear decisions and managing emotions effectively.
- **Neurotransmitter Imbalance:** Anxiety can disrupt the balance of neurotransmitters in the brain, particularly serotonin, dopamine, and gamma-aminobutyric acid (GABA). These imbalances can exacerbate anxiety symptoms and contribute to a cycle of anxiety and negative thought patterns.

Even though anxiety can harm your brain, you have the capacity to repair it and calm your central nervous system, enabling you to handle anxiety effectively. As you set out on this path, you'll discover the power to change and have the opportunity to shape a better, more wholesome future for your brain and, by extension, for yourself. With appropriate interventions, you will learn effective coping strategies and techniques to promote a healthier brain function and overall well-being.

As you explore the content of this book, you'll discover strategies that empower you to heal your brain and develop a strong sense of appreciation for it. These techniques will inspire you to make your brain's well-being your top priority and protect it from harm. A brain that is healthy and free from anxiety plays a vital role in creating a more satisfying life, unlocking a wide range of benefits and opportunities.

To get a handle on anxiety, the first step is to truly understand how it appears in your life and understand how it affects you. We'll examine the various ways anxiety can manifest, and then we'll dig into methods that can help you in changing how you feel and achieving lasting control of your life.

Understanding Anxiety

To start on this journey of change, you need to first get a firm grasp of how anxiety shows up in your life.

As mentioned previously, anxiety isn't just about worrying too much or feeling nervous – it shows up in various ways. Intrusive thoughts, feeling drained, intense guilt or shame, irrational beliefs, perfectionist tendencies, excessive worrying, and even repetitive behaviors are some of the ways anxiety takes hold. And it's not only about how it affects you personally; it also can negatively impact your relationships and even play a part in creating addictive behaviors.

Before I address the different types of anxiety, let me first establish a clear definition of the term.

According to the **Diagnostic and Statistical Manual of Mental Disorders** (DSM), anxiety is *"the excessive worry and apprehensive expectations, occurring more days than not for at least 6 months, about a number of events or activities, such as work or school performance"*.

*"It is also a state of **chronic, excessive dread or fear of everyday situations**. It encompasses not just worry but also intrusive thoughts, physical symptoms like sweating and trembling, and a tendency to avoid certain situations due to apprehension"*.

It is marked by a sense of uncertainty regarding the actuality and nature of the perceived threat, *accompanied by self-doubt about our ability to handle it.* This emotional complexity leaves you feeling overwhelmed by fear, triggering physical and bodily reactions such as increased heart rate, sweating, and tension.

It is important to recognize that anxiety is not an isolated feeling; it is often interconnected with past traumatic experiences and the fear response associated with the fight-or-flight mechanism.

Understanding anxiety extends beyond the surface level of fear. While fear is often related to the fight or flight response or past traumatic experiences, anxiety can also stem from suppressed emotions such as anger, frustration, humiliation, and indecisiveness. Failure to express these emotions healthily can trigger anxiety.

For example, anxiety might have its origins in emotions we pushed away a while back, making it hard to figure out why we're feeling anxious. When we don't deal with our emotions and neglect taking care of ourselves, it can keep anxiety going and make it tough to get better at managing it. We MUST address the underlying emotions and lifestyle patterns associated with anxiety.

As long as your emotions remain suppressed and not dealt with, you will continue to struggle with anxiety. Also, if you overlook the well-being of your mind and body and neglect taking time for rest, anxiety will persist. Prioritizing self-care and enhancing your lifestyle are crucial steps in addressing and overcoming anxiety.

Remember, it's normal for everyone to feel anxious sometimes. But when anxiety starts getting in the way of your normal life, that's when it becomes a *disorder*. As anxiety's persistence increases, so does the intensity, frequency, and duration of its symptoms, creating a spectrum of severity.

In my view, anxiety exists on this spectrum, ranging from mild to extreme. I, too, continue to experience anxiety from time to time, but I have learned to manage it, knowing that unchecked anxiety can lead to problems in various aspects of my life. In severe cases, anxiety can be life-impairing and disabling.

THE ANXIETY SPECTRUM

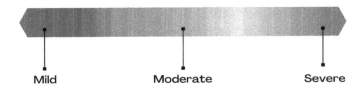

Mild   Moderate   Severe

As we dive deep into the intricacies of anxiety, we start to uncover its hidden layers and the various ways it affects our lives. With this knowledge, we can clear the way for healing, gain personal growth, and improve our ability to bounce back from challenges.

In the upcoming sections, you'll better understand anxiety and equip yourself with crucial insights and strategies. The road to mental well-being might be tough, but it offers the potential for transformation. By embracing this journey of self-discovery and empowerment, you set on a path that can significantly reshape your relationship with anxiety, helping you face life's trials with greater calmness and inner strength.

Types of Anxiety

In order to better understand anxiety, we must explore the various types of anxiety disorders, such as Generalized Anxiety Disorder, Panic Disorders, Agoraphobia, Social

Anxiety Disorder, Specific Phobia, Separation Anxiety Disorder, Post-Traumatic Stress Disorder (PTSD), Obsessive-Compulsive Disorder (OCD), and Illness Anxiety Disorder.

Generalized Anxiety Disorder:

Generalized Anxiety Disorder is the most common diagnosis of anxiety. It is characterized by excessive and uncontrollable worrying that becomes difficult to manage, causing distress and significantly impairing daily functioning.

To receive a diagnosis of Generalized Anxiety Disorder, individuals must exhibit at least three symptoms associated with worrying, such as restlessness, irritability, poor concentration, and difficulty sleeping.

Statistics show that over 6.8 million people, roughly 3.1 percent of the population, suffer from Generalized Anxiety Disorder. Women are twice as likely as men to have this condition, but it is important to note that the actual numbers for men might be higher, as men are less likely to report anxiety symptoms to their doctors.

Generalized Anxiety Disorder often coexists with other disorders and can lead individuals to experience excessive and inappropriate worry persistently for several months or even longer.

While it's normal for everyone to feel anxious occasionally, those with Generalized Anxiety Disorder tend to worry about numerous things and do so more frequently than those without the condition. Their worries can become intense and unrelenting. Despite being aware that their excessive worrying is unhealthy, individuals with Generalized Anxiety Disorder often feel powerless to control it.

They may find themselves worrying about seemingly minor things, such as being late for appointments, speaking in groups, or completing daily chores on time. The overwhelming nature of their anxiety can stand in the way of their ability to lead a fulfilling life.

Panic Disorders

You or someone you know may have encountered Panic Disorders, which are characterized by recurrent and unexpected surges of severe anxiety known as "panic attacks." These attacks are often accompanied by anticipatory anxiety between episodes.

Approximately six million people, accounting for 2.7 percent of the population, suffer from Panic Attacks. Panic disorders often coexist with depression. Interestingly, women outnumber men in panic disorder cases by a 2-to-1 ratio, possibly because men are less likely to report symptoms of Panic Disorder to their doctors.

Panic attacks manifest as discrete episodes of intense fear and discomfort, accompanied by multiple physical or mental anxiety symptoms. These attacks typically reach their peak within 10 minutes and can last anywhere from 30 to 45 minutes.

Frequently, individuals who experience panic attacks develop a fear of having them in the future. While some panic attacks may be triggered by obvious immediate dangers, at other times, they seemingly occur "out of the blue" without any apparent reason.

During a panic attack, the individual is engulfed by a profound sense of fear and foreboding. They may also feel an urge to escape the intense sensations and symptoms, with a prevailing fear of losing control or even thoughts of dying.

These distressing episodes can significantly impact a person's well-being and daily life.

To learn more about how to prevent a panic attack, check out "Intervention for Panic Attacks" in Chapter 3.

Agoraphobia

Agoraphobia is characterized by the fear of experiencing panic attacks in places or situations where escape could be challenging or assistance might not be readily available. These places or situations may include crowds, outdoor settings, or using public transportation.

Individuals with agoraphobia may feel intense anxiety or panic in crowded places like shopping malls, movie theaters, or busy streets. They fear that they won't be able to escape or get help if they have a panic attack. They might also avoid using buses, trains, or planes due to the fear of being trapped and unable to escape if anxiety or panic sets in. Elevators or small, enclosed spaces can also evoke feelings of being trapped, leading to anxiety for someone with agoraphobia.

Some individuals may fear open spaces like parks or wide streets because they feel exposed and vulnerable to potential danger. Social gatherings or parties could also trigger anxiety due to the fear of experiencing a panic attack in a public setting.

People with agoraphobia might find it difficult to leave their home alone, as they fear having a panic attack without someone there to help or comfort them. They may also avoid long-distance travel, such as road trips, due to the fear of being far from familiar surroundings or help. Exploring new locations, even if they are not particularly crowded, could cause anxiety due to the unfamiliarity and uncertainty.

It's notable that around two-thirds of individuals with panic disorders will eventually develop agoraphobia. This condition can lead to significant limitations in daily life and social interactions, as individuals may avoid certain places or activities to prevent the occurrence of panic attacks.

Social Anxiety Disorder

Social Anxiety Disorder impacts roughly fifteen million individuals, making up about 6.8 percent of the population. Interestingly, this condition affects both men and women equally. The key characteristic of Social Anxiety Disorder lies in an intense and irrational fear of receiving negative evaluations from others. Those struggling with social anxiety are not necessarily afraid of people themselves, but rather, they are worried about how others might perceive them and react to their actions.

The fear of rejection and judgment is particularly pronounced in individuals with social anxiety. This fear can be so overpowering that it can disrupt their capacity to carry out everyday tasks, especially in social situations. Simple activities like eating in front of others or visiting public venues like stores or fitness centers can become overwhelming and believed to be beyond their ability to manage.

Estimations suggest that roughly one in ten individuals experience social anxiety. When left unattended, this condition can significantly curtail a person's potential and quality of life, obstructing their ability to fully engage in various facets of life.

31

Specific Phobia

Specific Phobia affects around nineteen million individuals, accounting for approximately 8.7 percent of the population. Women are twice as likely to be affected compared to men.

Fear is a natural and essential instinct that helps to keep us safe. However, phobias are characterized by extreme and often *irrational* fears that appear unusually intense. Among anxiety disorders, specific phobias are the most common. These phobias involve an excessive and unreasonable fear of particular animals, objects, or situations. For example, some people experience a DEATHLY fear of butterflies, which may be difficult for butterfly enthusiasts to relate to but is a genuine fear for some individuals.

Others fear specific objects or situations such as going to the dentist, riding elevators, flying, or seeing blood. Fear of heights, confined spaces, or situations with limited escape options are also common examples of specific phobias.

For instance, I used to be TERRIFIED of going down on escalators, and it took me many years to overcome this fear. Specific phobias can significantly impact a person's daily life, causing distress and avoidance of the feared stimuli.

Separation Anxiety Disorder

Separation Anxiety Disorder often originates from attachment experiences.

In adults, this disorder is characterized by a deep-seated fear or anxiety related to being separated from individuals to whom one is emotionally attached. Common features include experiencing excessive distress when facing separation from home or anticipating such separation. There is a persistent and overwhelming concern about potential harm befalling the attachment figures or events that may lead to separation, such as moving or traveling.

An example that illustrates this is one of my patients who continues to reside with her parents and has a strong aversion to getting married due to her separation anxiety disorder. Despite numerous attempts to leave home for work or college, she finds herself returning home within hours each time, unable to cope with the anxiety and fear associated with being apart from her primary caregivers.

Post-Traumatic Stress Disorder: PTSD

Around 7.7 million individuals, making up 3.5 percent of the population, suffer from Post-Traumatic Stress Disorder (PTSD). Women are more likely to be affected than men, and one of the most common triggers for PTSD is rape.

Moreover, childhood sexual abuse is a strong predictor of the likelihood of developing PTSD throughout one's life. PTSD is characterized by exposure to actual or threatened death, serious injury, or physical harm to oneself or loved ones. This exposure can lead to persistent intrusive thoughts, such as flashbacks, dreams, or vivid recollections of the traumatic event.

People with PTSD often go to great lengths to avoid activities or thoughts associated with the trauma. This disorder negatively impacts overall cognitive functioning, mood, sleep, and can lead to an exaggerated startle response.

Individuals with PTSD tend to be hypervigilant, finding it difficult to relax or let their guard down. They constantly experience anxiety, worry, and an underlying sense of fear or trepidation. Feeling constantly unsafe or at risk, they may even avoid social interactions unrelated to their trauma. In some cases, individuals struggling with PTSD may engage in risky or destructive behaviors as a way to cope with their distress.

Obsessive-Compulsive Disorder: OCD

Approximately 2.2 million individuals, roughly 1 percent of the population, suffer from severe Obsessive-Compulsive Disorder (OCD). OCD is equally prevalent among men and women, and interestingly, about one-third of adults with OCD experienced their first symptoms during childhood.

I view OCD, along with most anxiety-based disorders, as a spectrum disorder, where there may be OCD thoughts and behaviors causing distress that might not reach the level of a diagnosable condition.

If you find yourself struggling with an overly critical and overanxious mind that has difficulty shutting down at night, or if you have trouble letting go of intrusive and irrational thoughts and feelings, if you tend to react strongly in relationships, taking things personally and catastrophizing situations beyond your control, you might be dealing with **OCD traits** and fall on the spectrum of OCD, but might not meet the diagnosis criteria of OCD.

Despite being overwhelmed and frustrated by these traits, you might still be considered highly functioning and not treated for the OCD symptoms. This is one of reasons it can take up to 10 years to get an official diagnosis of OCD and get the help that you need.

OCD is a mental health diagnosis related to a glitch in the brain that keeps you fixated on unwanted and irrational thoughts and beliefs. Left untreated or unmanaged, these thoughts and beliefs can create immense stress and overwhelm.

Typically, OCD is characterized by recurrent obsessive thoughts and images, which may or may not be connected to impulses or accompanied by repetitive physical or mental rituals like counting, touching, or washing.

While many people experience worries, those struggling with OCD feel they cannot stop worrying, fearing that something terrible will happen if they do not perform their rituals.

The strong desire *to feel safe from harm lies at the core of obsessive-compulsive disorder*.

This "harm" associated with OCD extends beyond physical harm; it can also manifest as fear of judgment, ridicule, feelings of inadequacy, or concerns about not being clean enough, among other things.

Those with OCD believe they must be constantly vigilant against potential dangers and do whatever it takes to avoid them. These obsessions can be distressing and time-consuming, interfering with daily social and work functions.

Common obsessions might revolve around fears of contamination, germs, or accidents. OCD thoughts and obsessions can even impact religious practices and sexual matters. Common rituals involve excessive washing, checking, cleaning, counting, and touching.

Obsessive-Compulsive Personality Disorder (OCPD), is often confused with OCD. Although OCPD shares certain characteristics with OCD, they differ in significant ways. It's important to understand the differences between them to avoid confusion.

OCD is an anxiety disorder characterized by the presence of obsessions (unwanted intrusive thoughts) and compulsions (repetitive behaviors or mental acts performed to alleviate distress). These obsessions and compulsions can significantly interfere with daily life and cause marked distress.

OCPD, on the other hand, is a personality disorder characterized by a pervasive pattern of perfectionism, preoccupation with orderliness, and a need for control. Individuals with OCPD may focus excessively on rules, details, and organization, often at the expense of flexibility and spontaneity. Rigidity in OCPD means that individuals tend to stick very strictly to their own way of doing things and have a very difficult time adapting to changes or different ways of thinking.

Getting an OCPD diagnosis is often difficult. The challenge lies in the fact that those meeting the criteria for OCPD are often not diagnosed because they don't perceive their extreme symptoms of rigidity and control as problematic. They consider their behavior justified and expect others to conform to their way of thinking. While there is some overlap with OCD symptoms like excessive cleaning, worrying, and irrational thoughts, individuals with OCPD require extreme control to manage their symptoms but lack insight into why they act this way.

Dealing with individuals lacking insight into their harmful behavior can be frustrating and challenging. Reasoning with someone who lacks this awareness becomes an uphill battle.

My initial contact with OCD was through dealing with OCPD, and I assumed all individuals with OCD were similar. Since I didn't exhibit such extreme behaviors, I considered myself fortunate and blessed to have evaded this aspect of the genetic inheritance. In hindsight, having this awareness earlier could have profoundly impacted my life and how I managed my anxiety and OCD.

Scrupulosity is a specific subtypes of OCD that revolves around excessive and irrational concerns about committing religious or moral sins. Individuals with scrupulosity may constantly worry about being morally impure, blasphemous, or violating religious laws or principles.

They may become preoccupied with thoughts of punishment or divine retribution for perceived wrongdoings, even if they are unintentional or inconsequential.

Illness Anxiety Disorder or Hypochondriasis

Illness anxiety disorder is characterized by excessive preoccupation with the fear of having a serious illness. Individuals with this disorder become overly focused on health-related issues, constantly checking symptoms on the internet, and experiencing heightened alarm regarding their personal health status.

Anxiety can coexist with other disorders such as depression, Attention Deficit Disorder (ADD), Bipolar Disorder, Schizophrenia, substance use disorders, and physical illnesses. In such cases, it is essential to address all co-occurring conditions.

The connection between the mind and body is crucial in managing anxiety because anxiety can affect us both mentally and physically. When we experience stress, our body activates the fight or flight response, which is an automatic reaction designed to keep us safe from immediate threats. However, in our modern lives filled with stress, this response can be triggered frequently, causing stress to accumulate within our bodies. This chronic activation of the fight or flight response can contribute to various health problems, such as heart disease, digestive disorders, and even autoimmune disorders. It's essential to recognize and address this mind-body connection to effectively manage anxiety and promote overall well-being.

Growing up, I personally struggled with social anxiety and OCD. As a professional working with young patients, I've observed many children who struggle with anxiety ask for help in overcoming it. On the other end of the spectrum, I've also seen many elderly individuals finally decide to regain control over their anxiety.

I remember one patient who was overly dependent on medication to manage his anxiety. Unfortunately, he had to stop taking the medication due to health concerns. This caused a lot of distress because he hadn't developed healthy coping methods and had become overly reliant on (and possibly addicted to) his anxiety medication. However, with our joint efforts to build healthier coping skills and improve his lifestyle, he ended up going through an incredible transformation.

Not only did he effectively learn how to manage his anxiety, but he also significantly reduced his reliance on medication. The family was thrilled with the positive changes, and he felt more in control and empowered than ever before. This case demonstrates the power of proven strategies and support in effectively managing and controlling anxiety. It's really encouraging to see my patients making progress and breaking down the stigma around anxiety.

CASE STUDY: From Being On the Verge Of Being Expelled to Becoming Student Of the Month!

When I think about this first step of **awareness**, it reminds me of an 8-year-old patient I once worked with. She was struggling with major behavior problems both at school and at home, and her parents were too overwhelmed to handle her frequent meltdowns. It was a frustrating situation for everyone involved.

Even her teachers and the school staff were frustrated by her stubborn behavior and her refusal to do what was expected of her. During our first family meeting, it became clear that this young girl was actually battling anxiety, and her mind was getting stuck on some irrational thoughts and beliefs. Unfortunately, her parents, unaware of the underlying anxiety, unintentionally reinforced her fears instead of helping her find ways to calm her overactive fight or flight response

Once I explained to the family what anxiety looks like and how it can affect a person, things started to change for the better. They became more open to implementing the treatment plan we put together for their daughter. It was a real turning point for this little girl, who was on the verge of being moved to a special classroom for emotionally troubled students. Instead, she went through an amazing transformation and became much more cooperative both at home and in school. Even her teacher was pleasantly surprised at how quickly her attitude improved.

The change was so significant that even the teachers were curious about what had brought it on. In the end, they nominated her for Student of the Month, which really showed how far she had come. Recognizing her anxiety and taking the right approach led to a heartwarming success story for this young girl and her family.

Calm Within

CHAPTER 2: Prioritizing Mental Health

Your present circumstances don't determine where you go;

they merely determine where you start

~Nido Qubein

Taking care of our mental and physical health is really important, especially in today's world. We can't just wait for someone else to do it for us – we need to take control and do the work ourselves to make sure we stay mentally strong and healthy.

Gaining mental strength starts by stopping self-sabotaging behaviors like avoiding or suppressing difficult emotions, neglecting self-care, and isolating ourselves, all of which make our anxiety worse. When we don't manage our anxiety, it messes with our ability to think clearly and make smart choices. Plus, if we let stress build up, it weakens our immune system, making us more likely to get sick – which is the opposite of what we want.

During the Coronavirus Pandemic of 2020, the world went through a big transformation. The mandatory lockdowns forced us to look inside ourselves and think. At first, the pandemic made a lot of people scared and anxious. But it also made many of us focus on our mental health. We started creating routines and doing things to take better care of ourselves, like meditating and going out in nature. These new routines and level of structure provided a sense of control in an otherwise uncertain and uncontrolled moment in time. It also

41

provided a real opportunity for us to experience first hand the importance of mental health.

By placing a priority on your mental health, you make a commitment to your overall well-being. While dedicating time to focus on your mental health may require effort, it is important to recognize that dealing with mental illness can also be time-consuming. Embracing the multifaceted strategies discussed in this book has the potential to create a lasting impact on your anxiety management. It is important to note that this approach does not offer an instant remedy; instead, it involves making lifestyle adjustments that empower you to take control over your anxiety. It is about gaining an understanding of how your brain works and equipping yourself with the tools to lead anxiety, rather than allowing it to control you.

My main focus here is to calm your natural response that triggers the fight, flight, or freeze reactions, ultimately restoring a sense of balance and peace to your mind. The fight/flight/freeze response is an instinctive reaction that activates when you perceive danger, whether real or imagined. By activating your sympathetic nervous system, your body is preparing for survival by taking action in the face of genuine threats. However, your body does not differentiate between reality and fantasy, and is not meant to stay in this heightened state for prolonged periods of time. Sadly, our modern lifestyles subject us to stressors that can activate our fight or flight response throughout the day, even for minor concerns, and this response often lingers. While our nervous system typically needs 2 to 4 hours to reset, the constant stressors of today's world make it almost impossible to achieve this necessary recovery.

Committing to put your mental well-being at the forefront of your priorities plays a crucial role in maintaining your overall wellness. Similar to taking care of your physical health, nurturing your mental well-being requires dedication, active participation, and a willingness to be patient as you progress gradually. The 3 step AIM program will provide you with the strategies you need to not only prioritize but improve your mental health.

Here are some important points to consider when it comes to prioritizing your mental health:

- **Self-awareness and Recognition:** The first step in prioritizing your mental health is acknowledging its significance and recognizing when you might be struggling. Being attuned to your emotions, thoughts, and behaviors allows you to identify any signs of distress or change in your mental well-being.
- **Breaking Stigmas:** Sometimes, the reluctance to prioritize mental health can be influenced by societal stigmas and misconceptions surrounding mental illnesses. By breaking down these stigmas and understanding that *mental health is as vital as physical health*, you can overcome the barriers that might stand in the way of seeking help and support.
- **Building Healthy Habits:** Prioritizing mental health involves cultivating healthy habits that contribute to emotional well-being. These may include regular exercise, maintaining a balanced diet, getting enough sleep, and finding healthy ways to cope with stress.
- **Time for Self-Care:** Engaging in self-care activities is not indulgence but rather a necessary practice for mental health maintenance. Taking time to do things you enjoy, practice relaxation techniques, or participate

in hobbies can help reduce stress and improve mental clarity.

- **Establishing Boundaries:** Setting healthy boundaries in your personal and professional life is crucial for safeguarding your mental well-being. Learn to say no when necessary, avoid overcommitting, and create a space that allows you to recharge and rejuvenate.
- **Developing Coping Mechanisms:** Life inevitably brings challenges and stressors. Building healthy coping mechanisms, such as mindfulness, deep breathing exercises, or seeking support from loved ones, can assist in navigating difficult times and managing emotional turmoil.
- **Consistency and Patience:** Prioritizing mental health is a continuous journey that requires patience and persistence. It may take time to see significant changes, but consistent effort in self-care and seeking support will contribute to long-term improvements.
- **Removing Toxic Influences:** Identifying and distancing yourself from toxic relationships or environments that negatively impact your mental health is vital. Surrounding yourself with supportive and understanding individuals can be immensely beneficial.
- **Embracing Imperfection:** Acknowledge that nobody's mental health is flawless all the time. Just like physical health, there will be ups and downs, and that's perfectly okay. Embrace the journey, learn from setbacks, and celebrate your progress.

Remember, prioritizing your mental health is not a sign of weakness but an essential aspect of living a fulfilling and balanced life. By investing time and effort into caring for your mental well-being, you can build resilience, foster personal growth, and create a stronger foundation for your overall health and happiness. The upcoming chapters will dive deeper in each of the sections mentioned in order to help you prioritize your mental health.

Create Your Baseline

Measurement is the first step that leads to control and eventually to improvement. If you can't measure something, you can't understand it.
If you can't understand it, you can't control it.
If you can't control it, you can't improve it
~ H. James Harrington

Creating a baseline at the beginning of your journey towards healing is very important because it gives you a way to gauge your progress as time goes on. It offers a crystal-clear reference point to see your starting point and how much you've improved. This foundation lets you objectively evaluate your initial status and document the modifications and enhancements as you move forward.

Not only does charting your progress keep your motivation high, but it also offers invaluable insights into the effectiveness of the methods and tactics you're putting into action. Whether it's about keeping tabs on your anxiety levels, observing specific behaviors, or assessing your overall wellness, having a baseline permits you to celebrate your achievements and appreciate the positive changes you've made.

When establishing a baseline, it's important to identify the key aspects that you plan to measure. These indicators serve as reference points, allowing you to track your progress and evaluate the effectiveness of your efforts over time. Here are some important factors to consider measuring:

- **Frequency of Panic Attacks:** Keeping track of the number of panic attacks you experience helps you understand the severity of your anxiety and how it might be changing as you implement strategies to manage it.
- **Sleep Patterns:** Recording the time you go to bed and assessing the quality of your sleep helps you gauge the impact of your sleep habits on your overall well-being. This can be done by tracking how well-rested you feel upon waking and throughout the day. Keep a sleep journal by your bed and document the quality of your sleep daily for a week.
- **Dietary Choices:** Maintaining a food journal to document your dietary choices over the week provides insights into how your eating habits might be influencing your mood, energy levels, and overall health.
- **Stress Levels:** Regularly assessing your stress levels lets you monitor how external factors and coping mechanisms affect your emotional state. This could involve rating your stress on a scale or using a stress assessment tool.
- **Irritability:** Keeping track of how irritable you feel on a daily basis gives you a sense of how your anxiety is impacting your emotional responses to various situations.
- **Reactivity:** Monitoring how reactive you are to stressors or triggers helps you become more aware of your emotional responses and identify patterns of overreaction or underreaction.

By diligently recording and analyzing these factors, you'll be equipped to gain a deeper understanding of your baseline state. As you progress in your journey to manage anxiety and enhance well-being, these measurements will serve as valuable tools to celebrate your achievements and make informed adjustments to your strategies. Remember, the baseline is not only a starting point but a compass guiding you toward positive change and growth.

Family History

To gain a deeper understanding of the roots of your anxiety, it is important to engage in some reflection and explore your family's history in relation to anxiety. Let us dive into how anxiety has manifested within your familial context. Anxiety often has a significant genetic influence, similar to traits such as eye or hair color, and is frequently passed down from one generation to the next. Developing a comprehensive understanding of anxiety's presence in your family history is vital for achieving long-term control over it, as it offers valuable perspective.

It is important to note that not everyone in your family may have received a formal anxiety diagnosis, as many individuals may experience anxiety without seeking professional help. However, they may exhibit noticeable signs of anxiety that you can now recognize and understand.

In certain families, anxiety can be so pervasive that it becomes the accepted norm, while in others, you may observe extreme behaviors that deviate from the usual. Additionally, anxiety can manifest differently among various family members. For example, one individual may exhibit excessive worry, while another may resort to self-medication through drugs or alcohol.

47

To regain control over your anxiety, it is important to understand how and why it has been affecting your life. By exploring its presence in your family history, you can identify patterns and behaviors that may be influencing you. Armed with this understanding, you can take proactive measures to confront anxiety and reclaim control over your own life.

Family Questionnaire

To gain a deeper understanding of your genetic connection to anxiety, a valuable tool at your disposal is the Family History Questionnaire. By downloading and utilizing this questionnaire, you can begin the process of uncovering the underlying causes of your anxiety.

To access the questionnaire, please visit **https://www.transforminganxiety.com/family-history** and begin answering the questions regarding your family's history with anxiety.

As you actively participate in the questionnaire and dive deeper into your understanding of anxiety, you will gradually gain valuable insights into the role it has played in your life so far. Take this opportunity to document memories that date back to your earliest experiences, where you either experienced anxiety yourself or witnessed events that left you feeling uneasy. These memories may include a range of situations, such as shows you watched, accidents you encountered, or conflicts you witnessed.

Make an effort to remember as many details as possible about your early school experiences. If possible, have a conversation with your parents about the type of early childhood you had.

Explore whether you were an intense and demanding child or if you tended to be more passive and shy. Gathering this information can provide valuable insights into your early development and help shed light on your experiences and personality traits during that time.

Take a moment to reflect on your relationships with your parents and siblings. Consider whether these relationships were healthy and nurturing during your childhood. Additionally, think about your childhood friendships and whether there were any close friendships that ended for various reasons. Reflecting on these aspects can provide valuable insights into your experiences and relationships during your childhood years.

By completing this questionnaire and journaling, as well as exploring both your personal and familial history, you will gain valuable insights into the factors that contribute to your anxiety. This understanding will empower you to address the underlying causes and help you make significant progress in managing and overcoming anxiety. With this heightened sense of awareness and knowledge, you will be ready to navigate your anxiety journey with greater confidence and success.

In addition to the questionnaire, you may find it beneficial to create a modified family tree where you can identify relatives and their struggles or history of mental illness. This exercise will offer further insight into your own experiences. You do not need to be overly concerned about specific details for each family member. Simply jot down everything you remember about them, as it can contribute to a clearer understanding of your familial context.

Baselines/Family History

For example:

- Who in your extended family was kind and loving, and who was harsh with discipline?
- Who in your extended family had very strict expectations, or was very rigid in their thoughts and behaviors?
- Who struggled with personal relationship issues?

The important takeaway is that even if certain individuals have not received an official anxiety diagnosis, it does not negate the potential impact of anxiety on different aspects of their lives. Anxiety can still affect areas such as relationships, career aspirations, addictions, and overall well-being, regardless of a formal diagnosis.

Let's take the example of my grandfather, who was never officially diagnosed with anxiety or OCD, yet his life was influenced by anxiety-related tendencies. He had a reputation for being extremely neat and meticulous about cleanliness, and he had a rigid approach to tasks. While I cherished him and never witnessed his anger, he was also known for having a volatile temper. Understanding his history was pivotal for me, as it provided context for my own experiences with anxiety. I also observed anxiety manifesting in distinct ways among his children and grandchildren, highlighting the importance of exploring how anxiety impacts different members of your own family.

It is important to pay attention to your family's experiences and how anxiety may have shaped their lives. It is not uncommon for individuals struggling with drug or alcohol dependence to have an underlying history of anxiety or other mental health issues, leading them to resort to substances as a form of self-medication. In certain ethnically diverse cultures, there may be a higher level of acceptance regarding the use of alcohol or prescription pain medication as coping mechanisms, rather than acknowledging and seeking help for mental disorders.

Take the time to document your observations and engage in meaningful conversations with your parents or relatives to gather information about your family's history with mental disorders. By actively seeking this knowledge, you can gain a deeper understanding of the mental health landscape within your family and how it may have influenced your own experiences.

Additionally, it is important to critically examine your current life situation, which encompasses aspects such as your relationship history, past or present school experiences, current work status, and social connections. By identifying the sources of anxiety in your life, you can gain valuable insights into how it personally affects you.

Explore your current emotional stressors related to work, family, and social connections by watching the video when you visit **https://www.transforminganxiety.com/family-history** on how to create a baseline.

Aim to provide as much detail as possible.

Here are some common sources of anxiety that you should be attentive to and see if they apply to your life.

For example:

- Are you being affected by past suppressed emotions or trauma?
- Is the news or current events causing you anxiety?
- Are you dealing with negative or toxic relationships?
- Does the current state of the environment upset you?
- Are you feeling overwhelmed or distracted by technology, which perpetuates your disconnect with your emotions?
- Do you keep yourself overly busy or overextended?

It is not uncommon for many of my patients to initially overlook the connection between their current anxiety symptoms and past challenges. However, upon reflection, they often come to realize that anxiety has been a consistent presence in their lives, even if it manifested in more subtle ways.

Usually, when we perceive life's demands as manageable and feel a sense of control, anxiety tends to have less of an impact on us. In my personal experience, I only began associating my symptoms with anxiety after becoming a mother and feeling overwhelmed by the responsibilities. Looking back, I realized that anxiety had always been present in the background, influencing various aspects of my life in subtle ways.

Throughout our lives, we often inherit familial patterns that continue to influence and control us. However, it is vital to pay attention to these patterns and be aware of them.

Understanding the origins of anxiety is crucial, and to facilitate this understanding, I encourage you to engage in honest and introspective self-reflection. Keep a notebook nearby and make note of any thoughts, feelings, or memories that arise, no matter how seemingly insignificant they may be. This process can help uncover valuable insights and contribute to your journey of self-discovery.

While recognizing your past history in relation to anxiety is crucial, it is equally important not to overlook the impact of your current lifestyle on the severity of your anxiety. Make sure to include this information in your self-assessment form and journal. By doing so, you will develop a comprehensive understanding of how both past experiences and present circumstances contribute to your anxiety.

Always remember that you cannot make positive changes if you are unaware of the factors that influence your anxiety. Therefore, this process of self-exploration is crucial for your journey towards attaining greater control and overall well-being.

Common triggers and underlying factors contributing to anxiety

Now, let's address the common triggers and the underlying factors that contribute to your anxiety. As you start this journey of internal healing and transformation, you will begin to witness positive changes in your external world as well.

Just imagine a life where anxiety no longer dominates your thoughts, where you can experience a newfound sense of freedom and inner peace.

The truth is, you have more control over your anxiety than you may currently realize. Your daily actions play a crucial role in either alleviating or intensifying your anxiety. However, we live in a society that often encourages dependence on external sources. My aim is to educate and empower you, so that you no longer rely on anyone or anything outside of yourself to regain control of your life. I will help you work towards cultivating self-reliance and empowering you to take charge of your own healing journey.

One of the factors that contributes to the intensity of your anxiety is related to your diet. Unfortunately, our dietary habits have significantly deteriorated over the past 50 years, exposing us to daily toxins that harm our gut microbiome and impact our brain. Maintaining a healthy gut microbiome is crucial because it releases neurochemicals that promote feelings of calm and control. Interestingly, many of these feel-good chemicals are not primarily found in the brain but are actually released in the gut, a fact that is not widely known. We will address the importance of caring for your gut microbiome in more detail in Chapter 3.

Our modern lifestyle has a detrimental impact on our anxiety levels as well. The fast-paced nature and constant stress leave little room for self-care and mindfulness. We often find ourselves lacking the luxury of dedicating two to four hours to reset our central nervous system, as chronic stress and repeated activation of the fight or flight response become the norm. Additionally, sleep deprivation or poor-quality sleep further contributes to the severity of anxiety symptoms. It is important to address these lifestyle factors and prioritize self-care practices in order to effectively manage anxiety.

Our jam-packed schedules often keep us trapped in a perpetual fight or flight mode, from the moment we wake up until bedtime. In our quest for immediate relief from anxiety, we tend to seek quick fixes. While these temporary solutions may provide temporary relief, they fail to address the underlying causes of anxiety. This desperate pursuit of instant relief has contributed to an epidemic of anxiety, where individuals become fixated on finding the next quick fix without exploring the root causes that need to be addressed for lasting change.

Recognizing the underlying cause of your anxiety is necessary for effective management and control. These root causes could be related to physical or gut health, unresolved emotional blockages, hormonal imbalances, or vitamin deficiencies, among other factors. Quick fixes may provide temporary relief, but they only mask the root issues. By moving beyond these temporary solutions, you can create a more sustainable and long-term approach to managing anxiety. This involves addressing your root causes and implementing strategies that promote lasting well-being and resilience.

Rather than relying solely on medication or meditation, addressing the root cause of your anxiety allows you to dive deeper and prioritize your overall health. By exploring the root causes of your anxiety, you can not only prevent potential underlying health issues but also effectively address any existing ones. Taking a holistic approach to your well-being empowers you to nurture your physical, mental, and emotional health, leading to a more comprehensive and sustainable solution for managing anxiety.

The Significance Of Fear In Anxiety

Anxiety is a thin stream of fear trickling through the mind.
If encouraged,
it cuts a channel into which all other thoughts are drained

~ Arthur Somers Roche

Let's explore the role fear plays in anxiety.

To effectively gain control over anxiety, it's important to have a deeper understanding of its underlying causes. It's interesting to note that around 95% of fears that contribute to anxiety are triggered unconsciously, silently limiting your progress towards achieving your goals.

Have you ever felt an invisible force standing in the way of your progress towards your dreams? It can feel as if there is this huge barrier standing between you and your goals. I felt this on numerous occasions before realizing fear and anxiety were holding me back.

What is certain is that *unchecked fears* have the potential to worsen your anxiety and ruin your chances of living the life you want. The specific type of fear doesn't matter—whether it's the fear of failure, public speaking, fear of being judged, shamed, embarrassment, or rejected—because beneath them all lies an unconscious trigger that shows up as fear.

Fear has the power to crush your dreams, interfere with your personal growth, and suppress your potential. Although fear is something we all experience, it has the ability to sabotage your actions and interfere with your progress towards achieving our goals and dreams.

56

Imagine your fear as if you are simultaneously pressing the brake and the gas pedal—resulting in spinning your wheels without any forward movement. This is why so many feel stuck.

The fear of judgment, being misunderstood, making mistakes, being wrong, or feeling shame is something that is universally experienced by all of us.

Fear plays a significant role in various aspects of our lives. From our earliest days, our well-meaning parents instill fear in us, cautioning us to be careful, not to talk to strangers, and to avoid risks. Reflecting on my own experiences as a parent, I made a conscious effort not to transfer my fears to my daughter, having been raised by an overly anxious mother who restricted our exploration and risk-taking. Recognizing the impact of fear can offer valuable insights into effectively managing anxiety.

As previously mentioned, fear had a profound impact on my life. When I was 19 years old, I made it my mission to conquer all of my fears before I turned 20. I was tired of being controlled by fear and the negative effects it had on my overall well-being. I made a conscious choice to confront my fears head-on and free myself from their grip. This journey was transformative, gradually enabling me to bypass the limitations imposed by fear and prioritize a life of empowerment and fulfillment.

Like many others, just thinking about fear brings up negative worst case scenarios and potential problems that *might* come up if we finally confront what scares us. Our minds tend to magnify the negatives while overlooking the positive outcomes that can result from facing our fears and pursuing our dreams. In these instances, it becomes important to focus on taking small, achievable steps forward. By recognizing and actively working to overcome our fears, we can experience a remarkable transformation. It takes courage to confront our fears, gain deeper understanding, and gather the strength to make positive changes.

One quote from Oprah Winfrey that truly inspires me is, "I have a lot of things to prove to myself. One is that I can live my life fearlessly." Despite facing past trauma and abuse, Oprah courageously paved her own way by confronting her fears. This journey not only made her relatable but also endeared her to people all around the world. Oprah's story serves as a powerful reminder that we too can overcome our fears and live life fearlessly.

In my attempts to confront my fears, I made a bold decision to take on my biggest anxieties: public speaking while dealing with social anxiety. These fears had really held me back in many aspects of life. Even though I knew it wouldn't be easy, I gathered the courage to sign up for a Drama class as an elective during my college days. It was quite an overwhelming experience for someone like me, but I felt it was a necessary step to take.

Speaking in front of the class and giving presentations had always been a real struggle for me, stirring up anxiety. However, I was determined not to allow my fears to hold me back, so I kept challenging myself. Even when my drama teacher gave me feedback on my acting skills, I didn't see it as a failure. Just taking those first steps to conquer my fear was very empowering.

While I might not have completely conquered my fear of public speaking, I managed to give speeches at state and national conferences, present in professional settings, and even address high-ranking government officials at the United States Health and Human Services Department in Washington DC. These experiences marked significant milestones in my personal growth and showed how far I had come in overcoming my fears. While I still get nervous during presentations, I now understand that I'll survive and that the initial 30 seconds of nerves will pass.

Despite my struggle with social anxiety, I eagerly accepted an invitation to the White House. It was an extraordinary opportunity that I couldn't allow fear to get in the way of. Even though I would be surrounded by unfamiliar faces in a room full of strangers, I refused to let fear dictate my actions. This remarkable opportunity was too valuable to let slip away, and I was determined to experience it fully.

Summoning every ounce of courage within me, I attended the event solo and found myself mingling with influential government officials, including none other than President Obama! Despite being very nervous throughout the evening, that night turned out to be an unforgettable and cherished experience. The memories I made that night will forever hold a special place in my heart, serving as a reminder of the incredible things that can happen when we push past our fears and fully embrace new opportunities.

When we make the decision to embrace change, the universe conspires to align and present us with opportunities and experiences that would have never materialized if we had given into fear and hesitated to take that leap of faith. It is in those moments of courage and determination that we open ourselves up to a world of possibilities, where growth and transformation become not only possible but inevitable. By trusting in ourselves and embracing change, we invite the universe to work in our favor, guiding us towards a future filled with extraordinary opportunities and meaningful experiences.

When facing fear, the ultimate objective is to *take action despite feeling afraid*. The goal should not be to completely eliminate fear, as it, much like anxiety, plays a significant role in our lives and serves a purpose. Instead, the primary goal is to *avoid being afraid of the fear itself.* As Erica Jong eloquently expresses, "I have not ceased being fearful, but I have ceased to let fear control me." Managing fear is about acknowledging our fears, embracing them, and refusing to let them dictate our actions and decisions. By doing so, we reclaim our power and pave the way for personal growth and empowerment.

Accepting fear as a natural part of life, especially the fear of change and the unknown, allows us to move forward despite the pounding in our hearts urging us to turn back.

Having personally experienced the paralyzing effects of fear, I wanted a different path for my daughter. Throughout her life, I actively encouraged her to take risks and created opportunities for her to confront her fears. Through these experiences, she not only developed resilience but also gained self-confidence. Witnessing her growth and newfound courage has reinforced the importance of embracing fear as a force for personal development and transformation.

Despite being naturally cautious and risk-averse, my daughter surprised me during a school retreat when she made the brave decision to climb a towering rock wall, even though she was visibly scared. Initially, I had agreed to join her in the climb, but after seeing the huge wall, I quietly chose not to, without revealing my own fear. Instead, I encouraged her to go and challenge herself, while I trusted in her abilities. With unwavering trust in me and inspired by my calm and confident demeanor, she gathered the courage to give it a try. Despite her fear, I kept reassuring her that she was capable and expressed how immensely proud I was of her.

As we witnessed her struggle during the climb, her classmates rallied around her from the ground below, offering words of encouragement and loudly cheering her on, which served as a powerful motivator for her to continue and reach the top. When she finally reached the top, you could feel her excitement and relief, and we all joined in celebrating her remarkable achievement. However, her journey was not yet complete; she now faced the challenge of ziplining back down, an experience she had never had before.

Amidst the height, our cheers grew even louder as she fearlessly ziplined to the other end. The exhilarating experience left her with a newfound sense of empowerment, instilling in her a profound lesson about her own capabilities.

It is important to note that in the face of real danger, I would never have urged her to take such a risk. My intention was simply to help her conquer her *irrational* fears, which often disguise themselves as genuine fears. By challenging these fears in a controlled and supportive environment, she was able to discover her inner strength and realize that she is capable of far more than she had ever imagined.

My determination to create this experience for my daughter was rooted in a haunting incident from my own past. During my time in graduate school, I participated in a similar retreat, but my outcome was very different. The purpose of the retreat was to confront and overcome our fears, but I found myself unable to overcome my own. This particular incident took place during a ropes course, an obstacle course where participants are harnessed and connected to overhead wires, navigating risky paths on thin cables.

Despite the reassurance from the instructors that the harness and cable would provide a safety net in case of a fall, the fear I experienced felt unbearable. Unfortunately, I didn't have the courage to even attempt the simplest, low-level course. My mind was gripped by paralyzing fear, and the weight of that regret has stayed with me for years.

Interestingly, years prior, I had successfully rappelled off the side of a mountain using the same type of harness—not just once, but twice! I vividly remember the intense fear that initially consumed me, but once I took that leap of faith, I found the courage to do it again. However, when faced with the ropes course, something inside me was triggered, and an overwhelming, *irrational* fear took hold. I was unable to conquer that fear on my own. Reflecting on this, I realized that maybe I needed the same kind of supportive encouragement that my daughter had received from her classmates during her climb.

It is crucial for us to be mindful of the fears we unintentionally pass on to our children. These fears extend beyond mere concerns about heights or public speaking; they can include the fears we unknowingly transfer regarding money, relationships, illness, and the challenges we can face in life. Our children absorb not only our words but also our attitudes and anxieties, shaping their own perceptions and beliefs. Therefore, it is important that we examine and address our own fears, so that we do not inadvertently burden our children with unnecessary anxieties that may block their growth and potential.

These fears we carry with us do not always stem solely from our parents; they can also be influenced by the media, politicians, well-intentioned relatives, doctors, and educators. While fear serves as a natural protective mechanism, excessive and irrational fear can stop us from living our lives to the fullest.

As mentioned earlier, anxiety itself is rooted in fear. It is important to recognize the sources of our fears and anxieties, and question their validity and impact on our well-being.

Anxiety includes a wide range of fears, such as the fear of failure, disappointing others, getting hurt, traveling, crowds, germs, losing control, and perhaps most significantly, the fear of not being perfect or not good enough. Those who struggle with anxiety often exhibit self-critical tendencies and set unrealistic expectations for themselves, which can ultimately lead to feelings of disappointment.

Frequently, these fears stem from unmet basic needs or a lack of secure attachment during childhood. However, it is important to note that the source of the fear is less significant than our commitment to addressing and transforming it. When fear dominates our lives, it becomes difficult to authentically express ourselves or experience self-love.

Understanding how fear affects us empowers us to keep moving forward on our path to healing and personal growth. It helps us rediscover our authentic selves and build a strong sense of self-acceptance and love. It is important to recognize and address these anxieties, have self-compassion and embrace a mindset that acknowledges our inherent worthiness, regardless of our perceived imperfections. By doing so, we can build a healthier and more fulfilling approach to life.

Take a moment to reflect on your life and consider how fear has influenced your actions and decisions.

If you are dealing with anxiety, fear often plays a prominent role in influencing your job choices, relationship decisions, or even avoidance of certain activities due to the fear of the unknown. While fear itself is neutral and cannot directly harm us, our interpretation of fear can be paralyzing. Fear ultimately stems from our sense of feeling unsafe in the world and is closely tied to our fight or flight response. Understanding the impact of fear on our decision-making processes can empower us to navigate these challenges with greater clarity and resilience, enabling us to make choices that align with our true desires and aspirations.

Unresolved and deeply rooted fear can stop us from embracing our authentic selves, as it often revolves around the core fear of being fully known with all our imperfections and weaknesses. This fear can originate from past experiences of abuse, trauma, or dysfunctional family relationships.

Additionally, fear can also manifest as an overwhelming need for control, driven by the belief that things will not be okay unless we have complete control over every aspect of our lives. The truth is that there is very little we can truly control.

Embracing uncertainty and releasing the need for excessive control may lead us to a more effortless and fulfilling life, where we can navigate challenges with greater ease and find a deeper sense of peace and contentment.

Similar to paddling upstream versus going with the flow, the relentless need for absolute control can make life more difficult. It may be time to remind ourselves that, despite our fear of uncertainty and the unknown, things will be okay and to allow life to unfold naturally. While feeling in control can provide a sense of temporary relief, it will not lead to lasting happiness. What if instead, our constant efforts to control every aspect of life actually make our lives more difficult? What if we choose to let go and trust in the natural flow of life? This process requires building trust and having faith—faith in the unfolding of events and the willingness to accept where they may lead us. By releasing our need for excessive control and embracing uncertainty and the unknown, we open ourselves up to new possibilities and a more peaceful existence.

Embracing the core belief that we _can_ handle anything that comes our way is very important.

As adults, it is important to remind ourselves that we have grown beyond the helpless children who were once at the mercy of adults' decisions, which may have instilled fear and anxiety within us. It is time to release the belief that we must constantly be in control, driven by the fear that others might ruin our lives.

We have the ability to shape our own futures and move through life with strength and belief in ourselves. By letting go of the need for excessive control, we can embrace a sense of freedom and trust in our own abilities to overcome challenges and create a fulfilling life on our own terms.

Keep reminding yourself that you are no longer that helpless child. You have grown into a capable and resilient adult, even if your inner child may not fully realize it yet. When faced with the inner "screaming child," it is important to treat ourselves with the same compassion and understanding that we would extend to any child. Let us speak kindly to ourselves, soothing our own fears and offering love and compassion. Engaging in enjoyable activities can also serve as a helpful distraction. By treating ourselves with care and compassion, we can promote a sense of inner peace and empowerment, allowing our true capabilities to shine through.

It is important to refrain from scolding or berating ourselves when we experience fear, and we should avoid dismissing our fears by simply telling ourselves to "get over it." Instead, in order to build a more empowered life, we must find ways to move through fear instead of allowing it to slow our progress. Embracing uncertainty and having faith in the journey can lead to a more fulfilling life experience.

Remember, fear will only maintain control over us if we allow it to do so. It is possible to manage anxiety by holding realistic and accurate thoughts about difficult situations. By adopting a balanced perspective, we can effectively address our fears and move forward with confidence and resilience. In Chapter 3, I will provide you with powerful strategies to harness your fear as fuel in the pursuit of your goals.

Fear Of Pain And Suffering

*A man who fears suffering
is already suffering from what he fears*
~Michel de Montaigne

It is common for all of us to engage in numbing behaviors, each with our own preferred agents. Whether it is food, work, social media, shopping, television, video games, pornography, or alcohol, these numbing agents can become addictive when we repeatedly and compulsively turn to them, using them as a means to escape or numb ourselves from potential pain and suffering rather than just calming our discomfort. It is possible that either we ourselves or someone close to us—a friend, family member, or colleague—is struggling with addiction. Regardless of who is affected, if we pay attention, we can witness the pain, suffering, and costs involved.

According to the National Council on Alcoholism and Drug Dependence, Inc., approximately 70 percent of the estimated 14.8 million Americans who use drugs are employed, resulting in substantial costs for employers each year. Numbing behaviors are not limited to a specific group; they are a shared human experience. The crucial aspect lies in understanding the extent to which we engage in these numbing behaviors ourselves. By recognizing and acknowledging our own tendencies towards numbing, we can begin to explore healthier coping mechanisms and build a greater sense of self-awareness.

When it comes to addiction, it goes beyond just easing discomfort—it can be similar to a tornado, causing widespread devastation in various aspects of our life. Even though engaging in numbing behaviors may not have the same severe consequences as full-blown addiction, it still carries significant and life-altering implications. This is because we cannot selectively numb our emotions. When we numb our darker emotions like sadness, anger, or despair, we are also inadvertently dulling the experience of the lighter emotions as well. In our attempt to lessen pain and discomfort, we unintentionally diminish the sensations of joy, love, belonging, and other emotions that give life its profound meaning. It is essential to recognize the interconnectedness of our emotions and to seek healthier ways of navigating and embracing the full spectrum of human experiences.

Imagine hard or difficult emotions as thorns on a rose bush, their sharp points poised to prick and cause discomfort or even pain when they come into contact with us. The mere thought or anticipation of these emotions can make us feel vulnerable, knowing that we will have to confront them. Faced with this pain and discomfort, our instinctive response is often to seek a quick escape rather than confronting it directly.

We tend to resort to numbing ourselves and searching for ways to quickly alleviate the pain, while seeking the fastest relief possible. However, it is important to recognize that by avoiding these emotions, we may miss out on valuable opportunities for growth and self-discovery. By embracing and working through these challenging emotions, we can develop resilience and gain a deeper understanding of ourselves.

In our desperate need to numb ourselves, we use various methods such as turning to alcohol, drugs, food, sex, relationships, money, work, caretaking, gambling, staying busy, creating chaos, shopping, excessive planning, being perfectionistic, constantly seeking change, or losing ourselves in the vastness of the internet. These numbing behaviors act as temporary distractions, providing momentary relief from the immediate discomfort. However, they fail to address the underlying emotions that require our attention and understanding.

> *Many of us spend our whole lives running from feeling with the mistaken belief that you can not bear the pain. But you have already borne the pain. What you have not done is feel all you are beyond that pain."*

> *~Kahlil Gibran*

In order to grow and heal, it is essential to recognize and embrace these difficult emotions, navigating through them rather than seeking quick escapes. By leaning into the discomfort and feeling your way through it, you open yourself up to valuable insights and build emotional growth and resilience. Just as tending to a rose bush requires effort and care, facing our difficult emotions may be challenging, but it allows us to fully appreciate the beauty and richness of life's experiences.

We can all agree that confronting whatever is chasing us saves us a significant amount of time and mental energy. Stepping into discomfort and facing your fears also presents an unexpected advantage—it turns out to be far less scary and intimidating than constantly glancing over your shoulder while trying to escape. In those moments, it is important to pause, take a deep breath, and bring your attention to what you are trying to avoid. By doing so, you can identify the necessary steps needed to courageously navigate through the fears that lie before you. Embracing discomfort will allow you to transform your fears and limitations, leading to personal growth and a greater sense of empowerment.

Whenever you find yourself engaging in behaviors such as hiding, pretending, avoiding, procrastinating, rationalizing, blaming, or being dishonest, it is important to remind yourself that running away from your fears and problems is a significant waste of your energy. Running away will usually lead you further away from what you really want. Instead, you must summon the courage to confront your fears and face the associated pain head-on. By doing so, you can make the important decision to embrace growth and pursue what truly matters to you. It is through this act of facing your fears that you feel empowered and create the opportunity for transformative change in your life.

Facing your fears head-on and dealing with discomfort directly will release you from the burden of avoidance, allowing you to move forward with a clearer sense of purpose and direction. When you bravely face difficult situations and stay determined, you will feel more empowered to navigate through tough times and find solutions that match your true goals and dreams. Taking charge in this way not only pushes you toward personal growth but also boosts your confidence and self-belief. Confronting challenges directly opens up new opportunities and sets you on a course for a richer and more meaningful life.

Vulnerability, resentment, and anxiety often play significant roles in driving numbing behaviors, with resentment frequently stemming from a lack of boundaries in relationships. The key to overcoming numbing lies in developing tools and practices that empower you to confront discomfort and allow emotions to flow through you, instead of looking for ways to escape from dealing with unpleasant feelings. Instead of searching for the quickest way to rid yourself of these emotions, begin by gaining an understanding of what these feelings are and where they originate from. By looking into their roots, you create self-awareness, which can lead to healing and growth.

It's really important to explore new activities or habits that help you face discomfort and deal with your feelings head-on. Instead of trying to numb these emotions, try to find what truly brings you joy and comfort in your own body. Look for activities that recharge you and replace numbing habits for habits that are healthier and more positive. By facing anxiety, embracing your emotions, and setting healthy boundaries in your relationships, you can build emotional strength and gain a deeper insight into yourself and others.

When you resort to numbing and avoid confronting pain and suffering, you unknowingly worsen your anxiety. Inside all of us, there's a basic fear of pain and suffering. But when you confront these fears directly and welcome the discomfort that comes with personal growth, you can rise above your worries and find a fresh sense of strength and calm within.

Dr. Brené Brown, a renowned social worker, author, and research professor at the University of Houston, emphasizes the importance of transforming and processing emotional pain. She says that if we don't deal with this pain, it can unintentionally affect others. This shows how important it is for us to heal ourselves and stop the cycle of passing down trauma as if it's a normal part of our culture. We need to heal ourselves to prevent generational trauma from continuing.

Louise Hay, a respected author and spiritual guide, also observed that "We are all victims of victims." This profound statement resonates with me, highlighting how, often unknowingly, we pass on our unresolved issues and pain to future generations. In doing so, we inadvertently perpetuate the cycle of dysfunction and suffering. Recognizing this pattern encourages us to take responsibility for our own healing and growth, breaking free from the chains of generational pain. When we actively work on our own healing, we can set in motion a positive chain reaction, building a legacy of resilience, compassion, and empowerment for future generations.

It is of vital importance that we *process our emotional pain* **and prevent it from transforming into physical pain.**

Chronic pain is often associated with anxiety-based disorders like PTSD and panic. Addressing and healing emotional wounds can help alleviate physical symptoms and contribute to your overall well-being. By breaking the cycle of pain and suffering, you can create healthier and more nurturing environments for future generations.

Yes…all pain is in your head but so is the relief!

Inside our brain, receptors are responsible for processing pain signals. They also trigger chemical and hormonal changes in our body to help us effectively manage the pain. Interestingly, our spinal cord acts as a pain gateway, communicating the intensity of pain to our brain. For example, if you accidentally step on a Lego in the middle of the night, your spinal cord quickly processes the information, signals your foot to lift off the Lego, and sends a message to your brain to initiate the necessary chemical reactions to address the pain. Truly amazing, right?

Afterward, your brain responds by creating inflammation in the area around your injured foot. This inflammation helps to make your foot more sensitive, which in turn helps to protect it from any additional harm. It also gives your foot the time it needs to heal. As your foot continues to heal, the pain signal eventually stops, allowing you to move around without any discomfort.

Our bodies are truly incredible and have amazing abilities to alleviate and heal the pain we experience. Yet, instead of trusting our bodies to do what's best, many of us spend a significant amount of time trying to avoid pain and suffering. It is important to remember that pain, whether physical or emotional, serves a purpose.

Despite our body's natural healing mechanisms, many people resort to numbing themselves with drugs and alcohol to escape pain and suffering. Opioids, marijuana, alcohol, and other substances are increasingly used for avoidance, leading to potential negative consequences.

For example, many individuals use marijuana to manage anxiety without fully realizing or considering the damaging long-term effects on their brains. Today's marijuana plants have much higher THC levels than they did 50 years ago, and this increase can lead to side effects such as paranoia and hallucinations. Long-term use may even cause cannabinoid hyperemesis syndrome, characterized by persistent bouts of vomiting.

Although marijuana might help with anxiety and sleep initially, there are safer alternatives for improving sleep and anxiety that don't involve its use. Topical CBD oil may also be helpful for pain, but it's essential to be aware of its THC content, which can cause positive drug test results.

Regarding pain, individuals with a history of abuse or trauma may be more sensitive, and their current experience of any injury may trigger past traumatic memories. Therefore, it's important to learn effective emotional coping techniques to manage pain and avoid dependence on substances that may do more harm than good for our bodies.

When it comes to chronic pain, **effective emotional coping strategies** have proven to be the only methods that truly help. Our interpretation of any situation can turn it into either a positive or negative experience. Often, I find that my negative beliefs about suffering are much worse than the actual suffering itself. For many individuals dealing with chronic pain, *catastrophizing* is one of the reasons why managing their pain becomes challenging. Catastrophizing involves having irrational thoughts that lead us to believe a situation is far worse than it actually is. Unfortunately, catastrophizing interferes with the healing process.

When we start to catastrophize, our *understanding and interpretation* of pain ends up interfering with our ability to overcome it. For this reason, I have shifted my focus to change my interpretation, avoid catastrophizing, and explore the potential benefits of suffering. By focusing on a more balanced perspective, we can find new ways to cope with chronic pain effectively.

While it's true that experiencing suffering can be unpleasant, it's important to recognize that it also serves an important role in our personal growth and progress. In fact, moments of suffering can create opportunities for us to pause, reflect, and make positive changes that elevate us to the next level in life.

Failed relationships, for example, teach us to value healthy ones, while illness allows us to appreciate wellness. Grief, on the other hand, strengthens us and demonstrates our capacity to move forward after loss.

Avoiding suffering might seem tempting, but in truth, it only prolongs the experience of pain and holds us back. *Pain is an inherent part of life.* Learning to face and deal with it in a healthy way allows you to move on faster and leads to a healthier life overall.

Maybe fear of pain and suffering is keeping you trapped in an unhealthy relationship, job, or lifestyle. The idea of facing suffering might be discouraging you from taking the necessary steps toward change. But imagine if you had the necessary tools to handle those emotions in a healthy way. By learning healthy emotional coping strategies, you not only manage anxiety but also gain the power to break free from those self-imposed limits while improving other areas of your life. The journey to self-improvement is often about embracing challenges head-on, and when you do, you'll find yourself opening doors to a more fulfilling and authentic life.

It's fascinating to discover how our unresolved emotions can have a significant impact on various aspects of our lives. Research has shown that individuals who experience higher levels of emotional distress *before undergoing surgery* tend to have more challenging outcomes in terms of healing and pain management afterward. These individuals often report higher levels of pain intensity, rely on more pain medication, face greater functional impairments, and require a longer time to recover. This prolonged recovery process can prolong their pain and suffering, highlighting the undeniable connection between emotional well-being and physical healing. It's clear that our mental state plays an important role in our body's ability to recover and thrive. By addressing emotional distress and learning effective coping strategies, we not only enhance our overall quality of life but also set the stage for better physical outcomes during challenging times like surgery.

It truly is astonishing how powerful our brain is when it comes to healing. By getting out of our own way and providing our brain with the opportunity to heal, it can work wonders in restoring our well-being. When we embrace suffering as a natural part of life's journey, we open ourselves up to a world of emotional growth and mental resilience.

The human brain is truly remarkable, constantly working to promote healing and alleviate our pain and suffering. Extensive research has shed light on the remarkable power of the brain to generate positive responses, even in situations where placebos, which do not contain any active ingredients, have been shown to contribute to the recovery from a range of ailments.

In one study, participants were divided into two groups. Group 1 received a bottle labeled "OBECALP #1," while the other group received a bottle labeled "OBECALP #2." Surprisingly, both groups showed significant improvement, with some even requesting refills.

Little did they know that "OBECALP" spelled backward is "Placebo"! While some people may dismiss the placebo effect, have you ever taken a moment to contemplate the immense power of your own brain to promote health and wellness simply through the use of a sugar pill?

Research has demonstrated that, on average, people show a 35-40 percent improvement rate with placebo pills compared to antidepressant medications, which have a slightly higher improvement rate of 40-42 percent. This indicates that our bodies play a major role in healing, yet we often attribute this inherent power to pharmaceutical companies or doctors. Our minds have this incredible power. The placebo effect highlights the ability of our minds to trigger healing responses within our bodies, even in the absence of active medical treatments.

Another study involving surgery is equally fascinating. Participants were divided into three groups: one receiving no treatment, another undergoing fake surgery (incision and restitch without any actual procedure), and the last receiving the actual surgery and treatment. The recovery rates were astonishing, with the fake surgery group recovering by 65%, the actual surgery group by 60%, and those receiving no treatment by 18%.

Participants' Groups	Recovery Rates
No Treatment	18%
Fake Surgery	65%
Actual Surgery	60%

These studies highlight the incredible power of our thoughts and beliefs. When we have faith in our caregivers and believe we are receiving the best care, recovery tends to be faster. It's important to pay attention to our thoughts and beliefs as they can lead us towards either wellness or illness.

Taking steps to limit our exposure to negative and anxiety-provoking content, such as what we watch on TV, can have a significant positive impact on our mental well-being.

Building a strong social support system is also equally important. People who feel emotionally supported report significantly less pain and require less pain medication. On the other hand, those feeling lonely tend to perceive their pain as worse and often *require more medication* at higher doses. As social beings, healthy social connections are necessary for maintaining our mental and physical well-being. It is important to recognize the power of our minds and the influence of positive emotional support in promoting wellness and recovery.

Our past experiences shape us, but it's important to let go of what no longer serves us and give ourselves the chance to heal. This takes effort and a willingness to face emotions like pain, anger, fear, and frustration head-on. Instead of burying these feelings, it helps to express and release them through journaling or open conversations. Healing might not happen as quickly as we want, but it unfolds when we trust the process. Releasing the need to control everything and having faith in the healing journey allows us to embrace change. This way, we make room for emotional growth, mental resilience, and renewed well-being.

Fear Of Uncertainty

When you walk to the edge of all the light you have and take
that first step into the darkness of the unknown, you must
believe that one of two things will happen.
There will be something solid for you to stand upon,
or you will be taught to fly!
~Patrick Overton

Given the current state of the world, it is understandable that many of us are struggling with the fear of the future and uncertainty. I, too, acknowledge my tendency towards such fears if I am not careful. However, it is important to remind ourselves that throughout history, societies have confronted various threats and uncertainties, and yet life has continued to move forward. This understanding is a reminder of our shared resilience as human beings and our ability to adapt and conquer challenges. The truth is that *the future is inherently uncertain*, and we are not guaranteed anything beyond this very moment. Learning to embrace uncertainty and releasing our need for excessive control is necessary.

How have societies, both past and present, handle such instability about the future?

In war-torn countries, individuals face the harsh reality of destruction on a regular basis, and yet they demonstrate remarkable resilience by finding joy in celebrating birthdays, forming marriages, raising children, and nurturing hope for the future. The global forced lockdown in 2020 provided us with a glimpse of this resilience. Despite the challenges we faced, we discovered innovative ways to celebrate birthdays virtually and continued to plan for our futures. These experiences serve as a powerful reminder that even in the face of adversity, the human spirit has the capacity to adapt, find joy, and maintain hope. Limiting exposure to negative news about pandemics, wars, climate change, death, and destruction is an important step in protecting our mental well-being. Constant exposure to negative information keeps our minds in a perpetual state of fight or flight.

In premodern societies, people didn't have to stress over the wide range of global issues we deal with today. They could concentrate on what was happening right around them. In comparison, we are now constantly hit with news and information from all over the world, which leaves us with little time to relax and recharge.

It's important that we recognize that the fear of uncertainty is a natural human emotion. It's okay to feel uncertain at times; it's part of being human. Accepting this fact can help you confront your fear more effectively. By purposefully cutting down on the constant flood of "breaking" news and intentionally seeking out positive information, we can bring back a feeling of balance and peace into our lives. These practices allow us to tune into the present moment, finding calm even in chaos. Taking care of our mental well-being and practicing mindfulness helps us tackle life's challenges with a clear and peaceful mindset.

You can also shift your perspective. Instead of seeing uncertainty as a threat, try to see it as an opportunity. Uncertain situations often bring new experiences, lessons, and possibilities. Embrace the idea that uncertainty can lead to personal growth and positive change.

Throughout this book, I focus on helping you become more emotionally resilient so that you can better cope with uncertain and unpredictable situations. Practicing mindfulness, meditating, or other stress-reduction techniques will strengthen your mental and emotional well-being. You will learn more about effective stress management techniques in chapter 3.

When dealing with uncertainty, it is also important to understand that not everything in life can be controlled or predicted. Setting unrealistic expectations for yourself or others can intensify fear and anxiety. As discussed previously, it's important to learn to go with the flow and adapt to changing circumstances.

By welcoming uncertainty, nurturing meaningful relationships and showing ourselves compassion, we can confidently face our fear of the unknown and build a strong sense of inner peace. With time, you will realize that everything in the universe is unfolding according to its own natural course. Surrendering to this reality is an act of humility, a recognition that life is full of mysteries that go beyond what our minds can understand.

Embracing uncertainty opens doors for growth and adaptation, even when life is unpredictable. Building positive connections with others offers us emotional support and a sense of community, reminding us that we're not alone in our struggles. Practicing self-compassion enables us to approach challenges with kindness and empathy, promoting a resilient mindset that empowers us to overcome obstacles and thrive. Together, these practices empower us to face the future with courage, knowing that we have the inner resources to navigate whatever comes our way.

How Trauma Influences Our Anxiety

We cannot have a world where everyone is a victim.
"I'm this way because my father made me this way. I'm this way
because my husband made me this way."
Yes, we are indeed formed by traumas that happen to us.
But then you must take charge, you must take over, you are
responsible

~ Camille Paglia

Trauma extends beyond extreme situations like war, accidents, or severe abuse. Its impact is widespread and not exclusive to combat soldiers or war refugees. Traumatic experiences can occur within families, among friends, and within communities. It's important to understand that trauma takes diverse forms and impacts individuals from all backgrounds.

Research from the Centers for Disease Control and Prevention provides insight into the extent of trauma in the U.S. population. Alarming figures indicate that a significant portion of people have encountered traumatic events. For instance, one out of five Americans has faced childhood sexual molestation, one in four has experienced parent-inflicted physical abuse with visible marks, and one in three couples has been impacted by domestic violence. Additionally, a considerable number of individuals have grown up with alcoholic parents, and many have witnessed abuse or physical violence directed at their mothers.

Throughout my life, I have encountered various traumatic experiences, such as physical abuse, sexual abuse, bullying, exposure to war, and forced migration. These challenging events have shaped me in profound ways. Fortunately, these difficult experiences have helped me become more compassionate. This transformation has allowed me to offer my patients, who have also endured similar hardships, a deeper level of understanding and support.

Even though we are inherently resilient, traumatic experiences can leave lasting marks on our lives, both as individuals and as a community. They can deeply affect our mental and emotional wellness, influencing our ability to build positive relationships, find happiness, and establish intimacy. Trauma can also negatively impact our biological and physiological health, causing disruptions in our immune system and overall stress response.

The repercussions of trauma extend beyond those directly impacted, affecting our families and loved ones deeply. For example, soldiers returning from war might unintentionally cause emotional turmoil for their spouses and children due to their anger, nightmares, or emotional detachment. Similarly, children of depressed mothers might develop feelings of insecurity and anxiety, while those exposed to family violence might face difficulties in forming stable and trusting relationships in their adult lives.

Trauma is inherently unbearable and overwhelming. Many individuals who have undergone trauma often try to bury those memories and act as though nothing happened. They invest significant energy into functioning while carrying the weight of fear and shame. Even well after the traumatic incident has passed, any hint of danger can reawaken the trauma, resulting in panic or a sense of losing control.

Both major traumas and low-level traumas can keep us feeling stuck, preventing us from moving forward in life. Acknowledging the role trauma has played in our lives is an essential step toward healing and growth. Sometimes, we may not even be aware of the traumatic experiences we carry, especially if they were minor or occurred a long time ago.

Childhood experiences with bullying, parental distress, family difficulties, and negative events can have a lasting impact on our lives as adults. Through active emotional processing, we create an opportunity to integrate and reconnect these emotions back into our bodies.

"Processed" vs. *"Unprocessed"* Emotions

So what does it mean when we say *"processed"* vs. *"unprocessed"* emotions? Unprocessed simply means that we haven't acknowledged, addressed, or released a disturbing or distressing emotion or experience. It implies that the feelings associated with the event remain stuck in our body, *unexpressed.*

Trauma is often less about the event itself, the specifics of what happened, and more about how it is *processed* within our body. This is why not every soldier who goes to war develops Post-Traumatic Stress Disorder (PTSD). Trauma often includes abuse, neglect, and catastrophic events, but it can also encompass any deeply distressing experience.

It is important to acknowledge that events we may not initially perceive as traumatic can still have a profound impact on us. For instance, experiences such as childhood bullying or hurtful comments from friends or family, which may seem less severe, can still result in significant trauma.

Sometimes, events that are significant or horrifying receive more attention and support from those around us, which can facilitate the *processing of emotions* and encourage the overall healing experience. However, it is equally important to acknowledge that seemingly less severe experiences, such as childhood bullying or hurtful comments, may not receive the same level of recognition or support, leading us to suppress or ignore them. Despite this, the emotional impact can still be significant, and it is crucial to validate and address these experiences in order to promote healing and well-being.

For example, experiencing a significant catastrophic event, such as a car accident or war, often prompts support and open discussion from those around us. However, in cases like sexual or physical abuse, there tends to be a silence and avoidance of conversation, which unfortunately deprives victims of the essential support and attention needed to fully process their traumatic experiences.

In order to progress in our healing, it is necessary to process the beliefs and emotions associated with the trauma. Our subconscious mind needs to know it's okay to relax and move forward in a safe environment. By actively engaging with and addressing the emotions and experiences tied to the trauma, we can free ourselves from the grip of unprocessed trauma and create a sense of well-being and resilience.

The initial step in healing unprocessed thoughts, feelings, and experiences is to acknowledge that *they happened and recognize their impact on you.*

It's important to not minimize or downplay the significance of these events.

Dr. Eva Eger, a trauma psychologist who survived the Holocaust's concentration camps at Auschwitz, shared her experience of dealing with triggers related to her trauma. She emphasizes that taking responsibility for her feelings was crucial in her healing journey. To move forward, she had to stop repressing and avoiding her emotions, avoid blaming others, and accept them as her own.

Acknowledging and accepting our emotions and experiences, even if painful, allows us to begin the process of healing. By facing these emotions head-on, we can work towards understanding, processing, and eventually releasing their hold on us.

Owning our feelings gives us the power to regain control over our emotions and lives, encouraging healing and personal development. Dr. Eger's mantra is a powerful tool for overcoming intense emotions that could overwhelm us, guiding us back to the present moment.

Her go-to phrase is "notice...accept...check...and stay."

Dr. Eger recommends that as a *first step,* you should simply notice and acknowledge the feelings you are experiencing. You can say to yourself, "aha! Here I go again... This is anger that I'm feeling... or this is jealousy... or sadness... whatever comes up, I'll notice and acknowledge it."

Dr. Eger refers to the 4 primary human emotions- sad, glad, mad, and scared-which form the foundation of our emotional experiences. Each of these emotions plays a unique role in how we perceive and respond to the world around us.

- **Sadness:** Sadness is an emotion that arises when we experience loss, disappointment, or a sense of longing. It is a natural response to events such as the death of a loved one, the end of a relationship, or unmet expectations. Sadness allows us to process and grieve, ultimately aiding in our emotional healing and growth.
- **Gladness:** Gladness, often associated with happiness and joy, is a positive emotion that arises from experiences of pleasure, success, or moments of connection with others. Feeling glad enhances our overall well-being and contributes to a positive outlook on life.
- **Anger (Mad):** Anger is an intense emotion that arises in response to perceived threats, injustices, or frustrations. While it can be uncomfortable, anger

serves an important purpose, signaling that our boundaries have been crossed or that something is not right. When channeled constructively, anger can motivate us to address issues, advocate for ourselves, and bring about positive changes.

- **Fear (Scared):** Fear is an emotion that arises in the face of perceived danger or threat. It triggers the body's fight-or-flight response, preparing us to either confront the danger or flee from it. As mentioned previously, while fear can protect us from harm, excessive or irrational fear can lead to anxiety and limit our ability to engage fully in life.

Embracing and understanding these primary emotions is essential for emotional well-being. They provide valuable information about our experiences, needs, and desires. When we acknowledge and express these emotions in a healthy way, we can build emotional resilience and lead more fulfilling lives. Understanding the complex interaction of these emotions helps us understand ourselves better and approach others with empathy and understanding.

Dr. Eger suggests that by narrowing our attention to these four foundational emotions, we can better monitor our internal experiences without becoming overwhelmed by their countless variations.

Dr. Eger's *second step* is to process these emotions by understanding them and making peace with their presence in our lives. Once we name the feeling, the next vital step is to *accept that these emotions belong to us.*

Although they might be triggered by external actions or words, they are ultimately our own emotions. Reacting with anger or lashing out at others won't make these emotions disappear; instead, we must take ownership and responsibility for them.

The *third step* involves releasing the emotions and any negative beliefs associated with them to encourage healing and moving forward. Unprocessed emotions often retain a "charge," manifesting as physical sensations like a pit in the stomach, fluttering in the chest, teary eyes, a racing heartbeat, or sweaty palms. Releasing these emotions and beliefs is necessary to free ourselves from their hold. You will learn more about releasing the emotional charge of emotions from your body in Chapter 4, which is all about Energy Medicine.

After accepting, naming, and releasing the emotion, it's important to go to *step 4* and check your body's response to it. Tuning into your feelings and being aware of how the emotions move through your body allows you to stay present with them until they pass or change. This process will help you realize that ***emotions are temporary and cannot harm you.***

Learning to respond to your emotions instead of reacting impulsively is the last step. By choosing to feel and accept your emotions, tolerating them, and staying present with them, you gain control over your responses and reduce the chance of acting out based on temporary emotional states.

In the end, practicing these steps will help you build emotional intelligence. This will make it easier for you to navigate your inner world, leading to better mental health and improved relationships with yourself and others.

It's important to recognize that **time alone doesn't heal trauma**; ***healing depends on how you use that time and what actions you take***.

Taking responsibility for your healing journey, being willing to take risks, and choosing to release old wounds and let go of past grief are all significant steps towards healing.

"Healing isn't about recovery, *but about discovery*"
~Dr. Eger

Healing is about discovering hope amidst hopelessness, finding answers in seemingly unanswerable situations, and realizing that *it's not what happens to us that matters most, but how we respond to it.*

We often yearn to understand the truth, searching for reasons and explanations for our experiences, hoping to bring order to our lives. Yet, constantly asking "WHY" can tie us to the past, preventing us from moving forward. Although we can't change the past or control the actions of others, *we can control how we react to these situations.*

Mourning is an essential part of healing, especially in the context of trauma, as it allows us to process emotional events and losses in our lives. However, if mourning persists indefinitely, it can become a way to avoid facing our grief fully. Staying in a perpetual state of mourning might lead to adopting a victim mentality and believing that we will never recover from the traumatic experience.

Grief, when processed and eventually released, allows us to heal and grow, helping us reclaim our lives and move beyond the traumatic event. It's important to strike a balance when it comes to mourning. While it is important to acknowledge and grieve our losses, we must also recognize when mourning ends up becoming prolonged and interfering with our ability to move forward.

Many people choose to linger in mourning, regardless of how painful it can be, since it acts as a protective shield, isolating them from their present responsibilities.

By engaging in the process of mourning, people can establish a protective space to shield themselves from facing the reality of their loss. Dr. Eger, who personally faced the anguish of losing her loved ones during the Holocaust, spent years avoiding her traumatic history before eventually confronting and processing it.

In her own words, she shares, "I used to think that if I let grief in... I would drown, but it's more like Moses and the Red Sea. Somehow the waters part, and you walk through it." This analogy reflects how, when we courageously confront our grief, we find a path forward and can emerge on the other side, transformed by our experience.

Accepting our losses and working through our feelings is an important part of the healing process. Though it may seem overwhelming, it ultimately leads to personal development and inner strength. Choosing to face our grief rather than avoiding it allows us to navigate the difficult emotions and gather the courage to move forward in life. As we experience the waves of grief, we discover our ability to heal and change, embracing our current life with enhanced wisdom and understanding

Dr. Eger firmly believes that living a fulfilling life is the most profound way to honor those who have passed away. During her time in Auschwitz, she learned that the greatest prison is the one we create in our own minds, but within our pocket, we already hold the key to freedom. This key lies in taking absolute responsibility for our lives, being willing to take risks, and liberating ourselves from self-judgment. Embracing ourselves with love, imperfections and all, makes us whole as human beings.

Running away from our past or resisting present pain only leads to self-imprisonment.

True freedom lies in accepting what is, forgiving ourselves, and opening our hearts to the miracles that exist in the present.

When facing trauma, it's necessary to recognize that we cannot change the past or undo what has been done, but we hold the power to shape how we live now. We start this journey by breaking down the mental prison, one brick at a time.

In our quest for freedom, we have the power to break free from the chains of the past, release the weight of self-criticism, and shatter the limits we set on ourselves. Embracing our own humanity and practicing self-compassion paves the way for an authentic, evolving, and fulfilling life.

By finding hope, seeking answers, and understanding that healing comes from how we choose to respond to our experiences, we can break free from the grip of perpetual mourning and embrace a more empowered outlook on life.

Letting go of the past and embracing our journey of healing opens the door to new possibilities and a brighter future. It is in this freedom that we honor the past while embracing the present and creating a more fulfilling life.

The Impact of Unprocessed Past Emotions on Anxiety

Our current levels of stress and anxiety can be closely linked to unprocessed emotions from our past. These lingering emotions can distort our perception of reality and make us more reactive to non-threatening events, keeping us trapped in a constant fight, flight, or freeze mode. There are many reasons why we get stuck in this mode, and one of them has to do with unprocessed or unresolved emotions that remain stuck in our bodies.

Past childhood experiences with abuse, trauma, or an environment that lacked safety can contribute to increased sensitivity within us. These experiences can contribute to our fundamental belief of inadequacy and result in lack of self trust. As a result, we might seek external validation instead of trusting our internal instincts. Unresolved trauma can also unconsciously drive us to repeat similar dysfunctional dynamics from our parent-child relationship to our grown-up romantic connections, often attracting partners who mirror the dysfunction we experienced with our caregivers.

These irrational thoughts and beliefs can become lodged in our bodies if not processed properly. When we tightly hold onto unpleasant emotions without finding an outlet for their release, it triggers a state of discomfort.

Try this exercise: consider making a tight fist with your hand for a few minutes to understand how this tension can feel over an extended period. The prolonged tightness can feel like a knife cutting into your palm. Holding onto unprocessed emotions for too long can strain your body. So, it's important to find healthy ways to release and let go of these feelings. Doing so can help lower your anxiety. Besides finding ways to release your emotions, it's important to take time to rest and help your body recover from stress. This also helps calm your fight or flight response.

Differentiating Between Triggers and Overwhelm

As human beings, we naturally experience a wide range of emotions, and feeling overwhelmed is one of them. Our emotions act as important signals that guide our decision-making and reinforce our fundamental values.

When we look back at 2020, it's clear that many people felt overwhelmed while dealing with the mandatory lockdowns related to Covid-19. The pandemic exacerbated symptoms of anxiety, hopelessness, despair, and fear.

However, feeling overwhelmed is different from being triggered. Getting triggered means feeling intense emotions linked to past trauma, brought on by current triggers like scents or sounds. The key difference between the two is the element of time.

Overwhelm is a response to a current event, occurring in the present moment. In contrast, being "triggered" involves a reaction and response rooted in past traumatic experiences that caused profound psychological pain. The main difference between feeling overwhelmed and being "triggered" is the presence of trauma and how profoundly it has impacted the individual's life.

For example, imagine a person who experienced a car accident in the past. In a stressful driving situation, they might feel overwhelmed due to the present circumstances and traffic conditions. However, if they come across a car accident scene, they may be triggered, and the traumatic memories and emotions from their own accident could resurface, causing a more intense emotional reaction.

When someone is "triggered," a person with a history of trauma is no longer reacting to the present situation but instead becomes transported back to the moment of their past trauma. This can manifest as flashbacks or somatic symptoms, such as pain, dizziness, or fainting, causing them to re-experience the traumatic event from the past in the current moment.

Experiencing triggers can re-traumatize a person and worsen their symptoms of Post-Traumatic Stress Disorder (PTSD), ranging from intrusive thoughts and nightmares to dissociation and self-harming tendencies. An essential part of experiencing a trigger is that it might go unnoticed by others, but for the person affected, it can activate their fight, flight, or freeze response, causing stress hormones to be released in the body.

In certain cases, the response to triggers can be intense and entirely involuntary, indicating the need to handle the situation with sensitivity and compassion. Distinguishing between feeling overwhelmed and being triggered is important for supporting those who have faced trauma, and making sure they receive the right care and understanding. Understanding triggers and being sensitive to them can help create a safer and more supportive environment for those dealing with past traumatic events.

Recently I have observed an increasing number of videos circulating on social media with the inclusion of a "trigger warning" label. These warnings serve as valuable and necessary tools for individuals who are struggling with past trauma. By providing these warnings, trauma survivors are given the option to avoid situations that might lead to re-traumatization.

It gives them the ability to manage distressing content, a vital part of healing from trauma. I encourage you to be thoughtful when sharing videos that might trigger someone with a trauma history. Using trigger warnings is a kind way to protect vulnerable individuals from further harm.

Choosing your words carefully and distinguishing between feeling overwhelmed and being triggered is also important. This awareness will enable you to offer the right support and empathy to those who've been through trauma, creating a safer, more understanding atmosphere for all.

CASE STUDY: From Suicidal To Transformational Speaker

The AIM Program has helped save and transform lives! I'm reminded by the remarkable story of one of my patients who came to me feeling suicidal due to severe anxiety. When I first met her, she was trapped in a cycle of negative and irrational thoughts, which eventually led to psychosis after weeks of neglecting her symptoms. Her family was deeply concerned and struggled to reach out to her.

Although she was on several medications, she wasn't experiencing any significant improvement. Her doctor kept increasing the dosage, but without much success. It took me several weeks of diligent effort to stabilize her emotionally, and it wasn't the medication that achieved this but rather my proven and effective strategies. We approached her healing from multiple angles, ensuring she felt supported on various levels. We addressed both current and past stressors, made lifestyle adjustments, taught her techniques to calm her fight or flight response, and most importantly, focused on resolving her unresolved trauma.

It took time for her to grasp and apply these strategies, but gradually, she started feeling more empowered. Once she achieved emotional stability and mastered the strategies, her transformation was unstoppable. She has now become my most significant success story. From being at the brink of wanting to end her life due to anxiety, she now attends conference workshops and shares her journey of overcoming anxiety to inspire and help others. Her transformation is genuinely powerful! Every time I see her, she radiates happiness, telling me how wonderful she continues to feel. In my years of working with countless patients and students, I've managed to develop a strategy that consistently produces great results.

CHAPTER 3: Putting Proven and Effective Strategies into Action

Before you say you can't do something...TRY IT

~Sakichi Toyoda

Now that you know about how anxiety can limit your life, it's time to implement proven and effective strategies to take charge of your anxiety. The second step of the AIM program is all about intervention. These strategies have been tried, tested, and shown to produce long term control of anxiety.

Throughout this book, you'll discover various effective tools and strategies that will empower you to confront anxiety head-on. By incorporating these techniques into your daily routine, you can experience profound changes and regain control over your life. The strategies include a wide range of approaches, allowing you to choose what works best for you. Some might be intuitive and easy to adopt, while others may require a bit more effort. Remember, there's no pressure to try them all at once. Take your time, experiment, and find strategies that are the most effective for you.

In the following pages you will explore the connection between your gut health and emotional well-being. Making dietary changes and understanding how the foods you consume can impact your mental state will be an important part of the process.

You will also learn about the profound impact of negative self-talk on anxiety. Changing how you speak to

95

yourself and adopting a positive outlook can create a ripple effect, transforming your mood and overall state of mind.

Later in the chapter you will be introduced to the power of mindfulness, emotional freedom techniques, and the art of letting go. These practices can free you from unnecessary stress and open the way for emotional healing.

Remember, the journey may be challenging at times, but it's also incredibly rewarding. As you implement these strategies and make positive changes in your life, you'll witness the remarkable transformation within yourself.

So, let's start this empowering journey, armed with these proven strategies, and step into a life of long-term anxiety control. The path ahead is bright, and the power to overcome anxiety lies within you.

The Importance of Investing in Your Mental Health

The success of this program is dependent on your willingness and commitment to invest in your mental health. Investing in your mental health involves making time for self-care and taking proactive steps to seek support while also implementing effective strategies and resources. This can mean setting aside time for activities that promote well-being, such as self-care practices. It can also involve dedicating money and time towards therapy, adopting a healthy diet that avoids toxins and pesticides, exploring self-help literature such as this book, or online resources like podcasts, blogs, or digital courses. When my patients commit to a set number of therapy sessions, they are actively investing in their healing and well-being, recognizing the value of seeking professional support and taking an active role in their mental health journey.

If you ignore or don't pay attention to your symptoms, they won't get better. Actually, they might get worse and could turn into even bigger mental health problems if left untreated.

Of course, it's normal to experience occasional anxiety, like before a speaking engagement or a job interview. However, if you struggle with uncontrolled or unmanaged anxiety, the anxious feelings can get worse and negatively impact your ability to work, complete tasks, or even socialize.

Investing in your mental health is very important for several reasons:

- **Overall Well-being:** Mental health significantly impacts your overall well-being and quality of life. When you prioritize your mental health, you are more likely to experience greater happiness, contentment, and fulfillment.
- **Improved Coping Skills:** Investing in your mental health equips you with better coping strategies to deal with life's challenges. You develop resilience and emotional strength, allowing you to navigate difficult situations more effectively.
- **Physical Health:** Mental health and physical health are interconnected. Taking care of your mental well-being can positively influence physical health outcomes, leading to better immune function, reduced stress-related illnesses, and improved overall health.
- **Enhanced Productivity:** A healthy mind fosters increased focus, concentration, and creativity. When you invest in your mental health, you can optimize your productivity and performance in various aspects of life, including work and personal pursuits.
- **Stress Management:** Prioritizing mental health helps in managing stress more effectively. By learning

healthy coping mechanisms, you can reduce the negative impact of stress on your mind and body.

- **Improved Relationships:** Mental well-being positively affects your relationships with others. Investing in your mental health allows you to communicate more effectively, build deeper connections, and maintain healthier interactions with friends, family, and colleagues.
- **Preventing Escalation:** Addressing mental health concerns early can prevent them from escalating into more severe conditions. Early intervention allows for timely treatment and support, potentially reducing the impact of mental health challenges on your life.
- **Breaking Stigma:** By prioritizing mental health, you contribute to breaking the stigma surrounding mental illness. It encourages open conversations and promotes a culture of empathy and support.
- **Increased Self-awareness:** Investing in your mental health involves introspection and self-awareness. Understanding your thoughts, emotions, and behaviors allows you to make positive changes and lead a more authentic and fulfilling life.
- **Empowerment:** Taking charge of your mental health empowers you to actively participate in your well-being. You become an advocate for your own mental wellness, making informed choices and seeking the support and resources you need.

Remember, investing in your mental health is not just an option but a necessary component of leading a happy, healthy, and balanced life. It is about making a powerful commitment to yourself to build a solid foundation for personal growth and resilience.

So congratulations on taking this important step towards investing in your mental health by reading this book. Now, continue this momentum by following the recommendations provided for improving both your mental and physical well-being. Your commitment to self-care and personal growth will pave the way for a healthier and happier life.

The Power of Journaling

Write what disturbs you, what you fear, what you have not been willing to speak about.
Be willing to be split open

~Natalie Goldberg

Journaling and paying attention to your thoughts and behaviors are necessary for gaining better control over your anxiety. Making journaling a regular practice provides you with a safe space to express your deepest feelings and thoughts, encouraging you to be your most authentic self.

Unlike in daily life, where we often wear masks to conform socially, in your journal, you can explore your darkest and most vulnerable thoughts without fear of hurting others. Also, as we interact with others, we can build up resentment or anger. If we don't find a way to release these emotions, they can build up and eventually overwhelm us, leaving us emotionally drained. This can result in our becoming more easily annoyed and reactive even during minor interactions.

Journaling is also a great place to start practicing gratitude. Gratitude is a powerful emotion that can significantly impact our lives, rewiring our brains and promoting a more positive outlook. When we practice gratitude regularly, it activates certain neural pathways in our brain, leading to long-lasting changes in our thought patterns and emotional well-being.

One of the key benefits of practicing gratitude is its ability to shift our focus from what is lacking in our lives to what we already have. In our fast-paced and very competitive world, it is easy to get caught up in the pursuit of wanting more, leading to feelings of dissatisfaction and unhappiness.

Gratitude helps us to appreciate the abundance in our lives, even with the simplest things. By acknowledging and being thankful for what we have, we create a sense of contentment and fulfillment, reducing feelings of stress and anxiety.

Gratitude can positively impact the way we perceive and interpret the events in our lives. When faced with challenges or setbacks, having a grateful mindset allows us to reframe these experiences in a more positive light. Instead of focusing on the negative aspects, we can look for the silver linings and see the valuable lessons to be learned. This optimistic perspective not only helps us cope better with adversity but also enhances our resilience and problem-solving abilities.

The act of practicing gratitude can also profoundly impact our brain's reward system, triggering the release of dopamine and other neurotransmitters associated with pleasure and well-being. This neurochemical release encourages the habit of gratitude, making it easier for us to maintain a positive mindset over time. As we consistently express gratitude, our brains become more focused on seeking out and identifying positive experiences, which builds up our resilience and allows us to navigate life's challenges more effectively.

It's truly amazing how the simple act of practicing gratitude can have such a powerful impact on our brains and our overall happiness. By regularly focusing on gratitude, we can rewire our brains' neural pathways and train our minds to see things in a more positive light. When you replace your fears and anxiety with gratitude, your immune system will get stronger, and you will be less reactive to your environment. This simple act will allow you to experience a genuine shift in your outlook on life.

In the next 30 days, as you end each journal entry, take a moment to express gratitude for three different things in your life. Observe how this simple practice gradually transforms your perspective, allowing you to focus on all the current blessings in your life.

Try it...

To begin journaling, start by writing about what's on your mind at that moment. If you are stuck, simply say, "I don't know what to write about." This simple statement will open up a non-threatening way for you to pour out your feelings and emotions.

Each time you write about your thoughts and feelings, you are also diffusing the emotional charge these emotions carry. Journaling is particularly helpful when you feel very angry at someone but cannot or *should not* express it to them directly. In your journal, you can vent your frustrations, use strong language, and honestly express your anger.

Allow yourself to feel these emotions without judgment or worry about how you "should" feel. Writing it all out in your journal helps you to diffuse the emotional intensity, leading to more rational and compassionate conversations when needed. If you fear someone might read your deepest thoughts in your journal, you can shred or rip up what you've written. The simple act of writing it all out is what matters in the end and it is what will help you feel better.

When journaling, imagine your mind as a container with a spout that can be opened to pour out its contents. Whether you choose to pour those contents into a glass or let them flow freely, the key is to regularly release your emotions. Holding onto your emotions or stuffing them can result in overwhelming tears, heightened emotional sensitivity, or outbursts of anger. Journaling serves as a healthy outlet to maintain a manageable emotional container, allowing you to manage your emotions more effectively and maintain a sense of emotional balance.

Use your journal to monitor how often you experience uncontrollable worry or get angry over minor issues. Keep track of how often anxiety disrupts your sleep or impacts your performance at work. Creating a baseline by using this information is important for effectively gauging your progress and understanding your starting point. This baseline will also help you to evaluate the extent of the progress you make over time.

If you have not created your baseline from chapter 2 yet, **go to https://www.transforminganxiety.com/family-history** and download the baseline form to get started.

In addition to using your journal to create your baseline, you can also use your journal to document your feelings and capture your recurring negative thoughts. Write down the negative chatter so that you can gradually recognize and address it.

Many of my patients, including myself in the past, did not pay close enough attention to our anxiety; we simply believed it was an inherent part of our identity. It was through this process of reflection and observation that we truly understood the extent to which anxiety was influencing our thoughts, actions, and overall well-being.

In my experience, I come across patients who are aware of their struggles with anxiety but have never taken the time to document their symptoms or track how their irrational thoughts and beliefs impact their lives. The act of documenting their anxiety often leaves them shocked by the extent to which it controls their daily experiences. Simply dedicating time to declutter your mind through journaling and gaining insight into your thoughts can make a tremendous difference in your willingness to address and confront your symptoms.

Here are 5 Journal Prompts to Get Your Started:

1.) **Write about a favorite part of your day.** At the end of each day, write down three things you're grateful for: choose something from your morning, something from your afternoon, and something from your evening. This is a great way to remind yourself of the good experiences, even when your boss is irritating you. This process also shows you that there's always some good in every part of the day!

2.) **Reflect on your life and document a successful moment in your past.** Write about a time you felt successful or achieved a goal and remember the details of how you felt and who helped you along the way.

3.) **Write about a favorite hobby or passion in your life.** How does this hobby make you feel and what is so special about it? Growing up my very favorite thing to do was go into a dark room and develop the pictures I had taken. What do you like about your hobby?

4.) **Write about one of your favorite memories or experiences in your life.** What about the experience was unique? Write about how you felt during the experience and what makes you feel grateful thinking about it?

5.) **Write about a failure or mistake that turned out to be a blessing.** What valuable lesson did you learn from the mistake and how did this failure or mistake improve your life?

The Empowering Approach of Cognitive Behavior Therapy (CBT)

*Peace is the result of retraining your mind to process life as it is,
rather than as you think it should be.*

~Wayne Dyer

Cognitive Behavioral Therapy (CBT) is a powerful therapeutic technique that provides behavioral strategies, which reshapes your perception of specific situations, ultimately reducing your anxiety. With CBT, you can learn skills that allow you to actively participate in your healing journey and feel equipped with supportive coping strategies, leading to improved overall functioning.

An important aspect of CBT focuses on addressing your thought patterns, commonly known as automatic thoughts. These automatic thoughts, especially the negative ones referred to as Automatic Negative Thoughts (ANTs), can contribute to feelings of depression, anxiety, and stress. Dr. Daniel Amen, a well-regarded psychiatrist, recommends "killing the ANTs" as a way to create happiness in your life.

Our brains sometimes trick us or twist the truth, and if we don't realize this, we might react as if these tricks are real. It's important to be aware of this so you can break down and change the false stories that pop up in your mind when you deal with Automatic Negative Thoughts (ANTs). By doing this, you can gain more control over your thoughts and build a more realistic and positive view of yourself and the world.

By recognizing and writing down the automatic negative thoughts, you can stop them in their tracks and gain control over your thought patterns. This process is similar to distinguishing weeds from plants in a garden – identifying irrational thoughts helps us manage them effectively.

Here's a step-by-step overview of how to use CBT to reframe your negative or irrational thoughts:

- **Identify Problematic Thoughts and Behaviors:** Begin by recognizing the thoughts, beliefs, and behaviors that contribute to your emotional distress or negative patterns. These might include automatic negative thoughts, irrational beliefs, or avoidance behaviors.
- **Identify Triggers (Antecedents):** Pinpoint the situations, events, or triggers that lead to your negative thoughts and emotions. These could be specific situations, people, places, or even certain times of the day.
- **Recognize Automatic Thoughts:** Become aware of the automatic thoughts that pop up in response to triggers. These thoughts are often rapid and automatic, and they might be distorted or unrealistic. Write down these thoughts as they come up.
- **Evaluate Automatic Thoughts:** Assess the accuracy and validity of your automatic thoughts. Challenge their logic and evidence. Are they based on facts or assumptions? Are there alternative ways to interpret the situation?
- **Reframe Negative Thoughts:** Replace negative and distorted thoughts with more rational and balanced ones. This process involves considering alternative perspectives and evidence that contradicts the negative thoughts.

- **Generate Rational Responses:** Develop rational and balanced responses to counter the negative thoughts. These responses should be realistic, logical, and supportive. Focus on empowering and constructive self-talk.
- **Behavioral Strategies:** Implement behavioral strategies to address avoidance behaviors or unhealthy coping mechanisms. Gradually face situations that trigger anxiety or distress to build resilience and confidence.
- **Test and Experiment:** Test your new beliefs and responses in real-life situations. Experiment with the revised thoughts and behaviors to see how they affect your emotions and reactions.
- **Record Progress:** Keep track of your progress by maintaining a journal or using worksheets. Note your triggers, automatic thoughts, revised thoughts, and the outcomes of implementing new strategies.
- **Practice and Consistency:** Like any skill, mastering CBT requires practice. Be consistent in applying the techniques and strategies you've learned. Repetition helps reinforce the positive changes you're making.
- **Adapt and Learn:** As you continue using CBT, you'll learn more about your thought patterns and behaviors. Adjust your strategies as needed and continue refining your approach.

Using CBT involves a few stages that can guide you in dealing with your thoughts and emotions in a positive way. At first, CBT helps you recognize how your thoughts impact your feelings and actions. Once you understand this connection, you can question your negative thoughts to see if they're accurate or if there's another way to see things. Then, you can try new ways of behaving to improve how you feel and react in certain situations. As you practice these new behaviors, you'll learn skills like relaxation and problem-solving, which help you handle difficult emotions, manage stress better, and reduce anxiety. Just keep practicing these skills and find ways to use them at various times in your life. It's important to continue using these skills to prevent old patterns from returning.

Here's an example involving Lucy to explain this better. Lucy's feeling upset because her boyfriend Mark didn't call when he said he would. The trigger here is Mark's missed call. The instant thought that pops up is that he might be with someone else or he doesn't care about her. Because of this thought, Lucy ends up feeling sad or hurt. She's thinking in extremes, imagining that things are either perfect or a complete disaster. She's taking Mark's behavior personally, as if he's automatically rejecting her, and she's imagining the situation as much worse than it might be.

Cognitive Behavioral Therapy (CBT) Example with Lucy

Stage	Description
Trigger/Event	Lucy's boyfriend Mark doesn't call her as promised
Automatic Thought	"Mark must be with someone else or he doesn't love me"
Emotional Response	Lucy feels sad, hurt, and exhibits black and white thinking. She personalizes Mark's behavior as automatic rejection and catastrophizes the situation.
Reframing Through CBT	Lucy applies CBT techniques. She considers alternative explanations: Mark might have been busy, his phone could have died, or he might have fallen asleep. She also realizes

	that even if Mark were cheating or ignoring her, she would be okay, and her life wouldn't end if the relationship didn't work out.
Result	The change in Lucy's thinking leads to increased happiness, positivity, and a sense of control over her life. She becomes less reactive to triggers, develops a more balanced perspective, and is better equipped to manage her emotions and responses.

This table breaks down Lucy's experience using CBT into different stages and descriptions.

The Antecedent-Behavior-Consequence (ABC) model is also a fundamental concept in CBT and is used to understand the triggers and responses to certain behaviors. It helps you identify patterns and gain insight into the connections between your thoughts, feelings, and actions.

The ABC model consists of three components:

- Antecedent: This refers to the event or situation that occurs before the behavior.
- Behavior: The behavior is your response or action in response to the antecedent.
- Consequence: The consequence is what follows the behavior, which can either reinforce or punish the behavior.

Let's demonstrate the ABC model with a few examples:

Examples of the ABC Model:

Example	Antecedent (A)	Behavior (B)	Consequence (C)
Social Anxiety	Attending a social gathering with unfamiliar people.	Feeling anxious, avoiding eye contact, and staying silent during the event.	Reducing immediate feelings of discomfort, but reinforcing the belief that social situations are threatening and should be avoided in the future.
Procrastination	Having an important task or deadline approaching.	Engaging in distractions like browsing social media or watching TV instead of working on the task.	Temporary relief from the stress of the task, but increased stress and pressure as the deadline approaches, leading to further procrastination

These examples demonstrate the ABC model in action. In the case of social anxiety, the antecedent triggers anxious behavior and avoidance, leading to temporary relief but reinforcing avoidance in the long term. With procrastination, the impending task leads to distraction and procrastination, providing temporary stress relief but ultimately worsening the cycle.

Reflecting on the previous examples provided, recall a past experience where you can identify the Antecedent, Behavior, and Consequence (ABC) of your actions. Then, assess whether the consequences rewarded or punished that particular behavior.

Antecedent: _____

Behavior: _____

Consequence: _____

By using the ABC model, you can become more aware of the patterns in your thoughts and behaviors. You can learn to identify and challenge unhelpful thoughts and behaviors, modify responses, and create healthier coping strategies. Understanding the ABC model helps you to gain insight into the triggers and consequences of your actions, enabling you to make positive changes and improve your emotional well-being.

Beliefs hold significant influence over our behavior, and harmful or irrational beliefs can interfere with our progress, leading to self-sabotage or persistent setbacks. These irrational or fear-based beliefs may involve a fear of change, overidentification with symptoms, or gaining benefits such as attention, love, or financial assistance from illness or anxiety. It is important to identify the underlying advantages or benefits of our anxiety before attempting to overcome it, all while refraining from self-judgment for having these beliefs.

Our early childhood experiences often shape our adaptive beliefs, serving a purpose for survival. However, as we mature and transition away from survival mode, some of these beliefs may become outdated or unnecessary. The initial step towards freeing ourselves from their grip is becoming aware of these beliefs. It is important to remember that beliefs are not necessarily facts, and with the help of CBT, we can challenge and release beliefs that no longer serve us.

Our beliefs have a powerful impact on our lives, as they shape our perceptions and greatly influence how we interact and respond to the world around us. These beliefs can stem from various sources, such as the opinions of others or our own interpretations of past experiences. However, what makes it challenging is that we are not always consciously aware of these beliefs.

I'll use this example to explain further: Picture yourself as a child, excitedly showing a drawing to your mom, seeking her approval. However, due to her preoccupation with work-related stress, she dismisses your artwork. As a child, unable to fully comprehend the context, you interpret her response as a sign that your drawing is terrible. In order to avoid the feeling of rejection or lack of appreciation, you decide to stop sharing your drawings in the future. Unaware of the underlying circumstances surrounding your mother's response, you hold onto the belief that she disliked your artwork. This belief inadvertently stifles your creativity and reinforces old patterns of response.

Similarly, I had an experience in 9th grade with my English teacher who harshly criticized my poetry. At the time, I had recently moved to the United States and was still in the process of learning English. Her criticism deeply impacted me, leading me to avoid poetry for years based on her feedback. In hindsight, I now recognize that I should not have internalized her criticism to such an extent. Instead, I should have been more compassionate towards myself and viewed my teacher's criticism in the context of my language learning journey.

Irrational or false beliefs can have a profound impact on a person's life goals and may even contribute to physical illness. Clinging to beliefs that prevent us from being true to ourselves, such as staying in toxic relationships or working in unethical environments, can manifest as physical illness.

However, by letting go of these negative or false beliefs, we can create healthier response patterns.

Harmful beliefs have the ability to distort our perception of reality, trapping us in limiting thoughts and behaviors. They act as a lens that blocks our growth and self-expression, preventing us from fully realizing our potential. Irrational and limiting beliefs can give rise to patterns of self-sabotage, impacting our health and overall well-being. The power of our beliefs can either influence the process of healing and recovery from illness, or contribute to poor health. Recognizing and challenging these harmful beliefs is essential for creating positive change and promoting our overall health and wellness.

The path to freedom involves releasing false and harmful beliefs. Start by acknowledging and embracing your stress. Beliefs have a tendency to manifest in various parts of our body, so it is essential to be attentive and tune into where in your body you are holding stress.

It is often said that *"You have to feel it to heal it."*

Emotions initially start as neurological or physiological responses, and then we engage in self-talk and add our interpretations. Try setting aside the thoughts and instead focus only on the sensations in your body. It's important to allow ourselves the opportunity to truly experience and acknowledge our bodily emotions. Interestingly, these emotions typically last for a relatively short period of time, around 90 seconds, as long as we don't rush to judgment or misinterpret them. However, it's quite common for our minds to quickly jump to conclusions and react, which can prolong the duration of the emotion.

One day, as I was scrolling through social media, I came across a post by a woman expressing her frustration over someone copying her work. What intrigued me was her concept of *"Never Wasting a Good Trigger."* Essentially, she aimed to view this trigger as an opportunity for personal growth and healing. Instead of suppressing or downplaying her emotions, she made the courageous decision to openly confront and process them on social media. This approach enabled her to directly address the situation rather than avoiding or dismissing it.

She narrates, "So, here's what I did—I allowed myself to experience all the emotions without judgment. I didn't criticize myself for feeling angry or upset. Instead, I embraced those feelings, recognizing their power and acknowledging the boundaries that were crossed. I tapped into my inner strength and confronted the person involved, expressing myself in the best possible way. And then, I moved forward."

WOW! What an empowering way to embrace difficult emotions and deal with the unpredictability of life!

She further adds, "Even though you can't control others' actions that you perceive as wrong, remember you are never powerless. Disconnect from the outcome, stay true to your voice, and gracefully move forward". Such profound and wise words!

The purpose of this book is to empower you with the knowledge required for healing. My objective is to provide you with the necessary tools and empower you to transform anxiety from something to be feared into something that can work for you. It is important to recognize that your beliefs and interpretations of events in your life have a physiological impact on your body. Your mind has the ability to influence the intricate biochemistry of your body, all driven by the power of your beliefs. Remember, your thoughts and beliefs have the potential to shape your physical well-being in profound ways. Keep harnessing the power of your mind to create positive change and unlock your full potential! A recommended book that dives deeper into this subject is "*The Biology of Belief*" by Bruce Lipton.

Understanding the origins of false and harmful beliefs is necessary for transforming and letting go of them. Sometimes, without even realizing it, we can sabotage our own healing for various reasons. One common reason is feeling insecure or uncertain about starting the healing process. We might also hold subconscious beliefs that our illness somehow protects us from certain situations. In order to explore the root cause of these irrational or harmful beliefs, you can start by asking yourself whether you are *willing* and believe you *deserve* to heal and be anxiety-free. You can also ask yourself if you are ready to *release* the negative beliefs in order to heal your anxiety?

It's completely normal for doubts and uncertainties to come up during the healing process, but it's important to address them honestly. You might find yourself feeling like everything is moving too quickly, or you may believe that there are specific tasks or goals you need to achieve before you can fully heal.

Take a moment to reflect on your own capacity to heal. It's completely natural to have doubts about your ability to overcome anxiety and let go of limiting beliefs. After battling anxiety and these beliefs for so long, it's understandable to question whether healing is even possible. Perhaps healthcare professionals have led you to believe that anxiety will always be a part of your life or that medication is the only solution. However, it's important to recognize the incredible power of your mind. The beliefs you hold, regardless of their nature, have the potential to shape your reality and become your truth. Therefore, it's important to focus on healthy and empowering thoughts while releasing the destructive limiting beliefs.

Take a moment to reflect on whether you genuinely have a heartfelt desire to heal. It's important to approach these questions with complete honesty. During this process, you may discover that there are hidden advantages or positive aspects associated with your anxiety that you're not yet ready to let go of. Subconsciously, you might feel a sense of protection that you're unwilling to release, even if you're not consciously aware of it at this moment. By exploring these deeper layers of your emotions and motivations, you can gain valuable insights that will help you in your healing journey. Remember, self-awareness is a powerful motivator for transformation and personal growth.

Try it...

Take this opportunity to journal out whatever comes up for you and honestly ask yourself whether you are ready to let go of these limiting beliefs and start your journey towards an anxiety free life.

When you struggle with the idea of letting go of your anxiety or healing in general, take time to write down your thoughts and feelings honestly, without judgment, and pay attention to what comes up. The goal of this exercise is to identify what no longer serves you and what keeps you stuck, preventing your progress in life.

Taking an honest look at these questions will lead you to a deeper understanding of your limiting beliefs and their impact on your anxiety. Begin by writing in an honest and non-judgmental manner. Let your thoughts flow freely onto the paper.

For example, some of the topics that may come up during this reflection are:

- Fear that your family might not be happy if you heal, or that you'll only be loved if you remain sick.
- Belief that you can only get your needs met when you are unwell.
- A perception that being happy and healthy simultaneously is impossible.
- The thought commonly expressed in therapy: "I'm too damaged to heal!"
- The idea (or fear) that healing might require you to live up to your full potential (e.g. go back to school, or take on new responsibilities), is creating resistance.
- Feelings of unworthiness or self-doubt that might arise as excuses.

Allow yourself to express everything that comes up without judgment. Show compassion towards yourself as you jot down these thoughts—no judgment allowed.

Write whatever comes to mind, no matter how ridiculous or absurd it may seem. This process is about exploring your inner thoughts and emotions without censoring yourself. Take a moment to ask yourself: "Why would a part of me believe I need to cling to this anxiety"? Consider who might be affected or hurt if you were to improve and heal. Even exploring the potential downsides of getting better can reveal valuable thoughts and emotions that may offer insight.

Continue journaling until you reach a deeper understanding. The ultimate goal here is to discover what no longer serves you, what no longer promotes a healthy life, and what holds you back from progressing forward. This list doesn't require you to act immediately or find solutions; it simply serves as a tool for self-discovery and reflection.

You can create an imaginary container to hold these thoughts and beliefs, allowing you to set them aside until you are prepared to address them fully later. I'll share more about the imaginary container in Chapter 4.

Feel free to return to journaling if more thoughts come up, and as always, end each entry with three different things you're grateful for. This practice will help maintain a positive outlook and encourage more gratitude in your life. Afterward, close your journal and carry on with the rest of your day.

Consistency Is The KEY To Wellness!

Starting the journey of improving mental health is similar to adopting a physical exercise routine. Just as consistent physical exercise has many advantages for managing anxiety and nurturing overall mental well-being, working on your mental health creates similar benefits.

Regular physical activity not only benefits your body but also has a profound impact on your mind. The connection between physical and mental well-being is powerful and can bring about significant transformations that help alleviate symptoms of anxiety. By incorporating a combination of physical and mental exercises into your routine, you create a path towards holistic well-being and create a more balanced and resilient state of mind.

Here are some of the key benefits of exercise on anxiety management:

- **Stress Reduction:** Physical exercise triggers the release of endorphins, the "feel-good" hormones, in the brain. These endorphins act as natural stress relievers, promoting a sense of well-being and reducing the levels of stress hormones like cortisol. Regular exercise helps to modulate the body's stress response, making it more resilient to anxiety-provoking situations.

- **Mood Enhancement:** Exercise has been shown to enhance mood and reduce feelings of depression and anxiety. Engaging in physical activity stimulates the production of neurotransmitters like serotonin and dopamine, which play crucial roles in regulating mood and promoting a positive outlook on life.

- **Distraction from Worries:** During exercise, you will often focus on the physical activity, diverting your attention from anxious thoughts and worries. This temporary distraction can provide relief from anxious rumination and create a sense of mental clarity.

- **Improved Sleep Quality:** Anxiety can interfere with sleep patterns, leading to insomnia and disrupted rest. Regular physical exercise can help improve sleep quality, making it easier for you to fall asleep and stay asleep. Better sleep, in turn, reduces anxiety and enhances overall well-being.

- **Increased Self-Esteem:** Achieving fitness goals and experiencing the positive effects of exercise can boost self-esteem and self-confidence. This improved self-perception can counteract negative thoughts associated with anxiety and promote a more positive self-image.

- **Social Interaction:** Participating in group exercises or team sports can provide opportunities for social interaction and support. Building connections with others who share similar interests can be beneficial for reducing feelings of isolation and loneliness, common triggers for anxiety.

- **Physical Relaxation:** Certain forms of exercise, such as yoga and tai chi, focus on deep breathing and physical relaxation. These practices can activate the body's relaxation response, calming the nervous system and reducing anxiety levels.
- **Long-Term Resilience:** Consistent exercise not only provides immediate relief from anxiety but also fosters long-term resilience against stress and anxiety. Regular physical activity helps you to develop coping skills and emotional regulation techniques, making you better equipped to handle life's challenges.

By integrating regular physical exercise with other evidence-based interventions, you can create a more comprehensive and impactful approach to managing anxiety. Similar to the importance of consistency in physical exercise, prioritizing your mental health consistently is the key to achieving lasting results. When you commit to prioritizing your mental health through various proven methods, you enhance your ability to successfully manage anxiety and gain lasting results.

Motion Is Lotion For Your Body

Recently, I participated in a program aimed at improving vision, and it revealed an intriguing insight: people with perfect vision approach life differently compared to those with impaired vision. To achieve optimal vision, it is necessary to engage in activities that people with perfect vision regularly practice. For instance, those with perfect vision move their head and body more, displaying a sense of relaxation and engagement with their environment. In contrast, people with impaired vision tend to be stiff and rigid in their neck and

120

shoulders, holding onto stress, and staring without blinking as often. Interestingly, eye movement actually promotes eye relaxation, while staring leads to stress and rigidity, ultimately resulting in poor vision.

It is fascinating to note that eye movement plays an important role in promoting eye relaxation. By allowing our eyes to move naturally and freely, we encourage a state of relaxation and ease within our visual system. On the other hand, fixing our gaze for extended periods can create tension and strain, negatively impacting our vision.

As the saying goes, "*motion is lotion,*" so, just like with our eye exercises, we must move our bodies every day. Movement is medicine for your physical and mental wellbeing and is essential for all parts of your body, from your eyes to your mind, joints, and muscles. People who lead sedentary lives tend to struggle in various aspects of their lives. They even say that sitting for extended periods is equivalent to smoking several packs of cigarettes a day.

The great news is that you don't need to engage in excessive exercise to experience its benefits. Even dedicating just 30 minutes to your favorite activity is enough to make a positive impact. If starting with 30 minutes feels challenging, you can begin with just 5 minutes and gradually increase your time by 2 minutes each day until you reach the desired 30-minute mark. It's remarkable how even as little as 12 to 30 minutes of exercise can stimulate the release of feel-good chemicals in your brain, with the exact duration depending on the intensity of the exercise.

The form of exercise you choose doesn't matter; you have the freedom to dance, engage in seated exercises if standing is challenging, or even utilize portable pedals while enjoying your favorite TV shows. The internet offers a wealth of exceptional free resources for chair yoga, traditional yoga, and weight exercises, providing you with a variety of options to choose from. Managing long-term anxiety involves more than just exercise; it involves reducing stress, adopting healthier eating habits, and ensuring sufficient rest. Regular exercise plays an important role in releasing stress, improving digestion, promoting relaxation, and enabling you to let go. Similar to the approach I took with my eye exercises, the key to gaining long-term control over anxiety is to embrace the habits and activities of individuals who do not experience anxiety.

People who do not experience anxiety often lead lives that are both active and balanced. They place importance on nourishing their bodies with healthy eating habits, engaging in regular exercise, embracing spiritual practices, journaling for self-reflection, and maintaining healthy and meaningful social connections. By making these habits a part of your life, you can feel in control of your anxiety. These habits work together to boost your overall well-being and build a solid foundation for emotional strength and a happier life. Just remember, when you add these positive habits to your daily routine, it can seriously change how you deal with anxiety and improve your overall mental health.

CASE Study: Gina

In my line of work, I am constantly inspired by the unwavering commitment and dedication exhibited by my patients during therapy. Witnessing their realization of the impact of anxiety on their lives and the revelation that they possess more control than they ever believed is truly awe-inspiring. Those patients who grasp the tools and guidance required for the next steps are the ones who experience remarkable improvements in a remarkably short span of time. It fills me with joy, and I can't help but do a little happy dance inside when my patients express how much better they feel. Witnessing the surprise in their eyes as they realize the possibilities they never knew existed reaffirms my commitment to creating a positive change. And so, I am driven to reach people all around the world and empower them to regain control of their lives despite anxiety's challenges. I aspire to be their guiding light, illuminating the path towards a life free from the chains of anxiety.

One of my most determined patients was Gina, a remarkable fighter whose potential was obscured by the grip of anxiety. Convinced that she couldn't face her anxiety alone, she relied heavily on anti-anxiety pills. The mere thought of confronting her anxious feelings filled her with anxiety itself. She had never allowed herself to sit with those feelings, resorting to numbing herself as a response to the unpredictable nature of anxiety.

However, with the incorporation of lifestyle changes such as diet, supplements, exercise, and meditation, Gina experienced a profound transformation. Gradually, she took charge of her anxiety and felt a newfound sense of control. With each session, she eagerly shared her progress and the positive changes rippling through her life.

Her relationships flourished, she earned recognition at work for her outstanding performance, and she felt a level of happiness she had never known before. Witnessing Gina's incredible journey further solidified my determination to ensure that everyone struggling with anxiety has the opportunity to experience such a positive transformation.

My ultimate goal is for you to recognize that gaining control of your life in the face of anxiety is entirely possible. Through the chapters in this book, I aim to provide the necessary tools and support, enabling you to start your healing journey towards freedom from anxiety's hold. Remember, you too can reclaim control of your life and thrive beyond anxiety's limits.

Calm Within

Stress Management: The Foundation Of Long-Term Anxiety Control

The truth is that stress doesn't come from your boss, your kids, your spouse, traffic jams, health challenges, or other circumstances.
It comes from your thoughts about your circumstances

~Andrew Bernstein

In today's fast-paced world, anxiety has become more prevalent and intense due to the constant stress we face. It's all too common to find ourselves feeling out of balance, neglecting self-care, and pushing ourselves to the limits without fully acknowledging the toll it takes on our well-being. The demands of our daily lives often leave us overwhelmed and disconnected from our true selves. It's important to recognize the impact this can have on our overall well-being and take proactive steps to restore balance, prioritize self-care, and reconnect with our inner selves. By doing so, we can navigate life's challenges with greater resilience and find a sense of harmony amidst the chaos.

Stress is a natural part of life, and in some ways, it can even be beneficial for our optimal functioning. However, when stress becomes overwhelming, it can have negative effects on our overall well-being. The key to managing stress effectively lies in how we interpret and perceive the stressful events we encounter. Stress itself is not inherently bad; it is our emotional reactions and beliefs surrounding stress that can contribute to negative physical and emotional responses. By adopting a positive mindset and learning healthy coping strategies, we can handle stress more effectively and minimize its detrimental impact on our lives. It's important to remember that it's not the presence of stress that defines its impact, but rather our interpretation and response to it that shape our well-being.

The current balance between stress and relaxation has been disrupted. To restore this balance, it is important to redefine our relationship with stress. Unhealthy emotional patterns, negative beliefs, and fears can significantly impact how we perceive and respond to stress. By adopting a healthier mindset and holding empowering beliefs, we can change our perspective on stress and develop more resilient coping mechanisms. It is through this transformative process that we can restore the harmony between stress and relaxation, leading to a more balanced and fulfilling life.

This shift in our perspective is the first step towards a more balanced and harmonious relationship with stress, ultimately promoting better overall well-being.

Imagine yourself navigating a series of challenging situations in a single day: a difficult interaction with a coworker, followed by a tense encounter with a teenage child or spouse, all while juggling a demanding commute and pressing work deadlines. This constant activation of the fight or flight response leaves us with limited opportunities to reset our nervous system. If we fail to actively take steps to release built up stress throughout the day, its effects can gradually accumulate within our bodies.

This accumulated stress can take a toll on our health, impacting blood pressure, increasing the risk of heart disease, and leading to digestive disorders, which have become increasingly common. The chronic low-level activation of the fight or flight response can even contribute to autoimmune disorders. It is necessary to prioritize moments of relaxation and stress release, allowing ourselves the necessary time and space to restore balance and prevent the buildup of stress from taking a toll on our overall well-being.

Interestingly, much of the stress we experience is a result of our *perception* of situations, rather than the situations themselves. Our thoughts, negative beliefs, and outlook on the external world significantly contribute to our overall stress levels. To address this, it's important to become aware of our thoughts and pay attention to that constant inner chatter in our minds. Recognizing and understanding our thought patterns can empower us to make positive changes and manage stress effectively.

Your brain and body are constantly seeking balance and trying to compensate for the late nights spent on social media, consuming fast food regularly, and spending extended periods sitting in front of screens or during daily commutes in rush hour traffic. However, without proper nutrition, rest, and time spent outdoors, your brain cannot function optimally. The delicate balance of mood and emotions is governed by the chemicals and hormones in our body, and this balance can easily be influenced by our daily activities. Poor sleep, heavily processed diets, and a lack of exercise can upset this balance, leading to negative effects on our well-being.

On the other hand, we have the power to positively impact this balance. Implementing lifestyle changes and prioritizing self care can promote mental wellness. Even doing something simple such as practicing kindness not only releases but also increases the feel-good chemical Serotonin in our brains. Simply witnessing acts of kindness also has the same positive effect on the *observer's brain*, which is truly remarkable.

Effective stress management can restore balance to our brain chemicals and hormones, promoting a sense of control. To effectively manage stress it is necessary to prioritize rest and relaxation. By allowing yourself dedicated time for rest and relaxation, you provide your mind and body with the opportunity to rejuvenate and recharge. Providing your body the proper nutrition also plays an important role in supporting your overall well-being. By fueling your body with nutritious foods, you provide it with the essential nutrients it needs to function optimally.

When you find yourself feeling stuck, you can take a moment and ask yourself an important question: "Am I too attached to my expectations of how things should be, instead of accepting the reality of how they actually are?" This type of question encourages you to explore whether your attachment to *specific outcomes* is limiting your ability to adapt and find solutions.

Personally, I've realized that trying to control outcomes always leads to disastrous results. The most important decision I ever made was to allow life to unfold naturally and accept it for what it is. Surprisingly, I've often found that what I *needed*, instead of what I wanted, tends to unfold.

Another source of stress in life comes from our need to control others, including attempting to control how they behave. However, it is important to recognize that trying to control the lives of others often leads to misery, and in some cases, it can be even more detrimental than trying to control our own lives. As a psychologist, I have come to understand that true change in individuals can only happen when they are willing to change themselves. It is not within our power to change others unless they themselves are open and receptive to transformation. Recognizing this truth is necessary for our own well-being and for building healthier relationships. Instead of trying to control others, we can focus on supporting and empowering them in their own personal growth journeys.

There are several common examples of how we often try to change others. These include offering help when it is not wanted or needed, sacrificing our own well-being to help others, seeking forgiveness, acknowledgment, or validation from others in order to find inner peace, and demanding that others behave in certain ways to ensure our own peace and happiness.

It is important to recognize that these behaviors are driven by fear and can stem from a need for control and external validation. These attempts also limit our personal growth and progress in life. We hold onto the belief that if others make mistakes, we'll be left to clean up the mess. We fear that their lack of validation or responsibility for hurting us reflects poorly on ourselves. We may even fear not getting what we want from others and ending up hurt or alone. While all of these fears are understandable, they are not healthy or necessary. True fulfillment and contentment comes from focusing on our own growth, self-care, and inner peace, instead of trying to change or control others. By shifting our focus inward, we can create a sense of empowerment and create healthier, more authentic connections with those around us.

It's also important to understand that people will love us to the best of their ability, and it has nothing to do with our lovability. To truly free ourselves, we must stop demanding that people behave according to our expectations. If a relationship is toxic or unhealthy, we can remove ourselves from it, but attempting to change someone else is futile. We must allow people to be who they are, not only for their sake but also for our own. They might not meet our ideal standards, and some may even be unpleasant, but we can still be okay with ourselves.

Maya Angelou's wisdom resonates with the idea that when someone shows you who they truly are, believe them.

When dealing with difficult or frustrating people, it's helpful to express our feelings in a journal. We can express our need for change but ultimately remind ourselves that we cannot change them; *we can only choose how we react to them.*

Fear not only intensifies stress by distorting your perception and fueling the need for control, but it also limits your ability to love yourself. It is necessary to take back control from fear by being more loving and compassionate with yourself. Take the time to train your mind, gently reassuring it that everything will be alright. By reinforcing the belief in your own abilities to handle any situation, you can help reduce fear and create a sense of empowerment.

The Importance of Self-Care

If you are driven and success oriented, the idea of engaging in activities that do not directly contribute to financial gains can trigger stress and anxiety. You may perceive such activities as conflicting with your life goals, convincing yourself that moments of relaxation, playful interactions without responsibilities, quality time with your partner, taking rejuvenating naps, pursuing hobbies in the garage, or going for a refreshing run, are just a waste of precious time. You may even question your need for sleep when you could be working.

It is time to let go of the belief that exhaustion, busyness, and constant productivity define your self-worth or serve as symbols of status. In reality, impressing others through constant work will not make you happy. Celebrating those who work non-stop, never take vacations, refuse to call in sick, or neglect self-care sends a dangerous message. These extreme behaviors are unsustainable and lead to detrimental effects such as adrenal fatigue, burnout, depression, and anxiety. It also perpetuates a culture of workaholism that harms everyone involved.

It is important to recognize that incorporating moments of rest, play, and self-care into your life is not counterproductive, but very necessary for maintaining a healthy work-life balance and sustaining long-term success. Engaging in play has a profound impact on your brain, as it nurtures empathy, enhances your ability to navigate social complexities, and fuels your creativity. Rest provides a cooling effect for your overworked mind. Therefore, it is very important to create firm boundaries that allow you to switch off from work at reasonable times and prioritize your own well-being and time with family. It is through a balanced approach that you can truly thrive and create a life that is both fulfilling and impactful.

Remember, prioritizing self-care and allowing yourself moments of rest and relaxation is not a sign of weakness, but rather a testament to your wisdom and commitment to living a truly meaningful life. By allowing yourself the space to recharge and engage in activities that bring you joy, you enhance your overall well-being and unlock your full potential.

To create a healthier and more sustainable life, it is necessary to prioritize the value of balance. Recognize that time dedicated to rest, play, and meaningful connections enhances your overall productivity and well-being. Unfortunately, many people mistakenly associate self-care with selfishness or laziness, but this perception couldn't be further from the truth. In our fast-paced and overwhelming lives, it is easy to neglect taking care of ourselves. However, ironically, the busier we become, the more necessary self-care becomes. It should not be viewed as just a reward, but as a necessary practice to prevent feeling overwhelmed and burnt out, which can ultimately lead to decreased productivity and efficiency.

Engaging in self-care offers numerous benefits, including reducing the negative effects of stress on our bodies and minds, allowing us to function at our optimal capacity. It recharges our batteries, helping us regain focus and enhancing our performance when we feel drained and overwhelmed.

Neglecting self-care can lead to a phenomenon known as *Morning Anxiety*, although it is not an official diagnosis. This occurs when we wake up feeling panicked and overwhelmed by the tasks and responsibilities that have accumulated due to our lack of self-care.

In the following sections, I will address the significance of sleep in greater detail and explore the negative consequences associated with insufficient rest. I will also introduce the Worry Time technique, which involves setting aside dedicated time before bedtime to address worries. This practice aims to promote restful sleep and potentially alleviate the experience of "morning anxiety." By implementing this technique, you can create a space to address concerns and anxieties, allowing your mind to find a sense of calm and facilitating a more peaceful and rejuvenating sleep.

If you find yourself waking up with feelings of fear and dread, it's important to understand that high stress levels can contribute to elevated cortisol levels. Although cortisol levels can increase due to stress, it's also normal for your levels to be higher in the morning compared to nighttime. If you're curious about your cortisol levels, a simple blood or saliva test can provide valuable insights. It's worth noting that some people may experience a surge in cortisol levels specifically in the morning, which can contribute to sensations of panic and anxiety.

To improve self-care, it's necessary to identify the level of stress in your life, make better food choices, prioritize sleep, and engage in activities like journaling, guided meditation, or deep breathing to promote calmness and control. Spending quality time with loved ones, scheduling massages, or creating spa time at home can also be beneficial.

Wondering how to prioritize self-care? Here are some effective ways to take care of yourself:

- **Recognize Stress:** Start by acknowledging the level of stress in your life. Identifying sources of stress can help you address them more effectively.
- **Better Food Choices:** Nourish your body with healthier food options. Proper nutrition plays a significant role in improving overall well-being.
- **Prioritize Sleep:** Make time for sufficient and restful sleep. A well-rested body and mind are better equipped to handle daily challenges.
- **Journaling and Meditation:** Engage in journaling to express your thoughts and emotions. Guided meditation or simple deep breathing exercises can promote a calmer and more centered state of mind. To participate in my FREE 21-Day Guided Meditation Challenge and explore various meditation practices, visit transforminganxiety.com/meditate
- **Socialization:** Spend quality time with friends and family you genuinely enjoy being with. Genuine human connections can boost your mood and reduce stress.
- **Massage and Spa Time:** Treat yourself to a massage session or create a relaxing spa experience at home with facials and baths.
- **Exercise or Dance:** Regular physical activity can empower you and reduce stress. If traditional exercise doesn't appeal to you, dancing is a fun and effective alternative. Research indicates that dancing can

improve brain function and memory, making it a great option for overall well-being.

Remember, the specific method you choose for self-care matters less than your commitment to regularly incorporate self-care practices into your life. Prioritizing your well-being enables you to be more present and effective in supporting those around you. So, choose one or two self-care activities that resonate with you and make a conscious effort to implement them regularly. By making self-care a priority, you can become a healthier and happier you.

Embrace the Chaos and Release Perfection

Life is inherently unpredictable, and it is important to embrace the possible chaos that comes with it. We all face challenges, and it is only natural for various factors such as family responsibilities, daily routines, and unexpected events to occasionally disrupt our plans. In the fast-paced world we live in, it is truly remarkable that we are able to navigate and function amidst the constant whirlwind of life. By acknowledging and accepting the unpredictability of life, we can create resiliency and become more adaptable, allowing us to face challenges with a sense of control and determination.

Yes, life can be messy and unpredictable, and instead of using our energy to fight this reality, we can learn to embrace and navigate the chaos in order to find a sense of peace and acceptance. It is essential to realize that the pursuit of perfection is neither attainable nor necessary. Instead of striving for an idealized notion of perfection, we can focus on embracing the imperfections and uncertainties of life, finding beauty and growth within them. By letting go of the need for perfection, we free ourselves from unnecessary pressure and

134

open ourselves up to a more authentic and fulfilling experience of life.

Next time you feel overwhelmed but can't find time to rest ask yourself:

- Does your house need to be immaculate all the time?
- Are you a bad parent if you choose self care and rest over being over involved 24/7?
- Do you have to control your emotions around your kids constantly?
- Are you a terrible parent or spouse if you occasionally lose your cool?

The answer is absolutely not.

We're only human, and it's natural to have moments of frustration or imperfection. It is perfectly okay if your house isn't always spotless and immaculate. Prioritizing self-care and making time for rest is not only acceptable but necessary for your overall well being. It is also normal to occasionally lose your emotional cool. It's important to remember that explosive emotions and occasional slip-ups are part of being human, as long as we learn and grow from them. However, if anger becomes a constant presence and leads to harmful behaviors, seeking help and support is necessary. It is unrealistic for anyone to expect you to be calm and composed at all times, free of any complicated or negative emotions.

Embracing our humanity means accepting and navigating the full range of emotions and imperfections that make us who we are. In fact, it is beneficial for your children to witness you making mistakes and then taking responsibility for them.

It is important for them to see that everyone is flawed and that it is a part of life to learn from our mistakes. Additionally, it is valuable for your children to observe you prioritizing your mental health and practicing self-care. By demonstrating the importance of self-care, you teach them the significance of nurturing their own well-being and establishing healthy boundaries. Your actions serve as a powerful example for them to follow as they navigate their own paths in life.

We all have our ways of dealing with life's chaos. Some may choose to ignore it, pretending it doesn't exist. However, ignoring the chaos does not make it disappear; it lingers like a cloud over our heads, adding to our stress and overwhelm. On the other hand, fighting against the chaos is not a winning strategy either. Believing that we can outperform or organize every aspect of our lives worsens our stress and leaves us feeling even more out of control.

Similarly, wallowing in misery and resorting to unhealthy coping mechanisms, such as substance use, may provide temporary relief, but they fail to address the underlying issues that need to be addressed. Using alcohol or drugs as a means of escape is not a sustainable solution. The pain and problems will persist even after the numbing effects wear off, leaving us to face reality once again.

We may try to silence or hide the difficult parts of our lives, seeking distractions to avoid facing them. However, this approach only leads to issues piling up and can become an unhealthy crutch on which we overly rely. Imagine it like a real broken bone; a crutch is essential in the immediate aftermath of the injury to help us move around. But it's crucial to use it for a short period and then gradually regain strength to walk on our own.

These challenges we encounter in life are like tests that help us build the strength needed to handle any situation. Just as school tests keep us engaged and force us to learn to avoid failure, life's struggles and stressors push us to grow and learn about our capabilities. Instead of numbing ourselves to avoid difficulties, facing challenges and dealing with them head on produce better long-term results.

We need to develop better habits to handle stress, as turning to substances like alcohol or pills might provide temporary relief but come at a high cost. As mentioned in chapter 2, instead of seeking quick escapes, it's important to confront life's challenges and emotions head-on. Building healthier coping strategies and facing the chaos with resilience will lead to long-term solutions and personal growth.

Remember, it's okay to stumble and fall; what matters is that we learn, grow, and continue moving forward with strength and determination. Embrace life's unpredictability and find ways to navigate through the chaos, knowing that you have the power to face whatever comes your way.

Choosing to ignore, fight, or wallow in our problems can create a false sense of control. While we do have some influence over certain aspects of our lives, we cannot control the actions of others or the unpredictable nature of life events.

Feeling out of control might tempt us to seek superficial ways to regain control, such as suppressing or stuffing our emotions, but this only adds to our overall stress. There are healthier ways to manage stress than suppressing or trying to minimize chaos. Personally, I've found that embracing the chaos without feeling the need to fix everything immediately helps me navigate through my stressors. It's okay to sit with the challenges, take a moment to rest if necessary, and then prioritize where to direct your energy and attention.

Instead of resorting to escape or numbing tactics, it is important to confront your challenges head-on and learn to manage stress in healthier ways. By doing so, you empower yourself to navigate the complexities of life with confidence and courage. Through facing your challenges directly, you will grow stronger, gain wisdom, and develop the inner strength needed to thrive in the face of adversity.

While it is true that some people might prioritize having a spotless house due to anxiety or personal preferences, it is important to *question whether it is truly necessary for it to be cleaned all the time.*

Personally, having a perfectly tidy house is not at the top of my priority list. Instead, I choose to allocate my resources towards saving money and invest in a cleaning service, which removes my sole responsibility of maintaining the entire house. Delegating cleaning tasks to other family members also helps in maintaining a clean home without feeling overwhelmed. Breaking up chores into manageable steps and setting a timer to create an end-point prevents me from feeling overwhelmed by the entire workload all at once.

To manage the cleaning tasks effectively, I adopt a strategy of dividing the house into sections, such as the living room and kitchen, followed by the bathroom and bedroom, and so on. I approach each section in focused bursts, whether it takes hours or even days, allowing myself to concentrate on one section at a time. As a reward for completing each section, I indulge in enjoyable activities like watching my favorite show or treating myself to a delicious lunch. Adding an uplifting soundtrack by playing music and turning up the stereo also adds a fun and energetic touch to the cleaning process. By breaking down the tasks, incorporating rewards, and infusing some enjoyment into the process, I find that cleaning becomes more manageable and even enjoyable. By finding a balance that works for me, I can maintain a clean and comfortable living environment without sacrificing my overall well-being and peace of mind.

I have found that this approach has been effective for my daughter as well. I assign her specific tasks, and upon completion, she earns rewards such as going out to lunch or enjoying a trip to the movies. She responds positively to this method of completing her chores, since it provides motivation and a sense of accomplishment. Additionally, it is important for us to be kind to ourselves and avoid self-criticism when mistakes or forgotten tasks occur. Finding humor in challenging situations and remembering to take deep breaths help us maintain a positive perspective and handle stress in healthier ways. By embracing a compassionate and lighthearted approach, we create an environment that promotes growth, resilience, and a more enjoyable experience in managing our responsibilities.

Remember, your mistakes are not catastrophic. Making a mistake or forgetting something will not cause the ground to open up and swallow you whole. When you feel overwhelmed, take a break and prioritize self-care. Simply take a moment to recharge yourself by relaxing or indulging in a nice cup of tea with a piece of chocolate. Taking these brief pauses will help you tackle the chaos when you have to dive back into it.

In your efforts to deal with the chaos and unpredictability of life, be sure to surround yourself with supportive and non-judgmental people. Avoid the so-called "mommy shamers" who constantly try to one-up each other. It's baffling why some people engage in such behavior. Instead, be open about your struggles and avoid putting others down. Let's promote a more compassionate and understanding world. Connect with people you can be honest with and share your challenges with them. You'll be surprised to find that so many others are also going through similar experiences.

Don't hesitate to ask for help!

It's important to acknowledge that even if you excel in certain areas, you don't have to shoulder the burden of doing everything by yourself. Embracing different perspectives and approaches to tasks can be very valuable. Trust me, there's more than one way to effectively accomplish a task. I remember a time when I found myself annoyed with my daughter's method of washing dishes. However, I realized the importance of allowing her to continue and improve at her own pace. It's necessary to resist the urge to take over tasks from others, as doing so can create conflict and discourage them from offering their help in the future. By encouraging collaboration and respecting different approaches, you can build stronger relationships and create a supportive community where everyone feels valued and motivated to contribute.

Stop pressuring yourself to do it all.

It is also important to prioritize what truly matters to you, instead of giving in to the expectations and opinions of others. Let go of judgmental opinions from friends, family, and neighbors, and instead, focus on what brings you joy and satisfaction in life.

Once you have identified your priorities, direct your attention towards what genuinely matters to you. Begin by prioritizing self-care and build on it. Engage in activities that nourish your mental and physical wellbeing, such as exercising, spending time with friends, resting, praying, and practicing meditation. These practices serve as powerful tools to build inner strength, enabling you to face any challenges that may arise with resilience and confidence. By staying true to yourself and investing in activities that align with your values and bring you joy, you create a solid foundation for a fulfilling and balanced life.

By acknowledging and nurturing your inner strength, you will find yourself less inclined to choose the path of least resistance in challenging situations. Building this strength is not a journey without effort, but it is undeniably worthwhile. To truly become the person you are meant to be, you must be willing to deconstruct certain aspects of yourself before you can rebuild and grow. While this process may be demanding and time-consuming, persevering through it will ultimately guide you towards becoming the person you were meant to be.

This process of embracing chaos reminds me of the incredible transformation a caterpillar undergoes to become a butterfly. Have you ever wondered what it takes for a butterfly to come into being?

The incredible transformation that a caterpillar undergoes, including its complete dissolution to embrace change, never fails to amaze me. Caterpillars are already remarkable and beautiful creatures in their own way, but if they were content with remaining as they are, they would never realize their full potential. Just imagine if a caterpillar decided that the journey of becoming a butterfly was too overwhelming and not worth it. In making that choice, it would miss out on discovering its true beauty and the freedom to soar through the skies. Similarly, we must choose to embrace our own transformations and not fear the process. Like the caterpillar, you too have the capacity to undergo remarkable growth and emerge as something even more beautiful and extraordinary.

The Power Of Self Talk

If you keep believing what you've been believing,
you'll keep achieving what you've been achieving

~ Source Unknown

Studies have discovered that the average person generates as many as 60,000 thoughts per day. Sadly, a significant portion of these thoughts tend to be negative—statements like *"I'll never lose weight,"* *"Nothing I do makes a difference,"* *"I'm inadequate,"* etc. This type of language reflects a mindset of victimhood, which can perpetuate a sense of being a victim.

To create a sense of empowerment when dealing with anxiety, it is important to adopt a mindset of resilience and success when talking to yourself. Use affirmations such as *"I am a winner,"* *"I can discover solutions to this challenge,"* and *"I have the intelligence to navigate this situation."*

Think of your subconscious mind as the crew on a ship, with you as the captain responsible for giving directions. The crew takes your orders very literally and lacks a sense of humor. So, when you make statements like "I can't attend that event; everyone will judge me," your subconscious crew responds by saying, "Understood. Stay home." However, if you communicate, "I can go for a little while. If I feel anxious, I'll find a way to leave gracefully," your crew will work towards making that outcome possible. This highlights the power of your subconscious mind and emphasizes the importance of being mindful and attentive to both your spoken and internal dialogues.

Unfortunately, many individuals are unaware of the negative self-talk they frequently engage in. However, when

142

you do catch yourself in the act of negative and self-defeating self-talk, it is important to pause and say "cancel, cancel!" This communicates to your subconscious mind (your crew) that you are revoking the previous order. In its place, substitute the negative statement with a positive alternative. For example, if you catch yourself saying, "I'm a terrible public speaker," immediately counteract it with "Cancel, cancel! I may not be a good public speaker *yet*, but I am committed to practicing and learning until I master the art." This practice effectively reshapes your thought patterns towards positivity and self confidence. By consciously redirecting your self-talk in this way, you can transform your mindset and create a more optimistic and confident outlook on yourself and your abilities.

Try this exercise and start challenging your negative self-talk:

- For *"Bad things will happen if I'm not perfect"* you can add "Cancel, cancel" and then say *"I don't need to be perfect for all to be well"*
- For *"No one will like the real me"* add "Cancel, cancel" and then say *"For others to like the real me, I have to like the real me, and the real me is GREAT!"*
- For *"I have nothing to offer if I'm imperfect"* add "Cancel, cancel" and then say *"The world needs to see REAL, and people will relate better to me because I'm not perfect or fake"*.
- For *"I need to be the perfect wife, husband, daughter, son, employee, or mother/father in order to be loved or lovable"* add "Cancel, cancel" and then say *"I don't need to be perfect, I just need to be good enough"*

Feel free to include your personal instances of negative self-talk into the mix. It's equally important to introduce affirmations into the equation.

"I _____" add
"Cancel, cancel" and then say
" _____ "

"I _____" add
"Cancel, cancel" and then say
" _____ "

Being vigilant about your subconscious mind is important for several reasons, including its direct impact on your anxiety levels and sleep quality. The way you talk to yourself has a profound influence on your overall well-being. Your body responds to your self-talk, and even a small change in how you communicate with yourself can result in significant positive changes in your life. By being mindful of your self-talk and making a conscious effort to create positive and empowering inner dialogue, you can effectively reduce anxiety and improve your sleep patterns. This awareness and intentional shift in self-talk can lead to remarkable improvements in your overall mental and physical well-being.

The groundbreaking work of Dr. Masaru Emoto, a Japanese scientist, has revolutionized our understanding of how our thoughts and intentions influence our existence.

As one of the most renowned water researchers in the world, Dr. Emoto spent over 20 years studying the scientific evidence of how the molecular structure in water transforms when exposed to human words, thoughts, sounds, and intentions.

Dr. Emoto's remarkable life's work is documented in the renowned New York Times Bestseller, "The Hidden Messages in Water." Within this book, Dr. Emoto presents compelling evidence that demonstrates how water responds to loving and compassionate human intentions, resulting in the formation of beautiful and harmonious molecular structures. On the other hand, when water is exposed to fearful and angry human intentions, it forms disconnected, disfigured, and what can be described as "unpleasant" physical molecular formations.

Utilizing Magnetic Resonance Analysis technology and high-speed photography, Dr. Emoto's research provides extraordinary insights into the deep interconnection between our thoughts and the physical body. His work emphasizes the significance of cultivating positive intentions and practicing compassionate self-talk to foster a more balanced and fulfilling life. Through his findings, we gain a greater understanding of the profound impact our thoughts and intentions can have on the world around us. Dr. Emoto's research serves as a powerful reminder of the transformative potential that lies within our own minds and the importance of nurturing positivity and compassion in our daily lives.

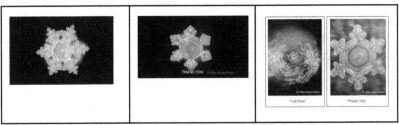

Google Images Dr. Emoto Water Crystals

In a groundbreaking study, Dr. Emoto made a remarkable discovery regarding the profound influence of words, *even when written on paper*, on the crystallization of water molecules. His research revealed that the crystallization patterns of water changed when exposed to negative words over a specific time period. Since then, other researchers have replicated this study using plants and bacteria, further highlighting the powerful impact that words can have on various living entities.

Given that water makes up approximately 70% of our bodies, it is truly remarkable to imagine the potential impact of experiencing negativity on a daily or even hourly basis. I encourage you to shift your attention towards challenging your automatic negative self-talk and being more mindful with your inner dialogue. The vocabulary we habitually use, especially when it leans towards negativity, can be draining and depleting. It is important to remember that you are constantly listening to yourself, so it is very important to be mindful and intentional with the words you choose. By consciously selecting positive and empowering language, you can support your well-being and create a more uplifting and fulfilling inner dialogue.

A helpful strategy is to reflect on how you speak to yourself and compare it to how you would talk to a sweet, innocent child. You wouldn't use hurtful or harsh language with a child, so why treat yourself any differently?

Let's imagine your anxiety as a toddler, experiencing intense emotions due to stress, uncertainty, and a lack of control over situations. Now, think about that same toddler trying to learn coloring or writing the alphabet. Would yelling, making fun, or name-calling encourage the toddler to complete the task with enthusiasm? Most likely not. We know that when children and adults feel good and loved, they tend to behave better. It's a fact. When dealing with a tantruming toddler, we understand that reacting with our own meltdown would only worsen the situation. Instead, we recognize the importance of responding with calmness and seeking to understand what the toddler needs. When faced with a toddler's needs, we naturally consider whether they're hungry, tired, in need of a diaper change, a hug, or simply someone to talk to in a soothing and positive manner.

Now, let's apply this same approach to ourselves by replacing negative self-talk with self-compassion. Just as we would speak gently and lovingly to a cute, helpless toddler learning a new task, we must adopt the same compassionate approach when speaking to ourselves. When faced with anxiety, approaching it with kindness, compassion, and a desire to understand its underlying needs can help create a more supportive and nurturing environment for ourselves.

We must change the language we use in our self-talk. Just as negative self-talk can be damaging and destructive for a toddler, it can have a similar impact on us. It is important to be mindful of these negative thoughts as they arise and challenge them. Practicing self-love means treating ourselves with kindness and accepting our imperfections.

Recognizing the impact of self-talk on your mood and anxiety is important, which is why you must take control of this internal dialogue. By adopting a kind and compassionate tone when speaking to yourself, you can nurture a more positive mindset. Remember, the way you speak to yourself matters, and by choosing uplifting and gentle words, you can build a healthier and more empowering relationship with yourself.

Embracing the idea that we don't need to be perfect and letting go of the expectation for others to be perfect is also necessary. Self-criticism is neither a healthy nor an effective way to encourage personal growth or improve our behavior. Instead, let us focus on self-compassion, understanding that we are all works in progress and that embracing our imperfections is part of our journey towards growth and self-acceptance. Remember, treating ourselves with the same compassion and care we would offer to a child learning something new can have a profound impact on our self-esteem and overall happiness.

Imagine if someone else subjected you to constant criticism on a daily basis. You would rightfully consider that as abuse. So, why would you willingly treat yourself in such a harsh manner? It is very important to be gentle with yourself, to forgive your mistakes, and to accept yourself for who you are. This approach will lead to healing and personal growth. Be sure to challenge those negative thoughts that come up and replace them with positive affirmations that nurture a healthier and more successful version of yourself. Whenever you notice your anxiety flaring up, take a moment to ask yourself what do you truly need in that moment and provide it to yourself with kindness and understanding, without resorting to self-criticism. Remember, you deserve the same compassion and care that you would offer to others.

It is important to be mindful of the impact that our words have on our ability towards achieving our goals. The language we use can either bring us closer to our goal or push us further away. When you catch yourself using negative words, take a moment to pause and consciously replace them with empowering language. By gaining mastery over your self-talk and adopting a more compassionate and empowering internal dialogue, you have the ability to positively influence your mood and reduce anxiety. Remember, the words we choose have the power to shape our mindset and ultimately impact our overall well-being and success.

Use the examples provided below as a helpful guide to modify your self-talk and empower yourself with more positive language. Start by directing your attention to the word "Anxiety." As discussed earlier, defining ourselves solely as anxious or having anxiety can often lead us to focus on the negative aspects and use it as an excuse to avoid exploring the deeper emotions underlying our anxiety. Instead of using the word "Anxiety," you can choose more neutral terms such as "Uneasy," "Discomfort," or "Emotional." These alternative words are easier to handle and do not carry the same negative connotations.

As an example, when experiencing feelings of anxiety, you can reframe your self-talk by saying, "*This situation is making me feel uneasy, and I'm curious to explore why that is.*" It is important to be mindful of how you associate yourself with the word "Anxiety" in phrases like "*My anxiety won't let me do x, y, z.*" This can inadvertently grant anxiety unnecessary power and perpetuate a focus on negative emotions rather than empowering ones. Instead, shift your language to focus on your personal power and growth by saying, "*I am working on managing my response to this situation*" or "*I am learning to navigate through these challenging emotions.*" By choosing empowering language, you reclaim control over your experiences and create a more positive and proactive mindset.

To create emotional distance from your anxiety, you can replace the phrase "My anxiety" with "The anxiety I'm feeling is bothering me." This subtle shift helps you to recognize that anxiety is not an inherent part of your identity, but rather a passing experience. Additionally, incorporating the word "yet" into your negative self-talk can promote a growth mindset. For example, instead of saying, "I don't have a good memory," you can reframe it as "I don't have a good memory...*yet.*" This simple addition acknowledges that your abilities and skills can improve over time with effort and practice.

It is important to be mindful of the words you use to describe yourself or how you present yourself online, such as in social media profile names, email addresses, gaming profiles, or personalized license plates. Avoid using words that

149

do not align with who you aspire to be. Instead, choose more motivational and inspirational descriptors that reflect your personal goals. For instance, instead of using names like "Lymegirl," "cancersurvivor," or "fibromyalgia4ever," consider changing them to names that embody positivity and personal growth.

It is important to remember that you cannot fully embody something while simultaneously distancing yourself from it. To create distance from draining and demeaning vocabulary, it is important to correct yourself immediately when you catch yourself using such language. By consciously choosing uplifting words and quickly correcting negative self-talk, you can transform your internal dialogue and embrace a more empowering mindset. Whenever you notice yourself using negative language, take a moment to rephrase the words, acknowledge them out loud, or even make a lighthearted joke about it. Remember, it is important to be kind to yourself and avoid being mean or harsh, as it will not improve the situation. By being self-compassionate and choosing positive language, you can create a more supportive and nurturing inner dialogue.

One of the most powerful techniques to nurture a strong sense of worthiness and self-confidence is through the consistent repetition of positive statements. By integrating these affirmations into your thought process, you can effectively replace any negative beliefs that may have influenced your subconscious mind over time. To start, create a list of ten to twenty statements that reinforce your belief in your own worth and your ability to shape the life you envision for yourself.

Here are several affirmation examples:

- I am worthy of love, success, and happiness.
- I believe in my abilities and trust in my potential.
- I am confident in my unique strengths and talents.
- I embrace challenges as opportunities for growth and learning.
- I am deserving of all the good things that come into my life.
- I am resilient and capable of overcoming any obstacles.
- I am grateful for the abundance and opportunities that surround me.
- I radiate positivity and attract positive experiences.
- I am in control of my thoughts, emotions, and actions.
- I am enough, just as I am, and I embrace my imperfections.

By consistently repeating these affirmations, you will gradually transform your internal beliefs, strengthening your sense of self-worth and enhancing your self-confidence.

My Powerful Lesson In Letting Go!

Have you ever experienced that moment of panic when you find yourself sinking in a pool? I vividly remember a similar situation from my high school days when someone threw me into a pool, and my lack of swimming skills made me feel like I was drowning.

In my panic, it took me a while to become aware of my surroundings and hear people urging me to simply stand up. To my surprise, I realized I was in the shallow end of the pool, and I could have easily stood up or even sat in the water. If I had been calm, I could have just floated, even in the deep end. It was a valuable lesson in surrendering to a difficult situation. By accepting it for what it was and allowing it to unfold, I could have handled it much better than if I had fought, controlled, and resisted it.

The same principle applies to other challenging situations in life. When we surrender and flow with them, rather than resisting and fighting, we can move past them much faster. It's like learning to float in the pool—it requires total surrender.

Surrendering doesn't mean giving up; it means letting go of the need to control everything. Trusting that everything will be okay, no matter what, creates a true and lasting sense of security. Attempting to control and manipulate every aspect of our lives may offer temporary relief, but true security comes from understanding that we will be okay regardless of external circumstances.

Embracing the flow of life opens up exciting opportunities where control won't be necessary. So, let go of the need to control it all, embrace the flow, and trust that life will unfold in ways that will lead you to growth and fulfillment.

Getting To The Root Of Fear

Whenever you experience fear, it's so important that you realize you weren't born with that fear. In fact, the only fears psychologists and neurologists believe we're naturally wired with are the *fear of falling* and *the fear of loud noises*—both being a protective mechanism. Every other fear you and I possess has been learned, and accumulated from experiences or influences in our lives.

As a child, I was inherently and genetically anxious and overly sensitive. However, when I immigrated to the United States after escaping a war-torn environment, while adapting to a new culture, learning a new language, and navigating new surroundings, my fears intensified, morphing into severe social anxiety that took years to overcome.

As mentioned previously, I've since learned effective techniques that have helped me transform my fears. This doesn't mean that all of my fears will completely vanish from my life. Personally, I still experience fear and moments of apprehension, but I've learned how to channel that fear into motivation, converting it into a driving force that propels me forward instead of holding me back.

I encourage you to also view fear as an ally and protector, which you can harness for your benefit instead of allowing it to dominate or intimidate you. So, while I still experience fear, I'm now able to channel that energy into taking inspired actions.

Remember, fear isn't your enemy or a problem in itself. Fear functions as an automatic circuit that triggers any thought associated with past or *imagined* experiences stored in your memory, which may potentially cause you harm or distress in some way. This circuit acts as an early-warning system, an alarm bell designed for your survival and protection.

So fear isn't something to be afraid of! In fact, fear can be your greatest ally.

Similar to anxiety, fear serves as an essential early warning system, protecting our safety and overall well-being. It plays a pivotal role in our survival, alerting us to potential dangers and enabling us to maintain a sense of security. Instead of allowing fear to intimidate us, it is important to recognize and appreciate its significance.

Manage Fear at The Subconscious Level

When your brain's fear response activates, remember this: the emotional trigger we call fear is actually being triggered in your subconscious mind.

The amygdala, which is the emotional center of your brain, plays a crucial role in regulating your emotions. When this circuit is activated, it prompts the retrieval of memories stored in your memory bank, including those from your past experiences, including childhood. This includes *any real or imagined incidents* stored in your memory bank—connected to instances where you were hurt physically, mentally, emotionally, or even financially. The level of importance you assign to any experience quickly triggers the emotional center of your brain.

When you perceive something as non-threatening and capable of bringing pleasure, you will naturally be motivated to take action. This prompts your brain to release feel-good chemicals such as serotonin, dopamine, and oxytocin. These chemicals are often associated with feelings of excitement and joy, encouraging you to dive into the experience.

However, if there's a negative association rooted in your subconscious, you will be *less likely* to take action. If there's a possibility of pain, loss, or discomfort, you'll slam on the brakes and refuse to take action.

This neurochemistry of fear acts as an *effect,* causing you to be reluctant to take action. This can also translate into a lack of motivation, often perceived as laziness or procrastination. Understanding the root causes of your procrastination is the key to overcoming it. Learn to understand the triggers and reasons for your procrastination, as well as the barriers that prevent you from completing tasks. Redirect your attention from the outcome (effect), which is procrastination, to the underlying cause, which could include avoidance of pain, sadness, or uncertainty.

When it comes to gaining long-term control over fear and anxiety, it is important to understand the underlying cause in order to avoid self-sabotage and the irrational belief that *change is beyond your capabilities.* Understanding the cause empowers you to take action and experience some level of success. However, without understanding the cause, you may unintentionally limit your progress (as I did when challenged by the ropes course).

Understanding the underlying cause will help you realize that fear holding you back is NOT YOUR FAULT!

When your subconscious mind receives information related to your desired actions but detects a link to past experiences of pain or discomfort, it activates the fear circuit. As a result, *your motivation circuit is deactivated,* causing your brain's motor cortex to essentially hit the brakes even when you are trying to move forward. In practical terms, this can look like you being eager to set goals, but continuing to feel stuck, without understanding the reasons why progress is not being made or why your potential is not being realized.

Without the understanding of how to reshape or retrain your mind, you may become trapped and increasingly frustrated by your perceived limitations. In certain cases, this situation can escalate to feelings of depression, self-loathing, or in extreme cases, even thoughts of suicide. To live a life of empowerment, it is necessary to train your mind and address your fears at the <u>subconscious</u> level. The steps below are a good place to start.

Step 1: "Calm Your Nervous System"
To begin, calm your nervous system by taking 3-4 deep breaths. Focus on inhaling deeply through your diaphragm rather than your chest. Inhale through your nose and exhale slowly through your mouth, as if blowing through a straw. This practice helps deactivate the fear or stress response center in your brain and prevents the amygdala from triggering the stress circuit. As a result, the sympathetic nervous system, responsible for fight, flight, or freeze reactions, is soothed. By taking these deep breaths, you will enter a state of calm and relaxed alpha brain wave activity. This is the state that will enhance your ability to retain information.

Step 2: "Define Your Outcome"
In your journal, take a moment to write down a specific outcome that you need or want to achieve today. Identify a goal that will bring meaning to your life. Additionally, you can explore your top 10 fears that may be sabotaging your progress towards achieving your goals. Select 2-3 of the most significant fears and explore their origins. Reflect on when and where these fears first started.

Step 3: Embrace Curiosity and Playfulness!
Approach this exercise with curiosity and a playful mindset. Engage your curiosity and explore like a child would. When you're curious and enjoying the process, your brain's neuroplasticity activates, and creates new connections and pathways.

Start by imagining the possibilities as if you were FREE from your fears. Consider where you could be today and how your life might be different with a clearer understanding or elimination of your fears. Reflect on the actions you could take if fear no longer held you back.

- What achievement becomes possible when fear stops controlling you?
- Would you have a thriving business or be in a happier relationship without fear as an obstacle?

Fear truly undermines our dreams. Countless individuals have unfulfilled goals and dreams because of fear. As mentioned earlier, I made a conscious decision to confront and conquer as many fears as I could before reaching the age of 20, freeing myself from the grip of fear. To overcome social anxiety, I pushed myself outside of my comfort zone and engaged in activities that I found intimidating. By facing these challenges head-on, I was able to overcome my social anxiety and grow as an individual. The crucial message here is that "*To succeed in life, you must triumph over fear.*" This leads to freedom without the subconscious barriers.

Courage is the Antidote to Fear. Courage and bravery counter fear. Yet, to embody these qualities, you must explore the unconscious realm of fear. Recognize your fears while remaining willing to act DESPITE them. Remember that fear is an effect, ***not the cause***, so eliminating fear itself wouldn't make sense. To change the *effect* of fear, you have to look for the cause.

Fear operates on a subconscious level, functioning automatically. It is important to address the underlying causes of your fear, empowering you to regain control of your life.

There are many ways fear gets triggered.

- Your irrational thoughts and beliefs can be a trigger for your fear response.
- Your lack of knowledge or lack of specific skills can also activate your fears.
- The absence of accurate information will activate your fear.

By addressing these factors, we can work towards overcoming fear and creating opportunities for personal growth.

Since fear is an *AUTOMATIC* and subconscious response, it's logical that deeply ingrained beliefs or experiences related to anything that could potentially cause you physical, emotional, mental, or financial harm would trigger this reaction, resulting in the EFFECT of fear.

Fear is the outcome—the underlying and subconscious beliefs are the cause.

The following process will help you address the CAUSE of your fear.

Recognize and Raise Awareness of Fear

The first step to understanding the underlying cause of your fear is to acknowledge and identify the *specific* fear that is holding you back. Similar to the overall foundation of the AIM Program, *awareness* plays a vital role in this process. When you are aware of your fears, you gain the ability to respond effectively. On the other hand, when fear consumes you, it can leave you feeling paralyzed and incapable of taking action. By creating awareness and understanding, you can begin to break free from the grip of fear and regain your ability to move forward.

In your journal jot down all the fears that come to mind during this step.

Awareness empowers choice,
and choice grants you the freedom you want.

Remember, all forms of freedom stem from awareness and choice—be it financial freedom, emotional freedom, or the freedom of time.

Reframing

The second step has to do with the triggers linked to those fears. Whenever we experience fear, it's often tied to memories of what we've seen, heard, read, or undergone during childhood or even in adulthood. These fears, for the most part, activate negative memories from our past.

Our fears set off a pattern either from the memory bank in our subconscious minds or, occasionally, from our external world. For instance, before 2020, COVID-19 wasn't in our awareness, but the shutdown and the ensuing concerns surrounding the virus awakened our fear of death and dying in our subconscious.

We're genetically programmed to instinctively stop in the face of any real or IMAGINED danger or pain and quickly move away from it. Our wiring is meant to protect us from anything that could potentially cause harm or danger in any form. When the fear center of our brain activates, our body initiates a chemical response, releasing stress hormones like cortisol and norepinephrine, and increasing our adrenaline levels.

In response to this chemical surge, our heart rate accelerates, digestion slows down, and blood flow is affected—all to ready us for a quick exit from the danger zone. This entire fight or flight sequence happens in a split second if we encounter an external threat, but the same reaction also occurs with internal or *imagined* thoughts! Facing an actual snake or even the simple *thought* of a snake has the potential to create the same reaction.

Think about panic attacks. For many individuals, it's a THOUGHT that triggers panic, often escalating into a full-blown attack.

In the case of many panic sufferers, the mere thought of having an attack precipitates one. If you don't *IDENTIFY THIS PATTERN*, challenge it, reframe it, or rescript it, it will persistently recur!

You are engaged in a continuous battle between the part of your brain striving to protect you from real or imagined threats and the rational part of your brain wanting more from life. This rational part of your brain acknowledges that irrational fears lack logic, but your body reacts to them regardless. The inner critic inside your brain is also activated, fueling negative self-talk that claims you are not good enough or smart enough.

Write this down in your journal and repeat it as often as you need to activate your rational brain.

"The meaning I attribute to anything, whether at a conscious or subconscious level, will ultimately determine my emotions and behaviors"

Your brain is a master at assigning meaning, so it's possible that you can DELIBERATELY be more in control and give things meaning that will cause you to be INSPIRED and TAKE ACTION instead of being FEARFUL, unmotivated, and procrastinate.

By consciously choosing empowering meanings, you can transform your mindset and propel yourself towards success. For example, let's say you encounter a setback in your business. Instead of interpreting it as a failure, you can choose to see it as a valuable learning experience that will ultimately lead to growth and improvement. This shift in perspective can inspire you to analyze what went wrong, make necessary adjustments, and take action towards achieving your goals.

Similarly, when faced with a challenging task, you can choose to view it as an opportunity to showcase your skills and capabilities. By assigning a meaning of excitement and personal growth to the task, you'll be more motivated to tackle it head-on and give it your best effort.

The meanings we've assigned to past experiences, whether through personal encounters, parental influence, educational experiences, or even media exposure, are the root of these automatic fears. Remember, the meanings we assign to situations have a profound impact on our emotions and actions. By consciously choosing empowering meanings, you can build a mindset that fuels inspiration, action, and ultimately, success.

Now shift from unwanted fear to freedom and success by writing in your journal
"I cannot change my fear by just thinking about changing my fear"

Changing your fear isn't a matter of just thinking about changing it. At its core, fear can exist either at a conscious or subconscious level, and just thinking about changing it won't change the fear itself.

Thinking about changing fear is similar to *just thinking about* changing the software on your computer and then wondering why the software isn't changing. To change the software in a computer, we must *reprogram* and alter the software INSIDE the computer. The same principle applies to our fears. We must address the root cause of fear and reprogram it at the subconscious level.

When you say you have a conscious fear of failure, that means that you are aware of that fear. But what about the subconscious fears that have been reinforced over the course of your life? What about those hidden beliefs that are holding you back? I cannot emphasize enough that "fear is a silent killer," especially at the subconscious level. These kinds of fears often manifest as anxiety or chronic stress, acting like an invisible force that holds you back, and you can't understand why it consistently shows up when you least expect it. This is often why so many individuals find themselves stuck and unable to succeed in their lives.

When fear controls you, even though it resides within you, it reinforces your self-perception as a fearful and disempowered person who either doesn't know how to overcome these fears or knows how but refuses to act. This cycle can lower your self-esteem and self-worth, even if you're aware and determined to break free.

For example, those who fear public speaking aren't truly afraid of speaking in public. Instead, they fear being embarrassed, ridiculed, or judged if they make mistakes or fail to deliver perfectly.

Their true fear centers on *the potential consequences of speaking*, based on the meaning they assign to public speaking. This meaning is the cause, and change occurs at the meaning level.

So if your fear of public speaking is rooted in self-image or based on low self-esteem, working on those areas *can be more effective* than just focusing on the fear itself. You can apply this approach to any type of fear you're struggling with.

Unchecked, these subconscious fears can not only undermine your dreams but also affect your relationships, finances, health, time, and energy. These fears can limit your chances of success. If left unaddressed, you'll constantly feel stuck and frustrated with yourself. Feeding your fears and allowing them to control you fuels more failure and solidifies a disempowered identity.

Whenever you're trapped in a comfort zone, repeatedly following the same pattern, chances are that fear is being triggered. It might be fear of embarrassment, fear of ridicule or judgment, or fear of inadequacy.

The space between your current state and your goals determines your success in achieving those goals. Accomplishing your goals often lies **beyond your comfort zone**.

Where Growth Happens

By *expanding* your comfort zone, you can achieve your goals. Initially stepping out of your comfort zone might trigger fear and panic. However, if you *gradually* widen that zone, much like a toddler walking away from their mother, fear and anxiety won't stop you. For example, a toddler's first steps away from their mother might be just a few feet, with frequent glances backward. Over time, these steps lengthen until the toddler plays confidently with friends. Now, picture suddenly removing the toddler far from their mother. Panic would surely set in, but gently expanding the comfort zone doesn't have the same impact.

The best way to expand your comfort zone is by taking consistent steps outside of what feels familiar and safe. Embracing new experiences, challenges, and pushing yourself slightly beyond your current boundaries gradually builds confidence and adaptability, leading to personal growth and a broader sense of comfort in new situations.

Recognizing your bravery and achievements plays a vital role in boosting your self-esteem. It sets the stage for personal growth and fulfillment, and courage is a quality that we all aspire to have more of. If you desire to overcome fear and experience true freedom, it's essential to step outside your comfort zone and put an end to self-sabotage.Recognizing your bravery and achievements plays a vital role in boosting your self-esteem. It sets the stage for personal growth and fulfillment, and courage is a quality that we all aspire to have more of. If you desire to overcome fear and experience true freedom, it's essential to step outside your comfort zone and put an end to self-sabotage.

For example, if you are afraid of taking a new job and choosing to stay with the familiar while avoiding the unknown, you are reinforcing your fear circuit. The goal here is to avoid strengthening the fear pathway. If speaking on stage will advance your career, focus on expanding your comfort zone, build courage, and address the root cause of your fear, instead of just focusing on the fear itself.

Even if you felt disempowered due to childhood experiences like bullying, you can change this as an adult by acknowledging that you're not that scared child anymore. Now, as an adult, you might seek new opportunities, which will require courage despite your brain flashing danger signals.

Transitioning from unwanted paralyzing fear to freedom and success involves the same mental training exercises we use to manage our anxiety in order to gain more control over our brain. So, when you procrastinate or feel self-doubt, feel stressed, or stuck in self-sabotaging behaviors, pause and calm your overactive brain with deep breaths. Inhale deeply through your nose, then exhale slowly through your mouth, as if blowing through a straw.

Taking a moment to pause and breathe allows you to enter a state of awareness, enabling you to identify disempowering negative thoughts. You can't transform these thoughts without first being aware of them. When you're calm and relaxed, with the fear center of your brain deactivated and the calm response circuit activated, you can appropriately respond to these thoughts.

Recognizing these negative thoughts, without any judgment, shame, blame, or guilt, places you in a state of pure awareness. In this calm state, you can reframe your beliefs, perceptions, and the meanings you attach to triggers that automatically set off your fear center.

For instance, if you hold the belief that being on stage might lead to embarrassment, consider reframing it as, "If I go on stage and make mistakes, I'll learn and improve, enhancing my communication skills." When I start to feel fear and anxiety rise inside, I quietly tell myself "When I'm nervous, be of service". I've been using this strategy frequently during my own live presentations.

When you engage in negative "What if..." thinking, or imagining worst case scenarios, you activate the fight, flight, or freeze response. But, you also have the ability to rewrite that script, changing the trajectory toward a positive direction. You can revisit that script, giving it an alternative meaning that aligns best with your desired outcome.

When you change the meaning,
you also change the feeling associated with it.

By changing "What if I embarrass myself on stage?" to "What if I learn and grow from this experience?" we evoke a different emotional response. This simple action, while in a calm state, consciously and subconsciously reshapes our neural pathways. Dr. Wayne Dyer remarked, "When you change the way you look at things, the things you look at change." When you change a negative "what if" into a positive one, you are actively assessing and *reframing* the patterns in your brain. By consistently practicing this mindset shift on a daily basis for 30, 60, or even 90 days, you take control of your thoughts and empower yourself.

It's said that it takes 30 to 60 days to reprogram your subconscious mind through *consistent repetition of positive affirmations* spoken *in the present tense*. Even in the face of fear, consistently affirming "I am calm and at peace in the presence of x, y, or z" (e.g. "I am calm in the presence of a snake") will gradually convince your brain and result in a calm response when confronted with the fear-inducing stimulus (snake).

No matter what you fear, consistently associating a state of calm with the stimuli that triggers your fear will condition your brain to maintain a sense of calm. This process requires *daily and consistent repetition* for a minimum of 30 days. By reframing the old fear-based script, you become ready to let go of the negative or fear-based thoughts that once held you back. Consciously and deliberately engaging in this practice alters the neural pathways in your brain, transforming your focus and motivation.

Retraining Your Mind

To eliminate these intrusive thoughts, you can enter a state of calm by *inhaling* positivity, peace, or joy, and *exhaling* the negative thoughts you wish to release, such as stress, fear, anger, or frustration. For example, you can inhale a sense of calm and exhale the fear of failure. Breathe out anything that no longer serves you. Repeat this process as often as necessary, maintaining a calm state of mind. By practicing this breathing and letting go exercise, you clear the way for *retraining* your brain, forming new habits that revolve around the actions necessary to achieve your goals. Affirmations, mindfulness practices, and guided meditations all play a significant role in the process of retraining your brain.

Incorporating these simple exercises into your daily routine can require as little as 10 minutes of your time. If you are unable to dedicate 10 to 15 minutes each day to transform your life, it is important to recognize that complaining about the lack of progress towards your goals or the realization of your desired life is counterproductive. Expecting change without putting in the necessary effort is unrealistic. Once you realize that your thoughts, fears, and stress are just subconscious patterns and that you have the power to reshape these patterns, therefore shifting your perspective and ultimately transforming your life, you will willingly invest the time needed to engage in this transformative process.

When you embrace these actions, you develop a deep sense of empowerment. This allows you to break free from emotional limitations and release yourself from the grip of fear.

Understanding Panic Attacks

It's crucial to remember that every symptom experienced during a panic attack is a natural and *harmless* part of your body's fight or flight response, triggered by your conscious or subconscious fears. These panic symptoms are a direct result of the hormone adrenaline, released by your adrenal glands when you perceive real or even imaginary danger.

If you tend to overestimate danger and consistently predict disastrous and catastrophic outcomes, your anxiety will intensify significantly. For instance, if you tell yourself that you'll be attacked while standing near a policeman on a calm day or on a very busy street with many bystanders, this belief might be unrealistic, as the chances of such events are very low.

This *overestimation of danger* can lead to panic attacks. As your panic escalates, it typically goes through several phases. Unrealistic self-statements (self-talk) keep you in a constant state of alarm. Your body responds with tension, increased heart rate, shortness of breath, and butterflies in your stomach. This chronic state of arousal makes you hypersensitive to any *hint* of possible danger, leading to heightened nerves that can trigger panic even in harmless situations. As a consequence, you may begin to fear the fear itself, anticipating panic attacks and trying to avoid them at all costs, which introduces a new fear.

It's possible to develop a fear not only of violence or criticism but also of the physical symptoms that fear triggers in your body. This fear can lead to resistance and fighting against any unusual bodily sensations. It's important to recognize that these physical sensations are a natural response to fear and anxiety. Ultimately, you become super sensitive to symptoms associated with panic, fearing any emotion or experience that reminds you of panic.

This avoidance can escalate over time, impacting various aspects of your life, such as avoiding going anywhere alone, avoiding work altogether, or avoiding social contact. Remember that adrenaline released during the fight or flight response is metabolized in your system within three minutes, and its effects can dissolve just as quickly. So, if you can stop the catastrophic predictions and redirect your negative self-talk, your panic attack will typically be over entirely within three minutes.

This can be done as simply as interrupting the loop of catastrophic thinking—for example, getting up and getting a drink of water will interrupt and break that loop. The important step to take is to stop and question any catastrophic predictions you find yourself making about your panic symptoms. By challenging and reframing these thoughts, you can break free from the grip of fear and anxiety.

Challenging catastrophic thinking during a panic attack is a necessary skill that can help you regain control over your overwhelming emotions and anxiety. Catastrophic thinking involves assuming the worst possible outcome in a situation, magnifying the negative aspects, and *underestimating your ability to cope*. This thought pattern can intensify panic attacks, making them more distressing. By actively challenging these thoughts, you can break free from the cycle of panic and anxiety.

For instance, consider someone who is experiencing a panic attack while driving. Their catastrophic thought might be, "I'm going to lose control of the car and get into a fatal accident."

To challenge this thought, they could ask themselves:

- **Is this thought based on evidence?** Have I ever lost control of the car in the past? Is there any reason to believe I will now?
- **What is the likelihood of this worst-case scenario happening?** How often do fatal accidents occur due to panic attacks? Am I overestimating the actual risk?
- **What evidence contradicts this catastrophic thought?** I have driven many times without any issues. I've taken safety precautions like maintaining my car and following traffic rules.
- **What's a more balanced perspective?** While I'm feeling anxious, it's unlikely that I'll suddenly lose control. If I do feel overwhelmed, I can pull over safely and take a break.

- **What have I successfully managed before?** I've handled difficult driving situations before without accidents. I have the skills to manage my panic and drive safely.

By challenging these catastrophic thoughts, you can begin to introduce a more rational and balanced perspective. This process helps in reducing the intensity of the panic attack and preventing it from spiraling into a cycle of escalating fear. Practice is key, and over time, you can become more skilled at recognizing and challenging catastrophic thinking, allowing you to manage panic attacks more effectively. If you find yourself resistant to letting go of difficult emotions, take a moment to reflect on why you might be holding onto them.

- What is the emotion serving to protect you from?
- Is there something it's helping you avoid or cope with?

Let's explore an example to illustrate this point: Suppose you experienced a panic attack before a class presentation, and your teacher excused you, allowing you to avoid the situation. In this scenario, you might subconsciously learn that panic attacks can protect you from challenging or uncomfortable situations.

Take some time to use your journal and recall all the details surrounding the onset of your panic attacks. It could be a childhood event or something more recent from last week. Write down these memories and observe how the fear or anxiety is serving to protect you in those situations.

Pay attention to what happened right before the initial onset of panic, what happened during, and what happened afterwards. Using the previous example, your fear of presentations happened before the panic, the teacher excusing you is the result of your panic, which allowed you to avoid the unpleasant situation.

By addressing the root causes and understanding the ways these emotions function as protective mechanisms, you can start to gain insight into your thought patterns and coping strategies. This self-awareness is a crucial step in learning how to release difficult emotions and develop healthier ways of handling challenges. Another effective strategy is to control anxiety-provoking situations in your environment. Surrounding yourself with supportive people, reducing social media usage, and limiting exposure to negative or fear-inducing content in the news can significantly improve your sense of control over your life. By taking these steps to calm your fight or flight response and creating a more supportive environment, you can better manage anxiety and regain a sense of control and peace in your life.

TRY IT...

The next time you experience panic, follow these steps to regain your composure:
- Take three deep breaths, inhaling through your nose and exhaling through your mouth.
- Sit with the feeling of panic and assess its intensity on a scale from 1 to 10, where 1 represents calmness and 10 indicates full-blown panic.

Now ground yourself using your senses:

1. Look around and identify **five different things you can see**, naming each of them. 👀

172

2. Listen carefully for **four things you can hear** in your surroundings. 👂

3. Pay attention to **three things you can smell** in your current environment. 👃

4. Identify **two things you can touch**, focusing on their textures and sensations. 🤚

5. Finally, explore **one thing you can taste**, savoring the flavor to anchor yourself in the present moment. 👄

By following these steps, you can center yourself and find relief from panic's overwhelming grip.

To break the cycle of panic and anxiety, consider engaging in the following activities:

- Take a nice (hot or cold) shower to shift your focus and calm your senses.
- Head to the fridge, grab a cool glass of water, and enjoy drinking it.
- Splash your face with cold water, re-energizing yourself in the process, as you rub your wet hands on the back of your neck to release tension.
- Hum a tune or sing a song, since that can activate your vagus nerve and calm your stress response.
- Go on a nice long walk, allowing nature and movement to calm your stress and anxiety.

By incorporating these actions into your routine, you can disrupt the pattern of panic and anxiety, promoting a sense of calm and well-being.

The Impact Of Sleep On Anxiety

Humans are not sleeping the way nature intended.
The number of sleep bouts,
the duration of sleep, and when sleep occurs
has all been comprehensively distorted by modernity

~Matthew Walker

Sleep plays a vital role in influencing our levels of anxiety. By prioritizing and improving our sleep hygiene, we can effectively manage anxiety and overall stress levels. When stress takes hold, it often interferes with our ability to fall or stay asleep at night. The constant worry and life's challenges can keep our minds active, leading to disrupted sleep patterns and leaving us feeling even more on edge the next day. However, by focusing on improving our sleep habits, we can create a foundation for better mental health and a calmer state of mind.

Studies indicate that more than 40 million Americans suffer from long-term sleep disorders, and even more encounter occasional sleep disruptions. With about 70% of adults facing daily stressors, it's not surprising that individuals, on average, are getting less sleep compared to previous decades.

The relationship between sleep problems and anxiety is bidirectional, with sleep disruptions causing anxiety and anxiety, in turn, affecting sleep quality. Both anxiety and sleep issues can profoundly impact our emotional, mental, and physical well-being.

Managing stress and anxiety effectively involves prioritizing sleep. Sleep's impact on our daily functioning is profound. Even a single weekend of disrupted sleep can throw our sleep cycle off balance. The brain, being a crucial organ, significantly influences our sleep patterns, and healthy sleep plays a vital role in regulating our moods.

Understanding the reasons behind our sleep and the fascinating processes that occur during this restorative state is necessary to fully appreciate its importance. Sleep serves multiple purposes beyond just rest. It plays a vital role in memory organization and learning, allowing our brains to process and consolidate information gathered throughout the day. Additionally, sleep acts as a period of rejuvenation for our cells, enabling them to repair and regenerate. During sleep, growth hormones are released, supporting the development and maintenance of our bones and muscles. Furthermore, sleep is essential for maintaining a healthy immune system, regulating body temperature, and keeping our blood pressure in check. By recognizing the multifaceted benefits of sleep, we can prioritize and optimize our sleep habits for overall well-being and energy.

The link between sleep and health is incredibly powerful, to the extent that sleep deprivation can be more harmful than food deprivation in certain cases. Insufficient sleep not only increases the risk of conditions such as depression, psychosis, stroke, and obesity but has also reached epidemic proportions due to modern lifestyle factors. The prevalence of sleeplessness has been amplified by the widespread use of electricity, television, computers, tablets, and smartphones, which disrupt our natural sleep patterns.

Our sleep cycles consist of several stages, each serving a distinct purpose in promoting the health of our brain and body. Ranging from light sleep to deep sleep, these stages play a vital role in memory consolidation, brain cleansing, and emotional processing. Particularly, the deep sleep stages, specifically stages 3 and 4, are of utmost importance as they facilitate cellular repair and restoration, contributing to overall well-being and rejuvenation. Understanding and valuing the significance of each sleep stage can help us prioritize quality sleep and optimize its benefits for our physical and cognitive health.

Research has uncovered the profound influence of sleep on traumatic memories. Delaying sleep shortly after experiencing a traumatic event may prevent the consolidation of these memories into long-term storage, suggesting the important role sleep plays in processing emotions and experiences.

To promote optimal sleep and effectively manage anxiety, it is essential to prioritize and maintain good sleep hygiene. While power naps and pharmaceutical interventions like antidepressants and sleeping pills may offer temporary relief, they are not sustainable long-term solutions. Instead, by recognizing and honoring the importance of sleep in our lives, we can pave the way for enhanced mental and physical well-being.

When we lack adequate sleep, we deny our bodies the chance to undergo essential repair and recovery processes. Our body's natural rhythm is intricately connected to the rising and setting of the sun. Sleep is influenced by the hormone melatonin, which helps regulate our internal clock on a daily basis. As the sun sets, our production of melatonin begins to increase, reaching its peak around 10 pm and remaining elevated until approximately 2 am. After 2 am, melatonin levels gradually decline, preparing our bodies for waking up and starting a new day. By understanding and aligning with this natural rhythm, we can optimize our sleep patterns and support our overall well-being.

During the peak hours of melatonin production, our bodies enter the deepest stage of sleep, facilitating crucial repair and resetting processes after a day's activities. To maintain optimal melatonin levels, it is important to minimize exposure to artificial lights before bedtime. Blue light, commonly emitted by electronic devices, serves a purpose in keeping us alert during the day but can interfere with melatonin production at night. Ideally, creating a completely dark sleeping environment is essential. However, if some light is necessary, using dim, redder light is less disruptive to our biological clock and can help promote better sleep quality. By being mindful of our light exposure and creating a sleep-friendly environment, we can support the natural sleep-wake cycle and enhance our overall sleep experience.

While sleeping pills and natural supplements like melatonin are often sought after to address decreased melatonin levels, it is important to be cautious. While these supplements may provide temporary relief in certain situations, such as resetting sleep cycles after jet lag or shift changes, they are not recommended for long-term use. It's important to note that melatonin, when taken as a supplement, can potentially disrupt the brain's natural production of the hormone, causing an imbalance of chemicals. Therefore, it is advisable to consult with a healthcare professional before considering the long-term use of such supplements and explore alternative strategies for improving sleep quality and addressing underlying sleep issues.

**Before we continue, it's important to address some significant side effects associated with melatonin usage. It is generally advised to avoid melatonin for individuals under the age of 20 due to potential risks, including impaired liver function, increased seizure activity, and exacerbation of

177

depression symptoms. If you are pregnant or breastfeeding, it is crucial to refrain from using melatonin as well. Additionally, melatonin can interact with certain blood pressure medications, so it is essential to consult with your doctor before considering melatonin if you are currently taking such medications. Prioritizing your health and seeking professional guidance ensures that you make informed decisions regarding the use of melatonin or any other supplements.

**Extended use of melatonin can potentially result in several side effects, such as dizziness, irritability, headaches, daytime sleepiness, mild depression, and stomach cramps. Furthermore, some individuals, including myself, have reported experiencing very vivid dreams while using melatonin. Personally, I tried melatonin once, but the intensity of the dreams was enough to discourage me from using it again. It is important to exercise caution when considering melatonin and to have a discussion with a healthcare professional about any potential risks and side effects before incorporating any new supplement into your routine.

While natural, it's important to acknowledge that even supplements like melatonin can have potential side effects. Therefore, it is important to use melatonin appropriately and for short-term purposes only. Instead of relying solely on supplements, prioritizing healthy sleep habits and creating a conducive sleep environment can be highly effective in maintaining a balanced sleep-wake cycle.

Let's recognize and appreciate the invaluable role that sleep plays in our lives and make it a priority to optimize our sleep habits. By doing so, we can enhance our ability to effectively manage stress and anxiety, ultimately leading to healthier and happier lives.

Try it….

To maintain optimal melatonin levels, the most effective approach is to disconnect from screens and electronics for at least an hour to two hours before bedtime. During this time, engaging in relaxing activities like taking a bath or shower can help lower your body temperature and promote faster sleep onset.

Instead of relying on screens, consider alternative activities such as reading a physical book or magazine, journaling, spending quality time with your partner, practicing yoga or QiGong, or listening to guided meditations to wind down before bed. These activities can help create a peaceful and calming environment, preparing your mind and body for a restful night's sleep.

To address sleep disturbances caused by worries, it can be helpful to practice a **Worry Time Exercise** around 7 pm or at a convenient time during the day. Set aside a specific period to sit in the living room and write down all your concerns in a notebook. This approach allows you to process and release your worries earlier in the day, preventing them from interfering with your relaxation when it's time to sleep. If you find yourself tossing and turning in bed for 45 minutes or longer, it's best to get out of bed and go to the living room. Take a moment to jot down what's keeping you awake, allowing your mind to unload any lingering thoughts and promoting a sense of calm before returning to bed. By implementing these strategies, you can create a healthier sleep environment and improve your chances of achieving a more restful night's sleep.

To train your sleep cycle gradually, it's important to avoid going to the bedroom until the time you typically fall asleep. To adjust your sleep schedule in a gradual manner, aim to go to bed 15 to 30 minutes earlier each night until you reach a reasonable bedtime, such as 10:00 pm. This gradual adjustment helps train your body to adopt a healthier sleep routine over time.

If you feel the need to take daytime naps, it's best to limit them to a maximum of 30 minutes. Longer naps can disrupt your sleep cycle, leaving you feeling groggy and impacting your ability to rest well at night. By implementing these strategies, you can gradually establish a more balanced and consistent sleep pattern for improved overall sleep quality.

Establishing a tranquil sleep environment is necessary for achieving a good night's sleep. Taking control of factors such as light, sound, and temperature in your bedroom can greatly contribute to creating a peaceful atmosphere. Dimming the lights, minimizing noise disturbances, and maintaining a cool temperature can enhance your ability to calm your mind and facilitate easier sleep onset. Incorporating guided meditation or tapping right before bed can also facilitate faster sleep onset. I'll address tapping in more detail in Chapter 4.

By prioritizing these elements, you can optimize your sleep environment and increase the likelihood of experiencing a peaceful and rejuvenating sleep.

Nurturing Gut Bacteria: Unraveling its Influence on Anxiety through Dietary Choices

If there's one thing to know about the human body; it's this: the human body has a ringmaster. This ringmaster controls your digestion, your immunity, your brain, your weight, your health and even your happiness. This ringmaster is the gut

~ **Nancy Mure**

The relationship between food and mood is undeniably strong and influential. The saying "you are what you eat" holds true not only for our physical health but also for our mental well-being. The foods we choose to consume have a profound impact on our mood, emotions, and overall mental state. When we indulge in a diet that is abundant in junk food, including sugary snacks, processed foods, and unhealthy fats, it can lead to fluctuations in blood sugar levels and a rapid rise and fall in energy. While these foods may provide temporary comfort or pleasure, they often lack the essential nutrients necessary to support brain and gut health. It is important to be mindful of the foods we consume and prioritize a balanced diet that nourishes both our body and mind.

By making conscious choices and opting for nutrient-rich foods, we can positively influence our mood and promote overall mental well-being. Consistently consuming excessive amounts of junk food over time can contribute to a range of negative effects on our mental health. These effects may include feelings of lethargy, irritability, increased anxiety, and even symptoms of depression. The lack of essential nutrients and the presence of unhealthy additives in junk food

181

can disrupt the delicate balance of chemicals in our brain, leading to these detrimental emotional and mental states. It is important to be mindful of our dietary choices and prioritize nourishing foods that support our overall well-being, both physically and mentally.

When we nourish our bodies with nutrient-dense foods, we provide them with essential vitamins, minerals, and omega-3 fatty acids that are crucial for supporting both brain and gut health. These nutrients play vital roles in the production of neurotransmitters, such as serotonin and dopamine, which are responsible for regulating our mood and emotions. By incorporating a diverse range of fruits, vegetables, whole grains, lean proteins, and healthy fats into our diet, we can promote a balanced and positive mood. These wholesome foods provide the building blocks necessary for optimal brain function and contribute to overall mental well-being. Making conscious choices to prioritize nutrient-rich options can have a profound impact on our mood and emotional state, allowing us to thrive both physically and mentally.

The gut and brain are intricately linked through a connection known as the gut-brain axis. The health of our gut can have a significant impact on our mood, and conversely, our mood can influence the state of our gut. A diet rich in fiber and probiotics, which can be found in foods like yogurt and fermented foods, can support a healthy gut microbiome. This, in turn, has a positive effect on our mood, reducing feelings of anxiety and stress.

By incorporating balanced meals that include complex carbohydrates, protein, and healthy fats, we can help stabilize our blood sugar levels. When blood sugar remains steady, it contributes to a more consistent and stable mood. On the other hand, sharp fluctuations in blood sugar can lead to mood swings and increased irritability. By prioritizing a diet that supports both gut health and stable blood sugar levels, we can build a healthier and more balanced mind-body connection.

Specific vitamins and minerals have distinct roles in regulating our mood. For instance, vitamin D has been linked to a reduced risk of depression, while adequate levels of B vitamins are essential for cognitive function and emotional well-being. Even proper hydration plays a significant role in mood regulation. Dehydration can contribute to feelings of fatigue and irritability, whereas staying adequately hydrated helps maintain mental clarity and a more positive outlook.

It is important to recognize that the food we consume has a profound impact on our mood and overall mental state. Opting for a well-balanced diet that emphasizes nutrient-rich whole foods and promotes gut health can have a transformative impact on our overall well-being.

By making mindful choices about the foods we consume, we can experience increased feelings of well-being, heightened energy levels, and a more stable emotional state. Nourishing our bodies with wholesome foods provides the essential nutrients and support necessary for optimal physical and mental health. Taking care of your gut and providing adequate nutrition for your brain and body can help you feel good, both physically and emotionally.

Love Your Gut Biome!

The connection between gut health and our mood has gained significant attention in the media and on social platforms. However, have you ever taken a moment to truly appreciate the remarkable influence of gut bacteria on anxiety management?

Within our intestinal tract, there exists a vast community of microscopic bacteria, collectively weighing around 3 pounds. This intricate network of both beneficial and less favorable bugs is often referred to as our "second brain" due to its crucial role in our overall well-being. Like dedicated little soldiers, these friendly bacteria tirelessly work to protect us from foreign invaders, assist in digestion, and maintain our mental and physical health.

It is truly awe-inspiring to consider the profound impact that these microorganisms have on our well-being.

In order for our gut bacteria to function at their best and maintain our overall health, they also need to be in a healthy and plentiful state. When our gut bacteria are not thriving, we experience the consequences. The intricate communication between this community of bacteria and the neurotransmitters present in our enteric nervous system has a profound impact on our emotions and feelings. It may come as a surprise, but over 80% of our feel-good neurotransmitter, serotonin, is actually located in our gut, rather than our brain. As a result, an unhealthy gut can block the release of serotonin, directly affecting our mood and overall well-being. Recognizing the significance of a healthy gut in maintaining optimal neurotransmitter function highlights the importance of nurturing our gut bacteria for improved emotional and mental health.

Thankfully, research indicates that maintaining a healthy gut can have a range of positive effects, including reducing inflammation and cortisol levels, enhancing stress resilience, improving memory, and even alleviating anxiety. Studies have shown that individuals with diverse and thriving gut microbes are less likely to experience depression or anxiety. By prioritizing the well-being of our delicate microbiome and nurturing a healthy gut, we can decrease our risk of developing depression and anxiety.

Many of us have grown up in environments that were excessively sterile, frequently relied on antibiotics, and consumed unhealthy foods, leading to an imbalance in our gut microbiome. However, making changes to our diet can have profound effects that extend far beyond just our waistline.

The choices we make regarding our diet have a significant impact on our anxiety levels, and it is crucial to understand the connection between gut bacteria and mental health. Opting for a diet that is abundant in nourishing foods like avocados, blueberries, broccoli, eggs, and green leafy vegetables can support a healthy brain and reduce reactivity in our daily lives. On the other hand, indulging in junk food and highly processed meals such as fast food burgers, fries, chips, and cookies can contribute to negative thought patterns and disrupt our emotional stability.

When it comes to managing anxiety, establishing a healthy tone for the day begins with a nutritious breakfast. Starting your morning with options that lack essential nutrients, such as cereal, donuts, pastries, or fast food egg muffins, can result in cravings for processed foods and sugar throughout the day. This is due to the rapid metabolism of sugar, which can lead to energy crashes. To maintain stable emotions, it is important to keep your blood sugar levels steady throughout the day. This can be achieved by consuming whole foods, including lean and healthy proteins from plant or animal sources such as eggs, wild Alaskan Salmon, chicken, tuna, lean cuts of beef, beans, lentils, chickpeas, garbanzo beans, quinoa, chia seeds, hemp seeds, almonds, peanuts, and sea vegetables like Spirulina.

Given that your brain primarily consists of fat, it is vital to include clean and healthy fats in your diet to support brain health. Incorporating sources such as avocados, olive oil, butter, ghee, and coconut oil can be beneficial. While certain diets advocate for low carbohydrate intake, completely eliminating carbs is not recommended for managing anxiety. Complex carbohydrates derived from whole grains, vegetables, and fruits are essential for providing sustained energy levels. If incorporating greens into your meals proves challenging, organic green vegetable powders can be added to drinks or smoothies as a convenient alternative. Additionally, raw nuts and seeds can serve as balanced snacks to help maintain stable blood sugar levels throughout the day.

When it comes to consuming sweets, it is important to be mindful of your overall sugar intake, as excessive consumption can contribute to issues such as insulin resistance, diabetes, and brain inflammation. Instead of relying on refined sugars, it is beneficial to choose natural sweeteners such as fruits, dates, raw honey, or alternatives like monk fruit or stevia. Additionally, dark chocolate with a minimum cocoa content of 70% can be enjoyed in moderation as a healthier option.

By opting for balanced meals and snacks that include a combination of complex carbohydrates, protein, and healthy fats, you can support stable blood sugar levels and promote a more consistent and balanced emotional state. Making mindful choices about your breakfast and subsequent meals can have a positive impact on your overall well-being and help manage anxiety more effectively.

Although you may depend on coffee for an energy boost, caffeine can worsen your anxiety. Drinking coffee first thing in the morning can also lead to increased cortisol levels. While coffee is a popular beverage that many people rely on to kick-start their day, its stimulating properties can have undesirable consequences for those susceptible to anxiety and stress. Before reaching for that cup of coffee first thing in the morning, consider the following:

- **Anxiety Trigger:** Coffee contains caffeine, a natural stimulant that blocks the neurotransmitter adenosine, responsible for promoting relaxation and sleepiness. By blocking adenosine, caffeine increases brain activity and stimulates the release of other neurotransmitters like dopamine and norepinephrine, which contribute to increased alertness and energy. However, for individuals prone to anxiety, this heightened brain activity can lead to increased nervousness, restlessness, and even panic attacks.
- **Cortisol Release:** Cortisol is a hormone that plays a crucial role in the body's response to stress. It is often referred to as the "stress hormone." When a person experiences stress, cortisol levels rise, preparing the body for the "fight or flight" response. While cortisol is a natural and necessary hormone, consistently elevated levels can be harmful. Drinking coffee first thing in the morning can trigger the release of cortisol even before any stressor is present, leading to an unnecessary and potentially harmful increase in stress hormone levels.
- **Disrupted Sleep Patterns:** Consuming coffee in the morning can impact sleep patterns, especially when the

187

habit is paired with a regular intake of caffeine throughout the day. Poor sleep quality and insufficient rest contribute to higher stress levels and can exacerbate feelings of anxiety and irritability.

- **Dependency and Tolerance:** Regular consumption of coffee can lead to tolerance, requiring higher amounts of caffeine to achieve the same stimulating effect. As a result, people may find themselves trapped in a cycle of dependency, where they rely on coffee to function optimally, even if it worsens their anxiety over time.
- **Digestive Issues:** For some individuals, especially those with sensitive stomachs or digestive disorders, coffee can irritate the gastrointestinal tract, leading to symptoms such as indigestion, acid reflux, or an upset stomach. These physical discomforts can also contribute to feelings of unease and anxiousness.
- **Blood Pressure Concerns:** Caffeine has been shown to temporarily raise blood pressure in some individuals. While this effect is usually mild and short-lived, people with pre-existing hypertension or cardiovascular issues may experience more significant increases in blood pressure, potentially heightening feelings of anxiety.

While moderate coffee consumption may not have negative effects on everyone, individuals who are prone to anxiety and stress should exercise caution, particularly when consuming coffee first thing in the morning. Limiting or avoiding caffeine intake can help reduce the risk of increased anxiety levels and the release of excess cortisol, promoting a more balanced and calmer start to your day. It is important to be mindful of how caffeine affects you individually and make choices that support your overall mental and emotional health.

If you want or need the benefits of caffeine without experiencing jitters, green tea extract supplements can provide a simultaneous calming and alert effect. Additionally, the polyphenols abundant in tea have been found to promote the growth of beneficial bacteria while reducing harmful pathogens in the gut, thereby supporting a balanced microbiome. Green and black tea, known for their theanine content, can serve as excellent alternatives to coffee. These teas enhance focus and alertness while promoting a state of calmness in the mind. By incorporating green or black tea into your routine, you can enjoy the benefits of caffeine while ensuring a balanced and tranquil state of being.

An additional effective method to support and nurture a healthy gut microbiome is by including probiotics in your diet. Probiotics are foods that have been cultured with strains of beneficial bacteria. Examples of probiotic-rich foods include yogurt, fermented vegetables, Kombucha, sauerkraut, and Kefir. However, it's important to note that not all yogurts are created equal, as many store-bought options are high in sugars and lack the beneficial bacteria you need. Choosing homemade yogurt or varieties that explicitly list strains such as Lactobacillus acidophilus and Bifidobacterium lactis can provide the desired health benefits. Incorporating these probiotic-rich foods into your diet can actively support the growth of beneficial bacteria in your gut, promoting a healthier and more balanced gut microbiome.

In addition to probiotic foods, incorporating prebiotic foods into your diet can also contribute to a thriving gut ecosystem where beneficial bacteria can flourish. Prebiotic-rich foods, such as onions and garlic, are abundant in fiber and provide nourishment for the bacteria in your gut. By consuming a combination of prebiotic and probiotic foods, you can support the development of a vibrant bacterial community, which is crucial for the optimal functioning of your "second brain." These dietary choices work together to create an environment that fosters the growth and diversity of beneficial bacteria, promoting overall gut health and well-being.

It is necessary to acknowledge that there is no universal approach when it comes to our microbiome. Whether you adhere to a strict vegetarian diet, follow the Paleo or keto diet, or find yourself somewhere in between, the key lies in consistently supporting your gut microbiome with the foods that work best for you. Nurturing your gut bacteria through a well-balanced diet can have a significant impact on managing anxiety and promoting overall mental well-being.

It is important to remember that addressing past traumas and taking charge of your emotions is necessary, but it can also feel overwhelming. It is okay if you're not ready to start that journey just yet. Each person's path is unique, and it's essential to prioritize self-care and take steps that feel comfortable and manageable for you at your own pace. However, there are proactive measures you can start taking right away to improve your mental health, beginning with making adjustments to your diet and prioritizing the nurturing of a healthy gut microbiome.

Start by giving priority to a nourishing breakfast and striving for balance in your overall diet. Choose foods that are rich in nutrients while avoiding those that may have been exposed to pesticides. Incorporate a wide variety of wholesome foods into your meals, while significantly reducing or ideally eliminating all junk food from your diet.

By embracing these dietary changes, you can initiate a positive shift in how you feel, supporting your emotional well-being in the process. Remember that every step, no matter how small, can contribute to significant progress on your journey towards improved mental health.

Importance of Reading Food Labels

Developing the habit of reading food labels for ingredients is an important step towards enhancing both your mental and physical health. In today's fast-paced world, where convenience and processed foods are readily available, it's easy to overlook the impact of our dietary choices on our overall well-being. However, by taking the time to check food labels, you can make more informed choices and regain control over your nutrition. This simple practice empowers you to be mindful of what you consume and enables you to prioritize foods that support your health and well-being.

Here are some key reasons why reading food labels for ingredients is essential for your overall health:

- **Awareness of Nutritional Content:** Food labels provide valuable information about the nutritional content of a product. By paying attention to the ingredients, you can identify the presence of essential nutrients, vitamins, minerals, and other beneficial components. This awareness allows you to select foods that contribute to your mental and physical well-being and avoid those high in unhealthy elements like added sugars, excessive sodium, and unhealthy fats.
- **Managing Allergies and Sensitivities:** For individuals with food allergies or sensitivities, reading labels is a matter of safety. Knowing the ingredients helps identify potential allergens and prevent adverse reactions. Consuming allergens unknowingly can lead to severe health consequences, so understanding food labels becomes a necessary precaution for those affected.

- **Reducing Consumption of Harmful Additives:** Many processed foods contain artificial preservatives, flavor enhancers, and colorants, which can have detrimental effects on your health. Some additives have been linked to hyperactivity in children, hormonal imbalances, and digestive issues. In order to protect your mental and physical well-being, reading food labels will empower you to avoid products made with harmful additives.
- **Supporting Healthy Eating Habits:** Reading food labels encourages conscious eating. When you understand the ingredients and their nutritional values, you can make better choices that align with your health goals. This practice helps you adopt a balanced and nutritious diet, promoting physical health and providing essential nutrients to support mental clarity and cognitive function.
- **Managing Weight and Energy Levels:** Excess consumption of unhealthy ingredients, such as added sugars and unhealthy fats, can lead to weight gain and energy fluctuations. By reading food labels, you can be mindful of your caloric intake and choose foods that fuel your body with sustained energy, helping you maintain a healthy weight and stable energy levels throughout the day.
- **Encouraging Transparency in the Food Industry:** As a consumer, your demand for clear and informative food labels pushes the food industry to become more transparent about their products. When you actively seek information about what you eat, companies are more likely to provide honest labeling and healthier product options.

Engaging in the practice of reading food labels for ingredients is a powerful tool that allows you to take control of your mental and physical health. By doing so, you empower yourself to make conscious choices about the foods you consume, ensuring that you are getting the necessary nutrients while avoiding harmful additives and allergens. This simple yet impactful habit promotes healthier eating habits, aids in weight management, and provides a sense of control and responsibility for your overall well-being.

It is vital to be mindful that the label "organic" does not automatically guarantee safety or superior ingredients. It's important to note that even organic products may contain highly inflammatory oils and additives that can have a negative impact on your gut microbiome. Therefore, it is necessary to read every label before making a purchase. By being an informed consumer, you can play a role in encouraging the food industry to prioritize health and transparency. This collective effort can lead to positive changes that benefit public health as a whole.

Stay vigilant and make conscious choices that align with your well-being, promoting a healthier food environment for everyone. By staying informed and attentive to food labels, you can make informed decisions that align with your health goals and contribute to your overall well-being.

Get A Blood Test!

Ordering a comprehensive blood test that includes measuring hormone levels, such Estrogen, Progesterone, Testosterone, DHEA, and Thyroid along with insulin, iron, and vitamin D is highly recommended for gaining a thorough understanding of both your mental and physical health. These tests provide valuable insights into the internal workings of your body, allowing you to identify potential imbalances and underlying health issues that may otherwise go unnoticed.

In my practice, I frequently encounter patients who experience significant anxiety and depression. Particularly among individuals aged 35 to 50, I have observed that these symptoms may be linked to natural hormonal changes associated with aging or lifestyle factors. In the case of these individuals, the solution does not involve prescribing antidepressants or anti-anxiety medications. Instead, achieving optimal health requires a focus on hormone balancing as a more suitable approach.

As a routine part of my practice, I strongly encourage all my patients, regardless of gender, to undergo a blood test and incorporate the results into their baseline assessment. By doing so, you can gain valuable insights into your hormone levels and work towards achieving a more balanced state of health. This personalized approach will allow you to address any underlying hormonal imbalances that may be contributing to your mental and physical well-being, leading to more targeted and effective treatment strategies.

Here are the key reasons why it is important to get regular blood tests :

- **Identifying Nutritional Deficiencies:** A complete blood test, including measurements of essential nutrients like iron and vitamin D, allows for the early detection of nutritional deficiencies. These deficiencies can have far-reaching effects on physical and mental well-being, leading to fatigue, cognitive impairments, mood disturbances, and compromised immune function. Addressing these deficiencies through appropriate supplementation or dietary adjustments can significantly improve overall health and vitality.

- **Assessing Thyroid Function:** The thyroid gland plays a central role in regulating metabolism, energy levels, and overall body function. Imbalances in thyroid hormones can lead to weight fluctuations, mood swings, sleep disturbances, and cognitive issues. By measuring thyroid hormone levels, health professionals can diagnose thyroid disorders such as hypothyroidism or hyperthyroidism and initiate timely interventions for optimal thyroid function.

- **Understanding Insulin Regulation:** Insulin is a crucial hormone that regulates blood sugar levels. Elevated insulin levels can indicate insulin resistance, a precursor to conditions like type 2 diabetes and metabolic syndrome. Monitoring insulin levels helps in the early detection and management of insulin-related issues, which can contribute to improved mental focus and overall physical health.

- **Evaluating Sex Hormone Levels:** Sex hormones, such as estrogen, progesterone, and testosterone, play significant roles in mood regulation, reproductive health, and overall vitality. Imbalances in these hormones can lead to menstrual irregularities, mood swings, reduced libido, and other health concerns. By assessing sex hormone levels, healthcare providers can tailor appropriate treatments and lifestyle adjustments to promote hormonal balance and well-being, for men and women.

- **Preventing Long-Term Health Complications:** Regular blood testing and hormone level measurements provide a proactive approach to health management. Detecting abnormalities early on enables healthcare professionals to implement preventive measures, potentially avoiding more severe health complications in the future.

- **Personalizing Treatment Plans:** Comprehensive blood tests and hormone assessments allow healthcare providers to create individualized treatment plans. A tailored approach takes into account your unique health profile, ensuring that interventions address specific needs and concerns, leading to more effective and sustainable outcomes.

- **Monitoring Progress and Health Trends:** Regular blood tests and hormone evaluations facilitate the tracking of health progress over time. These measurements provide valuable data on how lifestyle changes, medications, or other interventions impact your overall health, enabling adjustments to treatment plans as needed.

Iron deficiency alone can have a detrimental effect on anxiety levels. The link between iron deficiency and anxiety is a significant aspect of mental health that is often overlooked. Iron is an essential mineral that plays an important role in the production of hemoglobin, the protein responsible for transporting oxygen throughout the body. When the body lacks a sufficient amount of iron, it can result in a condition called iron deficiency anemia. This condition can contribute to increased feelings of anxiety. Recognizing the connection between iron deficiency and anxiety is essential in addressing mental health concerns and ensuring that individuals receive the necessary support and treatment to restore their iron levels and promote overall well-being.

Several studies have highlighted the relationship between iron deficiency and anxiety symptoms.

Here are some ways in which iron deficiency can contribute to anxiety:

- **Neurotransmitter Function:** Iron is involved in the synthesis and metabolism of various neurotransmitters in the brain, including serotonin, dopamine, and norepinephrine. These neurotransmitters play a key role in regulating mood, emotions, and stress response. When iron levels are low, the production of these neurotransmitters may be affected, potentially leading to increased anxiety and mood disturbances.
- **Oxygen Supply to the Brain:** As iron is essential for the formation of hemoglobin, which carries oxygen to body tissues, including the brain, iron deficiency can result in reduced oxygen supply to the brain. Insufficient oxygen levels in the brain may impair cognitive function and exacerbate feelings of unease and restlessness, contributing to anxiety.
- **HPA Axis Dysregulation:** The hypothalamic-pituitary-adrenal (HPA) axis is a complex system involved in the body's response to stress. Iron deficiency has been shown to disrupt the HPA axis, leading to increased cortisol levels and altered stress responses. Dysregulation of the HPA axis is associated with an increased risk of anxiety disorders.
- **Fatigue and Sleep Disturbances:** Iron deficiency anemia often leads to fatigue and weakness, which can contribute to sleep disturbances and an overall feeling of irritability and anxiety.

Taking steps to address iron deficiency, whether through dietary changes, iron supplementation, or medical interventions, can have a positive impact on symptoms of anxiety. However, it is recommended to consult with a healthcare professional before initiating any supplementation. They can provide guidance on the appropriate dosage and help confirm whether iron deficiency is indeed the underlying cause of the anxiety symptoms.

Iron deficiency can significantly affect mental health, especially in relation to symptoms of anxiety. By acknowledging and addressing iron deficiency, you can take proactive measures to enhance your overall well-being and alleviate anxiety-related concerns. Regular health check-ups and maintaining a balanced diet that includes iron-rich foods can play an important role in preventing and managing iron deficiency. Prioritizing your iron levels can contribute to a healthier mind and body, promoting a greater sense of well-being and reducing anxiety symptoms.

Obtaining a comprehensive blood test that includes measuring hormone levels such as insulin, thyroid, iron, vitamin D, and sex hormones is essential for gaining a holistic understanding of both mental and physical health. These tests play an important role in early detection, personalized treatment, and proactive health management. By undergoing these tests, you can take charge of your well-being and make informed decisions to support your overall vitality and quality of life. Regular monitoring of these factors empowers you to adopt a proactive approach to your health, promoting a sense of empowerment and well-being. By staying informed about your body's internal workings, you can take the necessary steps to optimize your health and lead a fulfilling and vibrant life.

Supplements For Anxiety

Vitamins and supplements play a vital role in promoting your overall well-being and helping you manage anxiety. While it's always best to obtain your essential vitamins from a balanced diet, it's not always practical in today's fast-paced world. Unhealthy eating habits and exposure to toxins can create nutrient gaps that may benefit from supplementation. Despite recent criticism surrounding certain vitamins, I firmly believe in their potential and encourage you to explore their potential for enhancing your health.

However, while considering vitamins, it's important to exercise caution when it comes to synthetic versions that contain unnecessary additives, as they may not provide the same level of effectiveness. Instead, opt for reputable companies that offer whole food-based vitamins, which are generally more readily absorbed by your body. Conducting thorough research is necessary to ensure you invest in high-quality products that will support your health without any potential harm.

Throughout my experience, I have observed encouraging results through the use of supplementation. While I refrain from endorsing specific vitamin brands, I suggest seeking guidance from reputable health food stores that offer *high-quality whole food-based multivitamins*. These multivitamins are typically made with real food, naturally colored and sweetened, and free from artificial preservatives. By opting for such products, you can ensure that you are making a choice that matches your health goals.

Besides starting with a high-quality, *food-based* multivitamin, I recommend supplementing with the following vitamins:

- **Magnesium:** Magnesium serves as a crucial element in various bodily functions, encompassing energy production, nervous system regulation, muscle contraction, bone health, and hormonal balance. Despite its multifaceted importance, many of us fail to acquire sufficient amounts through our diet alone. Incorporating magnesium supplements has revealed two prominent benefits - improved sleep quality and enhanced stress management. The impact of magnesium on overall well-being should not be underestimated, as it can significantly transform how you feel! Many individuals are deficient in magnesium due to changes in soil during food production. Getting at least 480 mg of magnesium daily can promote calmness, reduce restless leg syndrome, and aid sleep. You can also consume magnesium-rich foods like dark leafy greens, nuts, seeds, and dark chocolate, or use magnesium spray or take Epsom salt baths.

- **Vitamin D3 Plus Vitamin K2:** Vitamin D deficiency is widespread, impacting overall health. Check your vitamin D levels with a blood test and, if low, consider supplementing with vitamin D3 plus MK7 (vitamin K2) or consuming vitamin D-rich foods like Wild Alaskan Salmon, sardines, cod liver oil, tuna, egg yolks, or mushrooms. Sunlight exposure is beneficial as well.

- **Probiotics:** Maintaining a healthy gut microbiome is crucial for overall well-being and anxiety management. Incorporate fermented foods like yogurt, sauerkraut, Kombucha, and Kefir into your diet, or use a probiotic supplement with at least 5 billion active cultures.

High Quality Fish Oil:

High-quality fish oil and consuming fatty fish offer significant benefits for anxiety and overall mental well-being. Fish oil is a rich source of omega-3 fatty acids, specifically eicosapentaenoic acid (EPA) and docosahexaenoic acid (DHA), which plays an important role in brain health and function.

Some benefits of high quality fish oil include:

- **Reduced Anxiety Symptoms**: Studies have shown that omega-3 fatty acids can help reduce symptoms of anxiety. EPA, in particular, has been linked to a decrease in feelings of anxiety and stress. Regular consumption of high-quality fish oil or fatty fish can contribute to a calmer and more balanced mood.
- **Neurotransmitter Support**: Omega-3 fatty acids help support the production and functioning of neurotransmitters in the brain, including serotonin and dopamine. These neurotransmitters are essential for regulating emotions and mood, and imbalances can contribute to anxiety disorders.
- **Anti-inflammatory Properties**: Omega-3s have anti-inflammatory effects, and chronic inflammation has been associated with an increased risk of anxiety and mood disorders. By reducing inflammation in the brain, fish oil can help create a more favorable environment for emotional stability.
- **Improved Brain Function**: The brain is composed of a significant amount of fat, and omega-3 fatty acids are vital components of brain cell membranes. Regular intake of fish oil or fatty fish can support brain health, cognition, and memory, which may indirectly help with anxiety management.

- **Stress Response Regulation**: Omega-3 fatty acids can modulate the body's stress response by influencing the release of stress hormones like cortisol. By regulating these hormones, fish oil can potentially mitigate the impact of stress on anxiety levels.
- **Complementary Treatment**: While fish oil alone may not be a standalone treatment for anxiety disorders, it can be a valuable complementary approach alongside other therapies. Adding fish oil to a balanced treatment plan, including therapy, may enhance overall outcomes.

It's important to understand that the response to fish oil can vary from person to person, and its impact on anxiety may not be immediate. Consistency and long-term use are generally recommended to observe significant improvements in anxiety symptoms. If you are contemplating the use of fish oil supplements, it is recommended to select high-quality products from reputable sources to ensure their purity and potency. As with any dietary supplement, it is advisable to consult with a healthcare professional before incorporating fish oil into your daily routine, particularly if you have any pre-existing medical conditions or are taking other medications. Their expertise will help guide you in making an informed decision.

If you prefer to obtain vitamins directly from food, consider incorporating nutrient-rich options into your diet, such as leafy greens, nuts, seeds, lean proteins (chicken, turkey, wild Alaskan Salmon), and healthy fats like avocados, coconut oil, olive oil, and butter.

For sleep and anxiety management, consider the following options:

- **Teas:** Chamomile tea, Valerian Root Tea, and Golden Milk can promote relaxation and better sleep.
- **Passionflower:** Available as a pill or tincture, it can aid sleep, but avoid it if you're already taking other sleeping pills or drinking alcohol.
- **5-Hydroxytryptophan (5HTP):** An amino acid that can help with anxiety, but be cautious and consult your doctor before using it, especially if you're on antidepressants or other psychoactive medications.

Adaptogens

Adaptogens are a class of natural substances, typically herbs or mushrooms, that have been used for centuries in traditional medicine systems like Ayurveda and Traditional Chinese Medicine. These substances are known for their ability to help the body adapt and respond to stressors, both physical and mental, by promoting balance and resilience. Adaptogens work by modulating the body's stress response system, which includes the hypothalamic-pituitary-adrenal (HPA) axis and the sympathetic-adrenal-medullary (SAM) system. They help regulate the production and release of stress hormones like cortisol, while also supporting the body's overall physiological functions.

One of the key characteristics of adaptogens is their *ability to have a non-specific effect on the body*, meaning they can help normalize various bodily functions without causing any major disruptions. They work by exerting a balancing and harmonizing effect on different systems, such as the immune system, nervous system, and endocrine system.

Some well-known adaptogens include ashwagandha, rhodiola, ginseng, holy basil, and reishi mushroom. These adaptogenic substances are often consumed in the form of teas, tinctures, capsules, or powders.

Adaptogens are believed to offer a range of potential benefits, including increased energy and stamina, improved mental clarity and focus, enhanced immune function, reduced fatigue and burnout, and better overall stress management. However, it's important to note that individual responses to adaptogens may vary, and it's always advisable to consult with a healthcare professional before incorporating them into your routine, especially if you have any underlying health conditions or are taking medications.

Here's an overview of some popular adaptogens and how they can be used to manage anxiety and improve mood:

- **Ashwagandha (Withania somnifera):** Ashwagandha is well-regarded for its stress-reducing properties. It's believed to balance cortisol levels, a hormone released during stress, and support the nervous system. Ashwagandha is often used to alleviate anxiety, enhance relaxation, and improve mood. It can be consumed as a supplement or in powdered form.
- **Rhodiola (Rhodiola rosea):** Rhodiola is known for its adaptogenic properties that can help increase the body's resistance to stress. It's believed to support energy levels, reduce fatigue, and improve mood. Rhodiola may be particularly beneficial for individuals dealing with fatigue-related anxiety. It's available as a supplement or in extract form.
- **Maca (Lepidium meyenii):** Maca is considered an adaptogen due to its potential to enhance energy and

resilience. While not a direct stress-reducing herb, its ability to support energy levels and overall vitality can indirectly contribute to improved mood. Maca is often consumed as a powdered supplement or added to smoothies.

- **Holy Basil (Ocimum sanctum or Ocimum tenuiflorum):** Holy Basil, also known as Tulsi, has a long history of use in Ayurvedic medicine for its calming and stress-reducing effects. It's believed to promote relaxation, mental clarity, and emotional balance. Holy Basil can be consumed as a tea, tincture, or supplement.

How to Use Adaptogens to Manage Anxiety and Improve Mood:

- **Consult a Healthcare Professional:** Before incorporating adaptogens into your routine, especially if you're dealing with anxiety or mood disorders, it's important to consult a healthcare professional. They can provide personalized advice and ensure there are no interactions with any medications you might be taking.
- **Choose Quality Supplements:** If you decide to use adaptogen supplements, opt for high-quality products from reputable sources. Look for standardized extracts that provide consistent doses of active compounds.
- **Start with Low Doses:** When introducing adaptogens, start with lower doses and gradually increase as needed. This allows your body to adjust and minimizes the risk of adverse effects.
- **Monitor Effects:** Pay attention to how your body responds to the adaptogen. Some people might experience noticeable benefits, while others may not

notice significant changes. Be patient and give the adaptogen time to work.

- **Incorporate Regularly:** Consistency is key with adaptogens. Incorporate them into your daily routine to experience their potential benefits over time.
- **Combine with Healthy Lifestyle Practices:** Adaptogens work best when combined with a healthy lifestyle. Eating a balanced diet, engaging in regular physical activity, getting sufficient sleep, and practicing stress-reduction techniques (such as mindfulness and meditation) can amplify their effects.
- **Listen to Your Body:** As with any supplement, listen to your body's signals. If you experience any negative effects, discontinue use and consult a healthcare professional.

Adaptogens like Ashwagandha, Rhodiola, Maca, and Holy Basil offer a holistic approach to managing anxiety and improving mood. However, individual responses can vary, so it's important to find what works best for you under the guidance of a healthcare provider.

**Safety should always be your top priority, and it is always recommended to consult with a healthcare professional before trying any supplements, particularly if you have pre-existing health conditions or are taking medications. It's important to note that the term "natural" does not necessarily guarantee risk-free usage. Your well-being is of utmost importance, so it is advisable to choose the safest approach whenever possible and seek professional guidance when incorporating supplements into your routine. By doing so, you can ensure that you are making informed decisions that prioritize your health and safety.

Using Essential Oils For Managing Anxiety

Essential oils have gained recognition for their potential in helping to alleviate anxiety symptoms. These concentrated plant extracts are known for their aromatic properties and have been used for centuries in various traditional practices. When used in aromatherapy, certain essential oils have been found to promote relaxation, reduce stress, and create a calming effect on the mind and body. The inhalation or topical application of these oils can stimulate the limbic system, which plays a role in emotions and memory, leading to a sense of relaxation and emotional well-being.

Here are some potential benefits of essential oils for anxiety:

- **Relaxation and Stress Reduction:** Many essential oils have calming properties that can promote relaxation and reduce stress. When inhaled, certain essential oils can stimulate the olfactory system, which sends signals to the brain's limbic system, known to influence emotions and mood. Lavender, chamomile, and bergamot are some examples of essential oils with relaxing effects.
- **Improved Sleep:** Anxiety can often disrupt sleep patterns, leading to insomnia or poor sleep quality. Certain essential oils, like lavender and valerian, have sedative properties that may help improve sleep and reduce the impact of anxiety on restfulness.
- **Reduction of Nervousness:** Inhaling essential oils can have an immediate soothing effect on the mind and body. The aroma of oils like clary sage, ylang-ylang,

and frankincense can help reduce nervousness and promote a sense of well-being.

- **Alleviation of Physical Symptoms:** Anxiety can manifest physically, leading to symptoms like tense muscles, headaches, and gastrointestinal issues. Essential oils with analgesic and anti-inflammatory properties, such as peppermint and eucalyptus, can help relieve some of these physical discomforts associated with anxiety.
- **Mindfulness and Aromatherapy:** Incorporating essential oils into mindfulness practices or aromatherapy sessions can enhance the overall experience. The act of diffusing oils or applying them during massage can create a calming ambiance and promote a sense of balance and relaxation.
- **Non-Invasive and Low-Risk:** When used correctly and in moderation, essential oils are generally safe for most people. They offer a non-invasive and low-risk alternative to pharmaceutical interventions for anxiety. However, it's crucial to conduct a patch test and consult with a healthcare professional before using essential oils, especially if you have allergies or specific medical conditions.
- **Customizable and Versatile:** With various essential oils available, individuals can create blends that cater to their specific needs and preferences. Personalizing the scent and method of application allows for a tailored approach to anxiety management.

Several essential oils have shown potential in helping to alleviate anxiety symptoms. While essential oils can be a valuable tool in managing anxiety, it's important to remember that individual responses will vary.

It's always recommended to use high-quality oils, follow proper dilution guidelines, and consult with a healthcare professional if you have any underlying health conditions or are taking medications.

Here are some of the most commonly recommended essential oils for anxiety:

- **Lavender (Lavandula angustifolia):** Lavender is one of the most well-known essential oils for relaxation and stress reduction. Its soothing aroma is believed to promote calmness and help with sleep issues, making it beneficial for anxiety management.
- **Chamomile (Matricaria chamomilla or Chamaemelum nobile):** Chamomile has gentle sedative properties and is often used to reduce nervousness and promote relaxation. It can be particularly helpful for anxiety-related gastrointestinal symptoms.
- **Bergamot (Citrus bergamia):** Bergamot has a citrusy, uplifting scent and is known for its anxiety-reducing effects. It can help improve mood and promote a sense of well-being. However, it is phototoxic, so avoid direct sunlight after topical application.
- **Frankincense (Boswellia carterii):** Frankincense has a grounding and calming effect on the mind and body. It can be useful for reducing stress and anxiety, and it is often used in meditation practices.
- **Vetiver (Vetiveria zizanioides):** Vetiver has an earthy and woody aroma that is deeply relaxing. It is known to help with nervousness and restlessness, making it beneficial for anxiety management.

- **Ylang-Ylang (Cananga odorata):** Ylang-ylang has a sweet and floral scent that can help reduce feelings of tension and promote relaxation. It is often used to address anxiety and stress-related issues.
- **Clary Sage (Salvia sclarea):** Clary sage has antidepressant and anxiolytic properties, which can help reduce anxiety and improve mood. Its calming effects make it beneficial for stress management.
- **Rose (Rosa damascena):** Rose essential oil has a beautiful floral scent that can uplift the spirits and promote a sense of comfort and calmness. It is often used for anxiety, grief, and emotional support.
- **Neroli (Citrus aurantium var. amara):** Neroli has a sweet and citrusy aroma that is known for its calming effects. It can help reduce anxiety and promote relaxation.
- **Patchouli (Pogostemon cablin):** Patchouli has a rich, earthy scent that is grounding and can help reduce feelings of anxiousness and nervous tension.

When using essential oils for anxiety, there are several methods of application, including:

- Aromatherapy diffusers: Diffusing essential oils into the air to create a calming ambiance.
- Topical application: Diluting essential oils with a carrier oil (almond oil, fractionated coconut oil, or olive oil) and applying them to the skin through massage or direct application to pulse points.
- Inhalation: Inhaling the aroma of essential oils directly from the bottle or by adding a few drops to a tissue or inhaler.

It's important to note that while many people experience positive effects using essential oils for anxiety, individual responses may vary. What works well for one person may not have the same impact on another. Essential oils should also be used as a complementary tool alongside other anxiety management strategies, such as therapy, exercise, and lifestyle adjustments.

If you're considering using essential oils for anxiety, it's a good idea to start with small amounts and observe how your body responds.

Before using essential oils, it's crucial to conduct a patch test to check for any allergic reactions. Additionally, seek guidance from a qualified aromatherapist or healthcare professional to ensure you're using the right oils and methods for your specific needs, especially if you have specific medical conditions or are taking medications.

Calm Within

CHAPTER 4: Energy Medicine

Loving and accepting your body is the best way to cooperate with any intentions you might have for changing it. The intelligence of your body is remarkable.

~Donna Eden

To experience a deep and profound transformation in your life as you overcome anxiety, you must transform your energy. Energy *medicine* refers to a holistic approach to healing and well-being that recognizes the interconnectedness of our physical, mental, emotional, and spiritual health. It is based on the understanding that our bodies are composed of energy and that disruptions or imbalances in this energy can lead to various health issues. Energy medicine encompasses a wide range of modalities, including acupuncture, yoga, qigong, homeopathy, aromatherapy, reiki, and healing touch.

The underlying principle of energy medicine is that our bodies possess an innate ability to heal themselves, and by working with the body's energy system, we can support and enhance this natural healing process. Energy medicine recognizes that our thoughts, emotions, beliefs, and experiences can impact our energy field and overall well-being. By addressing and harmonizing these energetic aspects, energy medicine seeks to promote physical, emotional, and spiritual health.

Energy medicine has a profound and positive impact, offering relief from mental and emotional distress and even alleviating chronic physical pain. It is worth noting that athletes also recognize and utilize the power of energy medicine to

213

enhance their overall performance. By embracing energy transformation, you can unlock a world of possibilities for personal growth and well-being.

Look beneath the surface of the world, beyond the material trappings of life, and you'll encounter a universe of subtle and swirling energies. Though we may not fully comprehend their nature or mechanism, we acknowledge their presence, as they form the very essence of reality—including ourselves
~Cyndi Dale

Practice the art of listening to your body's messages with love and understanding. It's important to remember that even during times of anxiety, illness, or injury, your body is on your side. Your body is your wise and resilient companion supporting you on your journey to health. Through the practice of Energy Medicine, you can create a deeper awareness of how your energy aligns with your unique needs and requirements.

By responding to these energetic signals with compassion and honoring your true needs, such as rest, nourishing food, or exercise, you will unlock your inner strength and invite greater joy into your life. This process of self-care and self-discovery allows you to optimize your overall well-being and build a harmonious connection between your body, mind, and spirit. Embracing this journey of self-nurturing and self-empowerment will lead you to a place of balance, vitality, and profound fulfillment. Remember, you have the power to create a life of joy and well-being by listening to and honoring the needs of your whole being.

At the core of energy medicine is the belief in the interconnectedness of the body, where any shift or imbalance at one level can have an impact on all others. This practice recognizes that health issues develop when the flow of energy, known as "Qi" in Asian healing traditions, becomes blocked or disrupted. Asian healing traditions take a holistic approach, integrating physical, psychological, and spiritual methods to address these energetic imbalances and restore overall well-being.

In Chinese medicine, "Qi" is considered a mysterious and fundamental energy that aligns with properties similar to quantum mechanics. By embracing the principles of energy medicine, we can tap into the profound wisdom of these ancient traditions and unlock the potential for healing and harmony within ourselves.

The primary goal of energy medicine is to restore balance in both the energetic and physical bodies, nurturing the innate capacity for *self-healing*. Various techniques, such as acupuncture, tapping, and chakra clearing, are used to unblock energy channels and restore the smooth flow of Qi.

Personally, I have experienced the transformative power of energy medicine in my own healing with endometriosis. It played a pivotal role in restoring my hormonal balance and alleviating the pain associated with endometriosis. When faced with the diagnosis, I focused my attention on healing and rebalancing my energetic field, which in turn provided support and protection for my reproductive organs as I awaited surgery. Energy medicine offers a holistic approach to well-being, empowering you to actively participate in your healing process and create a balanced state of being.

Energy medicine also acknowledges the profound interconnectedness of our physical, mental, emotional, and spiritual levels. It includes a wide range of practices, including meditation, acupuncture, QiGong, Tai Chi, and the utilization of herbs and supplements from indigenous cultures and Eastern traditions.

What makes energy medicine truly appealing for me is its recognition and integration of the *mind-body connection*, understanding their mutual interaction and influence on each other. The essence of energy therapy lies in the intention to connect with the innate intelligence and wisdom of the body, promoting an internal state of balance, harmony, and wholeness.

Energy medicine has gained recognition and acceptance from reputable institutions such as Columbia University, Duke University, Yale, University of Pennsylvania, the Mayo Clinic, and the University of Arizona. These institutions have not only incorporated energy medicine into their clinical services but also conduct research in this field. They also offer courses and educational programs on various energy medicine practices, including reiki, healing touch, acupuncture, qigong, meditation, and mindfulness. This widespread acceptance and integration of energy medicine by reputable institutions further validates its efficacy and potential for promoting holistic well-being.

Energy Psychology, a therapeutic method that blends Eastern approaches with Western Psychology, has emerged as a relatively new and promising approach. One effective technique used by energy psychologists is Tapping or Emotional Freedom Technique (EFT), which we will address later in this chapter. Extensive research on energy psychology has consistently shown its effectiveness, with the majority of studies supporting its positive outcomes. As of 2014, only one study has presented contrasting results. This growing body of evidence highlights the potential of energy psychology as a valuable therapeutic modality that combines the best of both Eastern and Western traditions.

Energy medicine has emerged as a valuable treatment option for a wide range of issues, including depression, anxiety, trauma, pain, and stress. Research in energy psychology shows promising results, often showcasing its effectiveness in just a few treatment sessions for various psychological disorders. By equipping ourselves with the tools and techniques of energy medicine, we gain the ability to take charge of our health and well-being, creating a sense of empowerment throughout our healing journey. With energy medicine, we can tap into our innate capacity for healing and experience a profound transformation in our lives.

With the tools and techniques of energy medicine at our disposal, we have the power to actively take charge of our health and well-being, promoting a deep sense of empowerment. Our body's vibrational system is constantly changing, with the potential for both healing and disease ever-present.

This interconnectedness of our thoughts, emotions, and behaviors is often reflected in various aspects of our physical body, including the brain, heart, spinal cord, organs, blood, lymphoid tissue (our immunity), and the surrounding electromagnetic field. It is important to recognize that *unresolved chronic emotional stress* can manifest as physical illness, creating disruptions in our energy field. By addressing and resolving these energetic imbalances, we can promote healing and restore harmony within ourselves.

When we find ourselves consumed by obsessive or self-destructive thoughts and behaviors, we inadvertently drain our life energy (Qi), resulting in a depletion of vital cellular processes. This energy leakage often occurs when emotions like anger, anxiety, fear, depression, or sadness block our ability to move forward in life. Recognizing and addressing these energy leaks becomes important in our journey towards personal growth and healing. The field of medical research is increasingly supporting the understanding of our bodies in terms of energy fields and the impact of energy leaks.

217

For example, unresolved anger towards someone who has caused you harm can occupy a part of your spirit, impeding your ability to heal and move forward. In cases of severe abuse, spiritual and energy healers acknowledge the belief that a portion of a person's spirit may flee as a means of escaping the trauma, a notion that has also been recognized by certain realms of the medical field.

Often, we may not be consciously aware of the presence of energy leaks within us. However, these unhealed leaks can manifest in bodily distress, often appearing as pain or tightness. When our attention is drawn to these physical symptoms, it serves as a powerful signal that the healing needs to begin. By recognizing and actively addressing these energy imbalances, we pave the way for holistic healing and overall well-being.

In her brave sharing, this woman reveals her experience with unresolved trauma stemming from her history of sexual abuse:

"I realize now that I've spent my entire life trying not to remember that I was sexually abused. Now that I know it happened, I realize why I've never had a satisfactory relationship. I've always pushed people away. I didn't know how to be fully present in a relationship. But I didn't know any better. I'm grieving for who I was in my early life and the fact that it has taken me this long to remember and release the past. But finally the chronic knot in my stomach is gone. I feel free. I am so relieved."

Reflecting on her past, she realizes that she had spent her entire life trying to bury the memories of the abuse. Unaware of its impact, she struggled in her relationships, pushing people away and feeling unable to be fully present. The revelation of the abuse became a turning point, bringing clarity to her emotional struggles and allowing her to release the past. Although grieving for her younger self and the time it took to confront the truth, she finally experienced the relief of the chronic knot in her stomach vanishing, setting her free.

Remarkably, as she confronted and released the memories of abuse from her energy field, her sleep problems and depression also spontaneously cleared up. The majority of blockages within our vibrational systems are deeply rooted in our emotions, emphasizing the importance of genuinely feeling in order to start healing. Simple intellectual understanding of the problem is not enough; genuine emotional processing is necessary.

By honoring and addressing our emotions, we create a harmonious environment for the free and balanced flow of energy, promoting overall well-being and vitality. When our energy flow is vibrant and delicately balanced, and when we hold positive feelings towards ourselves, the risk of disease reduces significantly.

What's interesting is that environmental toxins, trans-fats, excess sugar, and alcohol, among other factors, don't necessarily lead to disease unless there are preexisting blockages in the body's energy system. An intriguing aspect of this phenomenon is exemplified by individuals who have engaged in harmful habits like smoking cigars, daily whiskey consumption, and a lack of exercise, yet still manage to live to a ripe old age.

Despite smoking heavily until the age of 90, my grandfather defied the odds and lived to the impressive age of 97. Although he eventually quit smoking, he then developed a habit of consuming substantial amounts of sugar and drinking soda on a daily basis. Such cases puzzle us as we seek to understand what protected them from the effects of their detrimental behaviors.

The presence of environmental or dietary risk factors can be compared to debris carried along in the body's energy flow. This debris remains relatively harmless as long as the energy stream remains unobstructed, much like how debris in a river flows freely until it encounters trees or rocks. However, when there is a blockage in the energy stream, these accumulations of debris can have detrimental effects over time, potentially leading to physical illness.

This analogy highlights the importance of maintaining a clear and balanced energy flow within the body, as it plays a significant role in supporting overall health and well-being. By addressing and removing any energetic blockages, we can promote a state of vitality and reduce the risk of illness associated with the accumulation of environmental or dietary factors.

Scientific research has also uncovered an interesting connection between the disruption of information flow between cells and the development of cancer within those cells. It is remarkable that emotions often become trapped at a childhood level, originating from moments when we were unable to fully experience and express them. Unresolved emotional issues from our past can contribute to the formation of energy blockages, ultimately impacting our overall health and well-being. By understanding this intricate interplay between our emotional states and the flow of energy within our bodies, we gain valuable insights into promoting a healthier and more balanced life.

By actively addressing and releasing these emotional blockages, we have the opportunity to create a more balanced energy flow within ourselves. This intentional practice not only enhances our emotional well-being but also strengthens our resilience. As a result, we can decrease the potential for disease and promote overall health and vitality.

Clinical psychologist Doris E. Cohen, Ph.D., highlights the significant influence of our inner child on our adult nervous system. She explains that unhealed fears from our childhood, which we were unable to fully process, can resurface and take control. This process serves a purpose: to bring healing to the unresolved aspects of ourselves.

For example, let's consider a woman who experienced abandonment by her father at the age of three. As an adult, whenever she enters a new relationship, she may find herself overwhelmed by a sense of impending doom—a manifestation of her inner three-year-old seeking resolution.

As a result, she unknowingly sabotages her relationships, inadvertently reenacting the experiences of abandonment from her past. This pattern continues until she becomes aware of the repetition and recognizes the influence of her scared inner child on her behavior.

Through this awareness, she can begin to provide comfort and healing to that inner child, breaking free from the cycle of unconscious repetition and building healthier and more fulfilling relationships. By addressing and nurturing the wounded aspects of herself, she opens the door to personal growth, self-compassion, and the potential for transformative change. By recognizing and addressing these inner child wounds, you can start your own journey of healing and growth, which will allow you to build healthier relationships and live a more fulfilling life.

In our mainstream Western culture, it is not uncommon to experience a disconnect between our intellectual knowledge as adults and our emotional reality and needs. It is possible to have an impressive academic background while simultaneously possessing an emotional body that reflects that of a two-year-old. Unexpressed and unacknowledged emotions from moments of fear or anger during early childhood can become energetically trapped, manifesting as repetitive patterns of behavior.

However, when we allow ourselves to *express*, *feel*, and *name* these emotions, they can flow through our energy system, leaving no unresolved emotional baggage behind.

Recognizing and acknowledging the dynamics of our inner child is of utmost importance in promoting healing and personal growth. By nurturing and tending to our inner child, we can become emotionally mature, which in turn contributes to healthier relationships and enhanced emotional well-being.

It is important to express and release any blocked emotions that may have become lodged within us. Additionally, it is essential to acknowledge that while these emotions and experiences may have impacted us, we are no longer helpless children, and it is time for our adult selves to take charge of our lives.

Researchers have demonstrated that emotions and experiences can leave imprints at the cellular level throughout our bodies, extending beyond the confines of the brain. This understanding emphasizes the importance of addressing and resolving these emotional imprints to promote holistic healing and overall well-being. These emotions have the potential to live within various parts of our body, creating a constant underlying presence that can significantly influence our perceptions and interpretations of the world around us.

By recognizing the impact of these stored emotions on our experiences, we gain a deeper understanding of how they shape our thoughts, beliefs, and interactions. This awareness allows us to consciously address and release these emotions, freeing ourselves from their lingering influence and opening the door to new perspectives and possibilities.

As previously discussed, these interpretations can often give rise to false or irrational beliefs that profoundly impact the way we navigate our lives. It is not uncommon for intense emotions to become trapped within our bodies, a prevalent phenomenon among humans.

In contrast, animals in the wild instinctively process and release the energy of stress or fear when faced with danger. They engage in physical activities such as shaking, trembling, or running, allowing them to transition out of the fight or flight mode and return to their natural state. This innate ability to discharge energy enables animals to maintain an energetic balance. Recognizing this distinction highlights the importance of actively engaging in practices that facilitate the release of trapped emotions within our own bodies, promoting a greater sense of well-being and alignment with our natural state.

Animals provide us with valuable lessons on how to effectively process and release emotions, enabling us to restore balance and move on in life. By recognizing the presence of blocked emotions within ourselves and then actively seeking ways to discharge them, we can initiate a transformative healing process. This conscious effort to release trapped emotions allows us to prioritize our emotional well-being and build a more harmonious existence. Drawing inspiration from the wisdom of animals, we can learn to navigate our emotions with intention, enabling personal growth, resilience, and a greater sense of inner peace.

Similar to animals, we also have the innate ability to process and release emotions when faced with stress or fear. However, we often learn, or are advised, to suppress or calm ourselves during such moments, inadvertently depriving ourselves of the natural energy release that can signal our survival and safety.

By allowing ourselves permission to purge this build up of energy during the stressful event, we send a reassuring message to our primitive brain that we have successfully overcome the threat and are now in a state of safety and security. This intentional release of energy sets the stage for effectively processing the associated emotion and releasing any unnecessary or lingering connections to the stressful event. By honoring this natural process, we empower ourselves to navigate emotions with greater resilience and encourage a healthier emotional response.

This process provides us with valuable tools to handle stress more effectively in the future, enhancing our resilience and promoting a greater sense of security within ourselves. By actively engaging in this energetic release, we create space for healing and growth. It is through this intentional practice that we can navigate life's challenges with greater ease and confidence, knowing that we have the inner resources to face them head-on.

However, when we are unable to effectively discharge and process the energy associated with a traumatic experience, the primitive part of our brain can *freeze that experience* within us. This unresolved energy has the potential to manifest as Post Traumatic Stress Disorder (PTSD), where the intense emotions we felt during the event remain unprocessed, vivid, and alive, impacting various aspects of our lives.

Recognizing the importance of emotional processing and the releasing of blocked energy becomes necessary in our healing journey. By actively addressing and discharging these emotions, we can let go of past burdens.

When we become disconnected from our emotions to the point where we no longer recognize the physical sensations linked to specific emotional feelings, we inadvertently give up control of our reactions instead of gaining it. Unbeknownst to us and without our conscious consent, our emotions start to influence our decision-making and behavior, while rational thinking becomes entangled and obscured. This lack of awareness and connection to our emotions can lead to a loss of control over our actions and choices, as our emotional responses take the lead. By establishing a deeper understanding and recognition of our emotions, we regain the ability to navigate our lives with greater clarity and intention.

By adopting a tea kettle approach, where you release pressure regularly, you can prevent the build-up of emotions and the potential for explosive reactions. This healthier way of handling emotions enables you to maintain a better emotional balance and navigate through challenging experiences more effectively. Embracing this practice of regular emotional release empowers you to cultivate a sense of inner peace and harmony. As you actively engage in your healing process, you pave the way for personal growth, resilience, and the possibility of living a life characterized by greater emotional well-being and contentment.

Embracing the analogy of a tea kettle, you practice the art of releasing steam and finding calmness, instead of allowing your emotions to build and eventually explode like a pressure cooker. Instead of suppressing your feelings, you grant yourself permission to express them in a healthy and constructive way. This can involve talking, screaming, shouting, engaging in physical activities like punching or kicking, running, journaling, or any other outlet that helps you release the pent-up pressure.

By adopting the tea kettle approach, you empower yourself to regain control over your emotions. Instead of allowing them to simmer and boil inside, you learn to release them in a way that promotes emotional well-being and builds a sense of inner balance.

During my younger years, I would deliberately choose to ride mildly thrilling roller coasters, providing myself with a socially acceptable environment to scream as loudly as possible. It was a way for me to release the pent-up pressure inside and find a healthy outlet for my emotions.

Next time you have an opportunity to release pent up pressure, do so! Don't allow it to build up unnecessarily. Find a constructive outlet, whether it's through screaming, engaging in physical activities, or any other means that allows you to release and let go. By actively releasing this pressure, you create space for emotional well-being and prevent unnecessary build-up. Embrace these opportunities to release any pent up energy as you experience the freedom that comes with it.

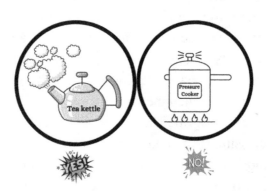

Tapping

Tapping, also known as Emotional Freedom Technique, or EFT, is an incredibly simple yet powerful energy medicine strategy that you can always access, with no cost to you.

EFT, developed in the 1990s by Stanford graduate Gary Craig, combines ancient Chinese acupressure principles with modern psychology. This technique utilizes the body's energy pathways, known as acupuncture meridians, which have been used in China for over 5000 years to move energy and remove blockages. When your body experiences imbalance, it often leads to physical and emotional symptoms caused by corresponding blockages.

Tapping works by simultaneously altering your brain, energy system, and overall body state. It's a remarkably effective tool to manage a wide range of emotions, such as anxiety, fears, traumatic memories, anger, and depression. There have been reports of those who have found success in using tapping for weight loss and eating disorders.

Tapping involves using your fingertips to gently tap on specific acupressure points, which helps release and relieve stuck thoughts and emotions. By doing so, direct signals are sent to the stress and fear center of your brain, bypassing the logical thinking frontal lobe.

This tapping process assists with releasing energy blockages and restoring balance, which ultimately reprograms your brain's relationship with stress. An additional benefit of tapping is that it allows you to process unprocessed emotions as a whole, instead of addressing one emotion at a time. It's a safe technique that can be done without re-traumatization, making it suitable for people of all ages, including kids.

You don't need to be precise with the tapping points, as the rhythmic motion creates a percussion effect that clears the blockages effectively. Think of tapping as a stress-relieving massage for both your body and mind, an approach Dr. Dawson Church beautifully describes.

Here are some essential points to remember when practicing Tapping:

- Calming yourself while acknowledging unpleasant emotions helps to disrupt and diffuse the negative charge in your body.
- Tapping is a valuable tool for releasing negative emotions.
- Don't be concerned about bringing up and holding onto negative emotions or thoughts. Tapping helps to clear them away.
- Focus on the stickiest details and emotions, and keep tapping until they are all cleared.
- Although it may not feel pleasant to confront negative and sticky emotions, it's necessary to allow yourself to feel them before you can effectively release them.
- There's a reason why these feelings keep resurfacing, so it's beneficial to bring them up and tap to let them go.
- If you experience intense emotions or feel worse during Tapping, don't worry; this is precisely the response you want. It is important to bring deep emotions to the surface to clear them effectively.
- Keep tapping until the emotion no longer have control over you.
- As a helpful tip, consider journaling your feelings first and then proceed with tapping them out.

By keeping these points in mind and practicing Tapping with patience and persistence, you can experience the positive transformation it can bring to your emotional well-being. The best part is that tapping is available to you 24 hours a day, seven days a week, providing a simple and accessible method to manage anxiety and promote emotional well-being. Give it a try and experience the profound power of EFT!

To learn how to tap and use it to manage your anxiety, visit: **https://www.transforminganxiety.com/tap** and get started right away! Be sure to check out the bonus **"Tapping For Deep Sleep"** video as well!

Thymus Tapping: Releasing Emotional Blocks and Balancing the Immune System

Thymus Tapping, a technique in Energy Medicine, along with Emotional Freedom Techniques (EFT), can help release unprocessed emotional blocks. The thymus gland, located in the center of your chest near the heart, is considered the emotional center in energy medicine and plays a crucial role in your immune system by producing T cells.

Observing gorillas, our closest animal relatives, we see them pound their chests when feeling unsafe or attacked. Similarly, humans often instinctively grab their chests when shocked or distressed.

By tapping on the thymus area, you can balance the body's energy and release negative emotions, and as a result supporting a healthier immune system.

Here's how to perform the Thymus Tap:

- Step 1: Create a list of unprocessed feelings.
- Step 2: Rate the intensity of each experience on a scale from 0 to 10, with 0 being no intensity and 10 being the highest.
- Step 3: Identify the emotion associated with each experience, using specific emotions such as abandoned, judged, attacked, betrayed, helpless, hopeless, frustrated, insecure, failure, rejected, angry, guilty, resentful, confused, unsafe, hurt, worried, shamed, overwhelmed, lonely, disappointed, or desperate.
- Step 4: While focusing on the emotion, take a deep breath and tap on your Thymus while saying, "Releasing this...(emotion)" or "Clearing this...(emotion)." Tap 5-7 times and then check how you feel. Continue tapping until the intensity level comes down to a 1 or 2.
- Step 5: Incorporate positive thoughts or affirmations. Use healthy emotions and thoughts like "I am able," "I feel abundant," "I am accepted," "I am appreciated," "I am brave," "I am joyful," and "I am protected." Repeat these affirmations until you feel better. Install at least 3 positive emotions.

Feelings that remain unprocessed can become trapped within our bodies, even after their initial purpose has been fulfilled. As we discussed earlier, animals in nature have a natural ability to process and discharge stress or fear energy through physical activities like shaking or running. However, humans are often discouraged from engaging in this way of releasing energy, resulting in the storage of emotions at the cellular level.

Releasing this trapped energy through tapping serves as a signal to your primitive brain that you are safe and have successfully navigated the stressful event. This process will empower you, support effective stress management, and promote a sense of security. By actively engaging in the release of trapped energy you can promote emotional well-being, enhance your ability to cope with stress, and cultivate a greater sense of inner stability.

Try It...

As part of a journal exercise, make a comprehensive list of memories and experiences that still bother you or affect you emotionally. Don't judge anything as insignificant or small. Processing each emotion or experience can be done through various methods, including Thymus Tapping, EFT, and journaling.

Assess the distress you feel related to the memory on a scale of 0 to 10, where 0 represents no distress and 10 signifies extreme distress.

- **0: No distress** - You feel completely calm and unaffected by the memory.
- **1-2: Minimal distress** - You experience very mild discomfort or unease.
- **3-4: Low distress** - You feel somewhat uncomfortable or upset, but it's manageable.
- **5-6: Moderate distress** - You are noticeably distressed, feeling uneasy and somewhat overwhelmed.
- **7-8: High distress** - You are significantly distressed, experiencing strong discomfort and emotional turmoil.

- **9: Very high distress** - You are nearly overwhelmed by distress, finding it extremely difficult to cope.
- **10: Extreme distress** - You are in extreme distress, unable to function or think clearly due to the intensity of your emotions.

Please choose a number on this scale that best represents the level of distress you currently feel related to the memory.

Choose either the EFT (Emotional Freedom Technique) or Thymus Tapping method, then start the tapping process. Continue tapping until your distress level decreases to around 1 or 2. Afterward, take some time to journal your thoughts regarding the exercise.

Keep in mind that processing emotions and beliefs is necessary for healing and moving forward. There are various techniques that can help you on this journey. For example, you can try using music, temporal tapping, shaking, or even writing down and then discarding the emotionally charged words to mentally let go of the associated thoughts. These techniques can help you release and process emotions in a healthy and productive way.

Qigong (Moving Meditation)

Qigong, known as a powerful moving meditation, is another energy medicine technique which can be practiced in just 10 minutes a day. Qigong offers numerous benefits for mental and physical well-being. Combining the words "Qi" (pronounced "chee" meaning vital energy) and "gong" (skill), Qigong translates to "the skill of cultivating your vital energy." This mind-body-spirit practice involves coordinated breathing, body movements, and meditation exercises, aiming to strengthen your mind and increase your energy reserves.

Qigong integrates posture, movement, breathing techniques, self-massage, sounds, and focused intent, improving mental and physical health. Qigong offers a range of styles, each with its own practical applications and unique theories about Qi. By practicing Qigong, you can experience the benefits of opening the flow of energy in your acupuncture meridians and strengthening your connection with the Life Force that exists beyond the physical realm.

When the breath, mind, and body are working together in synergy, with fluid, slow movements, dynamic stretches, coordinated rhythmic breathing, and specifically aligned postures, then we can harness the flow of our Qi—our vital energy

~Loffree

The gentle movements of Qigong will warm your tendons, ligaments, and muscles. It will tonify your vital organs and connective tissues, and promote body fluid circulation. Countless studies have shown Qigong's effectiveness in healing various health challenges, from physical ailments to emotional and mental stress.

Qigong practitioners focus on detecting and correcting imbalances in the body's bioelectric field caused by deep-seated emotions, trauma, poor diet, or lack of exercise. The practice helps balance your energy deficiencies and remove excess blockages, similar to getting an acupuncture treatment.

By combining slow, rhythmic full-body movements with coordinated breath, Qigong will calm your nervous system and promote mindfulness, making it an effective stress-reduction tool. It is considered one of the five branches of traditional Chinese medicine that support mental health and positive mood, alongside acupuncture, diet, herbs, and massage.

There is no one-size-fits-all approach to Qigong, and individuals may follow different styles according to their specific goals. For instance, Qigong can center and balance scattered energy in individuals with anxiety or increase energy for those struggling with depression.

Qigong is an evidence-based complementary therapy that effectively decreases negative mental health symptoms, making it a valuable addition to overall well-being. Popular Qigong instructors like Lee Holden and Marisa from Yoqi.com offer simple and easy-to-follow styles, but there are other more traditional teachers available as well. Search for Qigong instructors either online or in your local area. People use Qigong for various purposes, such as healing from physical illnesses, supporting addiction recovery, and reducing depression or anxiety symptoms.

Research has demonstrated that Qigong has a direct positive impact on anxiety, depression, stress, mood, and self-esteem. In randomized controlled trials, participants who practiced Qigong experienced significant reductions in anxiety compared to an active exercise group. Additionally, individuals who incorporated Qigong into their routine showed a remarkable decrease in depression symptoms, surpassing those who didn't practice it. One study found that Qigong led to reduced levels of circulating cortisol, the stress hormone, in participants who engaged in Qigong compared to a wait-list control group.

Qigong is a self-healing movement that can be practiced independently, offering the convenience of doing it wherever you are. Anxiety, stress, and depression are among the most common reasons why people turn to Qigong for relief. The practice alleviates these symptoms in a passive manner, meaning that you don't need to fully understand the techniques for them to be beneficial.

For more insights on how Qigong can help with anxiety, be sure to check out my interview with Qigong master Anthony Korahais, where he shares his personal journey of using Qigong to heal his anxiety.

▶ How To Use QiGong For Better Mental Health

https://www.youtube.com/@DrNafisaSekandari

Finding Peace: Spirituality and Grounding for Stress Management

In the pursuit of effective stress and anxiety management, we can adopt a multimodal approach that involves various strategies, including dietary adjustments, improved nutrition, better sleep patterns, and most importantly, grounding ourselves spiritually.

Spirituality serves as a pathway to connect with something greater than ourselves, providing a sense of purpose and peace. It's important to note that spirituality can include religious beliefs and practice, but it isn't limited to them.

In this section, we will explore relaxation exercises such as prayer, meditation, and yoga, all of which can be powerful tools for grounding and finding inner peace.

Prayer, in particular, has been found to have a powerful grounding effect on anxiety and mood. Regardless of your religious beliefs or background, research highlights the healing potential of prayer, benefiting both mental and physical well-being. Humans, it seems, are inherently wired for prayer and religious practices. Even in the absence of organized religion, humans will tend to find something to worship, whether material possessions or other pursuits.

Studies on Buddhist monks and Catholic nuns demonstrate how daily prayer and meditation practices can positively change and rewire the brain, leading to relaxation and mental clarity similar to progressive muscle relaxation exercises.

Meditation, a practice that has been embraced globally for thousands of years, gained significant popularity in the United States during the 1960s. Its simplicity and accessibility make it an ideal tool for individuals seeking to alleviate anxiety

236

and stress. Engaging in just a few minutes of meditation can bring about a sense of calmness and inner peace, offering emotional well-being and a range of overall health benefits. Importantly, the positive effects of meditation extend beyond the actual practice itself, enabling you to maintain a calmer disposition throughout your day. By incorporating meditation into your life, you can tap into its transformative power and cultivate a greater sense of balance, clarity, and serenity.

Meditation is a practice that requires no special equipment and can be easily incorporated into various settings. Whether you are taking a walk, riding a bus, waiting at a doctor's office, or even attending a challenging business meeting, you can engage in meditation.

To learn more about various meditation techniques, join my FREE 21 Day meditation challenge by visiting **transforminganxiety.com/meditate**

Similarly, yoga, which combines deep breathing, postures, and mental calmness, has been widely recognized for its benefits in managing anxiety and depression. One of the remarkable aspects of yoga is its adaptability to individual needs, allowing practitioners to customize their practice. By focusing inward and blocking out external distractions and comparisons with others, yoga encourages a sense of inner calmness. The goal is to find movements and postures that induce relaxation, keeping you grounded in the present moment and promoting a slower pace of life. Both meditation and yoga offer accessible and effective tools for encouraging mindfulness, reducing stress, and enhancing overall well-being.

By integrating spirituality and grounding practices such as prayer, meditation, and yoga into your stress management routine, you can discover a profound sense of peace and balance in your daily life. These practices offer you a way to connect with your inner self, establish mindfulness, and promote a deeper connection with the world around you. Through prayer, you can find solace and guidance, while meditation allows you to quiet your mind and find inner stillness. Yoga combines physical movement, breath awareness, and mental focus to promote a harmonious union of body, mind, and spirit. By incorporating these practices into your life, you can tap into a wellspring of inner strength, resilience, and peace, enhancing your overall well-being and navigating life's challenges with greater ease and grace.

Try it...

Mindfulness Exercises for the Whole Family:

Let's explore some simple mindfulness exercises that you can enjoy with your entire family.

1. **The Raisin Exercise:** Take your time and perform this exercise slowly. You can even add calming music if you like. Start by holding a raisin in your hand. Examine the raisin closely with your eyes, noticing its ridges, color (whether it's purple or black), and shape (oval or circular). Roll the raisin between your fingers, feeling its texture—soft or rough—and the ridges. Bring the raisin up to your nose, inhaling its scent. What does it smell like? Does it have a sweet aroma? Place the raisin on your tongue but refrain from biting it. Roll it around your mouth with your tongue, observing its taste and how it feels. Does your mouth water as you savor the taste? What thoughts come to mind as the raisin lingers in your mouth? This exercise can be a fun game,

especially with children at the dinner table, especially with unfamiliar or disliked foods. It teaches them to be more mindful.

2. **Elevator Breathing Exercise:** Picture an elevator ascending as you take a deep breath. Imagine it going up and up. Hold your breath for a count of three, and then exhale as you envision the elevator descending. Repeat this process 2-3 times. This exercise is suitable for children and adults alike, promoting relaxation and mindfulness.

3. **Upside Down Triangle Breathing:** Visualize an upside-down triangle with the long side on top instead of the bottom. Begin at the bottom peak and take a deep breath in for a count of 3. Hold your breath for 3 seconds as you move along the flat part, and then exhale for a count of 3 as you go down the other side. Repeat this cycle 2-3 times, focusing on the triangle's shape and your breath.

4. **Square Breathing:** This exercise is particularly useful for managing panic attacks. Envision a square with four sides. Start at the left side and breathe in for a count of 4. Hold your breath for 4 counts as you move across the top, then exhale for 4 counts as you descend the right side. Hold your breath for 4 counts as you slide along the bottom. Close your eyes and repeat this process 2-3 times, maintaining your focus on the square shape and your breath.

5. **The ONE Exercise:** In this exercise, you can choose any word that holds significance for you, such as "love," "God," or the name of someone you cherish. For our purposes, we will use the word "ONE" (O-N-E). Focus on the number or the word "ONE" as you breathe in, and then again as you breathe out. Practice this

exercise several times, solely concentrating on the word or the number "1."

Holding your breath during these exercises serves as a reminder to pause in life and take a moment for yourself. It allows you to stop, appreciate your surroundings, and find a sense of calm. Consistent practice of these mindfulness breathing exercises during moments of calm will train your brain and body to instantly find calmness during times of anxiety and panic. Muscles have memory, so when they have experienced calmness before, it becomes easier to access that state when anxiety is activated.

Embrace these mindfulness techniques as valuable tools to restore inner peace and cope with stress more effectively. By practicing these mindfulness exercises together, you can build a sense of presence and appreciation for the moment. Make it a delightful family activity that not only entertains but also nurtures mindfulness in each family member.

In addition to practicing meditation, yoga, and journaling, it's essential to prioritize outdoor time and embrace the nourishing benefits of sunlight.

Step outside and bask in the sunlight, especially during the early morning hours, as it helps reset your internal clock and nourish your eyes. However, avoid looking directly at the sun. Instead, face towards the sun with your eyes closed, engaging in 5-10 minutes of deep breathing to enhance the experience.

Use this time to include some light stretching exercises, either as a standalone routine or as an addition to your daily morning yoga or Qigong practice.

If anxiety creeps in, consider taking a soothing shower or holding an ice cube in your hand. These mindfulness activities can disrupt the anxiety loop in your brain, providing instant relief and comfort.

Also be sure to pay attention and focus on your self-talk and challenge any negative thoughts that arise. Recall in chapter 3, Dr. Emoto's study on the impact of negative words on water crystals, and be mindful of speaking kindly to yourself. Your mind and body are listening, so choose positive and uplifting words.

Maintain your journaling practice to track the progress you're making on your journey of self-improvement and inner well-being. Regular journaling can offer valuable insights and reinforce your commitment to personal growth.

By incorporating these outdoor activities and positive self-talk strategies into your routine alongside meditation, yoga, QiGong, and journaling, you'll create a holistic approach to nurturing your mind, body, and spirit.

EMDR

EMDR, which stands for Eye Movement Desensitization and Reprocessing, has emerged as a remarkable and highly effective tool for addressing anxiety and promoting mental health. Developed by Dr. Francine Shapiro, EMDR is a therapeutic approach specifically designed to facilitate healing from trauma and emotional distress associated with traumatic events.

EMDR was initially developed to treat post-traumatic stress disorder (PTSD) resulting from trauma. Since anxiety often has its roots in unresolved past experiences or distressing events, EMDR can help you process and release the emotional charge associated with these memories, leading to a reduction of your anxiety symptoms.

Through a structured process that incorporates bilateral stimulation, such as eye movements, taps, or sounds, EMDR helps you to reprocess traumatic memories and experiences, allowing for resolution and relief. This evidence-based therapy has gained recognition for its ability to bring about transformative healing and promote overall well-being.

Numerous studies have demonstrated that EMDR can provide the benefits of therapy much more rapidly than traditional psychotherapy for anxiety and trauma-related disorders. It has shown that the mind can indeed recover from psychological trauma similar to how the body heals from physical trauma. Through EMDR, the brain's information processing system naturally moves toward mental health and wellness.

When our energy system is blocked or imbalanced due to the impact of a disturbing event, emotional wounds can fester, leading to intense suffering. However, once that block is removed, the healing process can begin.

One remarkable aspect of EMDR is that it allows you to process intense emotions related to past trauma or fear *without the need* to discuss the intricate details or provide in depth explanations. During a session, both sides of the brain are activated in order to diffuse the emotional charge of the trauma.

EMDR is recognized as an evidence-based treatment by reputable organizations, including the American Psychological Association (APA), the World Health Organization (WHO), and the Department of Veterans Affairs (VA). Its efficacy has been supported by numerous research studies.

Over 30 studies have produced positive results on EMDR, with some revealing that 84%-90% of single-trauma victims no longer experience post-traumatic stress disorder after just three 90-minute sessions. Other studies funded by Kaiser Permanente found that after only six 50-minute sessions, 100%

of single-trauma victims and 77% of multiple trauma victims were no longer diagnosed with PTSD.

Combat veterans also benefited significantly from EMDR, with 77% being free of PTSD after 12 sessions. The effectiveness of EMDR in treating trauma has garnered worldwide recognition, making it an excellent approach to address everyday memories that contribute to issues like low self-esteem and feelings of powerlessness, leading individuals to seek therapy.

More than 100,000 clinicians worldwide utilize EMDR with their patients, and millions of individuals have successfully undergone treatment with this approach over the past 25 years. By following a detailed protocol and employing specific procedures, trained mental health professionals can help you activate your body's natural healing processes during EMDR therapy.

The unique approach of EMDR for healing trauma and emotional distress makes it particularly beneficial in managing anxiety-related issues and improving overall well-being.

Here are some reasons why EMDR is highly regarded as a great tool for anxiety and mental health:

- **Holistic Healing:** EMDR addresses not only the emotional and psychological aspects of anxiety but also incorporates physical and neurological elements. By tapping into the body's natural healing processes and the brain's information processing system, EMDR helps restore balance and resilience.
- **Versatility:** While initially developed for trauma, EMDR's effectiveness extends beyond PTSD. It has been successfully used to treat various anxiety disorders, phobias, panic attacks, and generalized

anxiety. Additionally, EMDR can address other mental health concerns such as depression and low self-esteem.

- **Safe and Well-Tolerated:** EMDR is considered a safe therapy when administered by trained professionals. It is generally well-tolerated by individuals, including those who may have difficulty with other forms of therapy.
- **Lasting Benefits:** EMDR not only helps individuals manage anxiety symptoms but also fosters lasting emotional resilience. By processing and releasing the emotional charge from past experiences, individuals are better equipped to cope with future stressors and challenges.

EMDR stands out as an exceptional tool for managing anxiety and promoting holistic healing due to its unique ability to address underlying trauma and negative emotions. This therapeutic approach has garnered worldwide recognition for its effectiveness in providing relief and healing to individuals struggling with anxiety-related issues.

The day before my engagement party, I decided to try EMDR therapy. I was on the verge of a panic attack due to the overwhelming possibility of being the center of attention. However, following just one EMDR session, I experienced a deep sense of calm and felt in control of my emotions.

If you find yourself struggling with long-standing trauma, it is important to seek the support of an experienced mental health professional who is not only trained in EMDR but also specialized in trauma work. With their guidance, you can begin a transformative journey towards healing, resilience, and enhanced overall mental well-being. EMDR offers hope and the potential for profound healing, allowing you to reclaim your life and find a renewed sense of inner peace.

EMDR and Energy Medicine techniques like Tapping share some common similarities, particularly in their approach to addressing emotional and psychological issues.

- **Mind-Body Connection:** Both EMDR and Energy Medicine techniques recognize the mind-body connection. They acknowledge that emotional distress and traumatic experiences can manifest physically as well, impacting the body's energy system.
- **Targeting Negative Emotions:** EMDR and Tapping/EFT focus on targeting negative emotions and distressing memories. They aim to release the emotional charge associated with these memories and experiences.
- **Bilateral Stimulation:** Both EMDR and some Energy Medicine techniques use bilateral stimulation. In EMDR, this involves rhythmic eye movements, while in Tapping/EFT, it involves tapping on specific acupressure points. Bilateral stimulation is believed to activate both hemispheres of the brain, facilitating the processing of emotions and memories.
- **Trauma Resolution:** Both modalities are effective in trauma resolution. EMDR is well-known for its effectiveness in treating post-traumatic stress disorder (PTSD), while Tapping/EFT has shown promising results in addressing trauma and emotional issues.
- **Disrupting Negative Thought Patterns:** EMDR and Energy Medicine techniques help disrupt negative thought patterns and beliefs associated with traumatic experiences. They aim to reprocess these thoughts and beliefs, leading to more adaptive and positive cognitions.

- **Self-empowerment:** Both modalities empower individuals to take an active role in their healing process. EMDR and Tapping/EFT often involve self-administered techniques that individuals can use outside of therapy sessions.
- **Non-invasive and Gentle:** EMDR and Energy Medicine techniques are non-invasive and generally considered safe. They do not require reliving traumatic events in great detail, making them more suitable for individuals who may find traditional talk therapies challenging.
- **Holistic Approach:** Both modalities take a holistic approach to healing, recognizing the interconnectedness of emotions, thoughts, and physical sensations. They address the whole person, considering the mind, body, and spirit in the healing process.

It is important to recognize that EMDR and Energy Medicine techniques, while sharing some similarities, are distinct therapeutic approaches. EMDR is an evidence-based therapy primarily utilized for the treatment of trauma-related conditions. On the other hand, Energy Medicine techniques encompass a broader range of practices that may involve tapping, acupressure, and other energy-based interventions. Each modality possesses its own unique strengths and applications. The choice of therapy depends on your specific needs, preferences, and the nature of the challenges you are facing. It is advisable to consult with a qualified professional who can guide you in selecting the most appropriate approach for your individual circumstances.

Try it...

While I'm not teaching EMDR in this book, I can teach you two strategies that you can begin using immediately.

Strategy 1: Creating a Safe Space

The concept of having a safe space for visualization is a technique commonly used in relaxation exercises and mindfulness practices to manage stress and anxiety.

This technique involves creating a mental image of a peaceful, calming, and secure environment that you can mentally retreat to whenever you're feeling overwhelmed or anxious. It serves as a mental refuge where you can find solace, recharge, and regain a sense of control over your emotions.

Here's how the concept generally works:

- **Choose Your Space:** Begin by selecting a place in your mind that makes you feel safe, relaxed, and at ease. It could be a real location you've been to, or an entirely imaginary place. The key is that it evokes feelings of comfort and security.
- **Details:** As you visualize your safe space, focus on the sensory details. What do you see, hear, smell, and feel in this environment? The more vivid and detailed your visualization, the more effective it can be in calming your mind.
- **Engage Your Senses:** Imagine yourself fully present in this space. Feel the textures, hear the sounds, and immerse yourself in the calming atmosphere. Engaging your senses helps create a deeper connection to the visualization.

247

- **Use in Times of Stress:** When you're feeling stressed, anxious, or overwhelmed, close your eyes and bring your safe space to mind. Imagine yourself stepping into this space, allowing the feelings of relaxation and tranquility to wash over you.
- **Breathe and Recharge:** Take slow, deep breaths as you immerse yourself in your safe space. Focus on the calming sensations and let go of the stress or anxiety you're experiencing. You can imagine spending a few moments or as much time as you need in this space.
- **Returning to the Present:** When you're ready, slowly bring your awareness back to the present moment. Open your eyes and carry the sense of calm and relaxation with you.

Having a safe space for visualization offers several benefits:

- **Immediate Relief:** It provides a quick way to reduce stress and anxiety in the moment.
- **Emotional Regulation:** It helps you manage overwhelming emotions by giving you a mental retreat to regain composure.
- **Cognitive Distraction:** Focusing on the details of your safe space can divert your attention from distressing thoughts.
- **Positive Association:** Repeated use creates a positive mental connection to relaxation and security.
- **Empowerment:** It gives you a tool to actively manage your emotional well-being.

Remember, the effectiveness of this technique comes with practice. Over time, you'll become more skilled at entering your safe space mentally, and it will become a valuable tool in your stress management toolkit.

Strategy 2: Creating a Container

This container is an imaginary exercise that helps you manage distressing thoughts and emotions that can't be resolved immediately. I want you to visualize a container of your choosing, one that perfectly suits your needs. It can be as large or as small as you want, it can even be magical. The key is to ensure that this container feels safe and secure, providing a sense of protection. To make the container secure, imagine placing an imaginary lock on the container, keeping it all safe until the time comes for you to revisit it. This visualization technique empowers you to create a space where you can temporarily set aside difficult thoughts and beliefs, granting you the freedom to explore and heal at your own pace.

The concept of having a safe imaginary container to put distressing thoughts or feelings to be processed later is a psychological strategy that aims to help you manage overwhelming emotions in a controlled and constructive manner. This technique is often used in therapies like EMDR, CBT or other mindfulness practices.

Imagine your mind as a space where different thoughts and emotions reside. Sometimes, particularly during times of stress, anxiety, or emotional turmoil, these thoughts and emotions can become too intense to deal with immediately. The idea behind the safe imaginary container is to create a mental space where you can temporarily set aside these distressing thoughts or feelings, allowing you to continue with your daily life without feeling completely overwhelmed.

Here's how the concept generally works:

- **Recognition:** First, you acknowledge the thoughts or emotions that are causing you distress. It's important not to suppress or ignore them, as that can lead to further emotional difficulties.
- **Container Creation:** In your imagination, visualize a secure and safe container. This could be a box, a vault, a room, or any other imagery that makes you feel like the thoughts and emotions are contained and controlled.
- **Placing Thoughts/Feelings:** As you experience distressing thoughts or emotions, mentally place them inside this container. Imagine sealing it shut and knowing that they are there, waiting to be addressed at a more suitable time.
- **Set a Time:** Choose a specific time when you will revisit the container to process the thoughts or emotions. This could be during a therapy session, a journaling session, or a designated "processing time" you set aside for yourself.
- **Temporary Relief:** By containing the thoughts and emotions in this way, you give yourself a temporary sense of relief. This allows you to continue with your day without being consumed by the distress.
- **Scheduled Processing:** When the scheduled time arrives, open the container in your imagination. Sit down and give yourself permission to process the thoughts and emotions within it. This could involve journaling, talking to a therapist, or engaging in other therapeutic practices.

The safe imaginary container technique can be a valuable tool when you find yourself feeling overwhelmed and need to concentrate on immediate tasks without disregarding or suppressing your emotions entirely. It provides a way to acknowledge your feelings while also creating a structured approach to address them when you feel better prepared to do so.

This technique can help promote emotional resilience and prevent your feelings from becoming unmanageable. It is important to remember that these strategies are not intended for avoidance or denial of difficult emotions. Instead, they serve as tools to help you in managing emotions and mental challenges, particularly in situations where immediate resolution may not be possible. By utilizing these techniques, you can navigate through difficult emotions with greater ease and work towards finding constructive resolutions when the time is right.

To fully benefit from EMDR, it is crucial to work with a trained mental health professional who has undergone extensive training and possesses expertise in this therapeutic approach. EMDR involves a structured and specialized process that requires a deep understanding of trauma and its impact on mental health. A trained professional will have the necessary skills to guide you through the EMDR process, ensuring your safety and providing appropriate support throughout the sessions. They will also possess the knowledge to tailor the therapy to your specific needs and circumstances, maximizing its effectiveness in addressing trauma-related conditions. By collaborating with a trained mental health professional, you can have confidence in the quality of care you receive and increase the likelihood of achieving positive outcomes through EMDR therapy.

It can also be beneficial to address any harmful and limiting beliefs that come up through journaling. Take the time to identify these beliefs and question their validity. Explore alternative beliefs that are empowering and positive, which can serve as replacements. Remember to always journal without judgment, allowing your thoughts and emotions to come up naturally. If you feel overwhelmed or past trauma becomes too much to handle during journaling, rely on the safe space and container exercises. If the overwhelm persists or becomes unmanageable, don't hesitate to seek the assistance of a trained mental health professional. They can provide the necessary support and guidance as you work towards healing, ensuring your well-being and helping you navigate through any difficulties that may arise.

Start Small but Start Now!

If, despite implementing the strategies discussed in the previous sections, you still find yourself feeling overwhelmed and burdened by anxiety, it may be necessary to address the root causes that may feel overwhelming. It is completely understandable to feel this way. However, the good news is that you can initiate positive changes without feeling the need to tackle everything all at once.

Start by focusing on simple yet impactful steps that can greatly enhance your mental well-being. By taking small, manageable actions, you can gradually make progress and experience significant improvements in your overall mental health. Remember, every positive step you take, no matter how small, contributes to your well-being and sets the foundation for long-lasting change. Improving your diet, engaging in physical activity, practicing gratitude, and focusing on what you can control are excellent starting points.

1. Nourish Your Body:
One of the foundations of mental health is a balanced diet. Start your day with a nutritious breakfast that includes lean protein, healthy carbohydrates, and healthy fats. A well-rounded breakfast can provide you with sustained energy, stabilize blood sugar levels, and positively impact your mood throughout the day.

2. Embrace Physical Activity:
Physical exercise is a powerful tool for reducing anxiety and stress. You don't need to commit to intense workouts right away. Begin with a manageable goal, like taking a 10-minute walk outside. The fresh air and movement will not only boost your mood but also help clear your mind.

3. Practice Gratitude:
When anxiety takes hold, it's easy to focus on negative thoughts and worries. Counteract this by deliberately incorporating gratitude into your daily routine. Each day, write down three things you're grateful for. This simple practice can shift your mindset, bringing attention to the positive aspects of your life and encouraging a sense of contentment.

4. Start Small, but Start Now:
Remember, you don't have to tackle everything at once. It's okay to start small and gradually build on your efforts. Focus on what you can control at this moment and take steps towards positive change. By starting with manageable actions, you'll create a sense of achievement and momentum that can motivate you to take further steps in your journey to improved mental health.

5. Listen to Your Body:
Be mindful of how your body responds to the changes you make. Pay attention to the positive shifts in your mood, energy levels, and overall well-being. Acknowledge any improvements, no matter how small, as they indicate progress in the right direction.

6. Seek Support:
If you feel that your anxiety is overwhelming and difficult to manage on your own, don't hesitate to seek support from friends, family, or mental health professionals. Talking about your feelings and experiences can provide comfort and validation. Additionally, a mental health professional can offer guidance tailored to your specific needs.

7. Be Patient and Compassionate:
Healing takes time, and progress may not always be linear. Be patient with yourself and practice self-compassion throughout the journey. Remember that it's okay to have setbacks; they are a natural part of growth and learning.

Each step you take, no matter how small, is a step towards a healthier and happier you. Take it one day at a time, and remember that seeking support and being kind to yourself are essential components of your journey to improved mental well-being.

CHAPTER 5: Mastering Long-Term Control

Your mental health is everything — prioritize it.
Make the time like your life depends on it, because it does

~ Mel Robbins

In the preceding chapters, we have explored a vast array of information and discussed various aspects concerning anxiety. I have faith that you have been diligently monitoring your progress and dedicating time to reflect on the areas that need additional focus. Now that you have gained insights into the significance of identifying your anxiety and applying effective techniques to alleviate it, let's move forward to Step 3 of the AIM program.

Step 3 centers around investing in your mental health and making it top priority. This involves dedicating consistent effort to build a healthy mind. While we are accustomed to giving attention to our physical well-being and engaging in regular workouts to maintain our physical fitness, we often overlook the importance of nurturing our mental well-being. It is very important to acknowledge the significance of tending to our minds and overall mental health. The insights you have gained from the preceding chapters should have equipped you with the necessary tools to quickly redirect your anxiety and refocus your energy.

As emphasized in chapter 1, the aim of this book was not to eliminate your anxiety entirely but rather to empower you to TRANSFORM IT into something that serves you instead of controlling you. As you move forward beyond this

255

book, discovering and embracing *your purpose* will become necessary if you want happiness and want to gain control over your anxiety.

Take a moment to ask yourself:
- What is your purpose in life?
- What brings you joy and motivates you to wake up every morning?

When you align with your purpose, you'll find a renewed sense of energy and determination in your life. Living with purpose empowers you to feel more in control and energized in your life.

Make your mental health a top priority and actively participate in regular maintenance for your health, becoming a strong advocate for your own well-being.

Following the dietary, sleep, and supplement recommendations will help you stay healthy, happy, and anxiety-free. Consider incorporating herbs and supplements into a natural, toxin-free lifestyle for physical and mental longevity.

Always keep in mind that learning and personal growth are ongoing journeys. My own exploration into natural and alternative medicine began when I was 26 and diagnosed with endometriosis, and it took me decades to truly master. Don't feel overwhelmed by the idea of understanding and absorbing everything all at once.

Each year, you will uncover new possibilities and opportunities for natural and alternative healing. To start, focus on essential supplements such as a high-quality, food-based multivitamin, beneficial fish oil, probiotics, and vitamin D. As necessary, you can gradually incorporate additional supplements like magnesium and adaptogens. However, it's important to keep things simple initially to avoid feeling overwhelmed. Remember, it's a gradual process of discovery and implementation.

Never forget that self-care is not a selfish act. It is essential to recharge and take care of yourself in order to show up as the best version of yourself for your loved ones. By prioritizing your mental health, you enhance your ability to care for others and become a positive force in their lives. Remember, taking care of yourself is not only beneficial for you but also for those around you.

Always keep in mind the valuable lesson from the airplane analogy: taking care of yourself enables you to be there for others.

If you're not familiar with this analogy, it draws a parallel between self-care and the safety instructions provided before a flight. Just as flight attendants instruct passengers to secure their own oxygen masks before assisting others in case of an emergency, this analogy emphasizes the importance of prioritizing self-care as a fundamental step in effectively caring for others or navigating life's challenges. Remember, by taking care of yourself *first*, you are better equipped to support and uplift those around you.

Here's how the analogy works:

In an airplane emergency, passengers are advised to put on their own oxygen masks before assisting others, even children. This is because if you aren't functioning at your best, you won't be able to help others effectively. Similarly, in life, you need to take care of your physical, mental, and emotional well-being first. If you're exhausted, stressed, or unwell, you won't be able to support or care for others optimally.

The analogy emphasizes that taking care of yourself isn't selfish—it's necessary. Engaging in self-care activities, setting boundaries, managing stress, and maintaining your overall health provide you with the strength and resilience needed to tackle challenges and support others when necessary.

Just as having oxygen ensures you can function in an emergency, practicing self-care builds your emotional and mental resilience.

As previously mentioned in Chapter 3, self care will prepare you to handle life's difficulties without becoming overwhelmed or burnt out. When you're well-cared for, you're more available, patient, and empathetic in your interactions with others. Prioritizing self-care enhances your ability to provide meaningful support. Neglecting self-care can lead to burnout, leaving you emotionally and physically drained. Prioritizing self-care can prevent this exhaustion and help you sustain your energy over the long term.

When others see you taking care of yourself, it can serve as a positive example, encouraging them to prioritize their own well-being. In essence, the airplane analogy emphasizes the idea that taking care of yourself is not only beneficial for you but also necessary for your ability to navigate life's challenges and care for others effectively. Just as ensuring your own oxygen mask is secured before assisting others ensures your well-being, prioritizing self-care ensures you're prepared to navigate life's demands while maintaining a healthy balance.

Recognize the power you have to change your life and create long-term wellness through your lifestyle choices. When you prioritize yourself and value self-care by ensuring sufficient sleep, consuming whole foods, reducing toxins, exercising, and meditating, you show your body that you care and want to take care of it in return for its care of you.

Your brain and body yearn for your happiness and diligently works to repair any damage when you provide the necessary building blocks for healing. View your anxiety symptoms as your body's cry for help, communicating that neglect and your destructive lifestyle practices are limiting its ability to function optimally.

As Maya Angelou said, "When you know better, you do better." This book has provided you with the knowledge and skills to make positive changes, leaving no room for the excuse of not knowing what to do. When you have control of anxiety and feel peace in your life, you have the ability to handle stress, improve your digestion, and navigate external challenges more effectively.

What we think or what we know, or what we believe is,
in the end, of little consequence.
The only consequence is what we do!
~John Ruskin

One of the key distinctions between individuals with anxiety and those without is that those without anxiety take action in life. If you want to live a life free from anxiety, it is important not only to be clear about your desires, turn those desires into measurable goals, break those goals down into actionable steps, and visualize and affirm your desired outcomes, but also to take decisive action.

Embrace a curious mindset and explore the various strategies listed in this book, and experiment to see what works best for you. If you find that a particular intervention or strategy doesn't resonate with you, don't hesitate to shift to the next one. Remember, it is through taking daily action and being open to exploration that you can pave the way to an anxiety-free life. Start by adding one new strategy each week, then gradually incorporate more, building momentum along the way.

Hope and positivity have incredible healing power. When you genuinely believe in your capacity to reshape your life, you'll witness astonishing positive changes. While you work on reaching your goals, keep in mind that striving for perfection isn't the ultimate goal. Recognize that not every action you take will result in precisely the outcome you're aiming for. Embrace the reality that some steps might not unfold as planned. Embracing mistakes, navigating close calls, and trying out new things are all vital aspects of the journey that ultimately leads to success. Remember, it's through consistency and a mindset of growth that you'll conquer obstacles and attain the outcomes you're aiming for.

Embrace the mindset that each action you take is like taking on an experiment or a journey of self-discovery. It's not about victory or defeat; it's about either achieving success or gaining valuable insights through the process. Remember you either win, or you learn. This outlook empowers you to act with courage, evaluate the outcomes, pivot if you must, and then fine tune your next moves based on the wisdom you gather. Growth comes from learning, adjusting, and moving forward.

At times, you might need to keep moving forward even when you are not motivated. Marie Forleo recently posted this quote "The secret to lasting motivation is MOTIVE. Make sure your 'why' is from your heart, not your ego". Once you know and are clear about your "Why" then you will be "motivated" to take action.

Keep focused on your positive results until you gather momentum and witness the positive changes that will fuel your motivation to stay on course. Keep in mind that every step, no matter how small, brings you closer to your desired goal of being mentally and physically healthy and in control of your life.

Throughout this book, I discussed how anxiety can serve a purpose, alerting us to potential threats. However, there can be flaws in the way our brains process anxiety, leading to false alarms. Given your history with anxiety, you might be familiar with the constant chatter or overwhelming panic it brings. You may find yourself believing irrational thoughts fueled by anxiety.

It is crucial to learn to differentiate
between genuine fear
and the false alarms triggered by anxiety.

By tuning into your intuition instead of giving into the panic of anxiety, you can effectively distinguish between genuine threats and exaggerated responses. Your intuition serves as a trustworthy guide, helping you navigate away from potentially dangerous situations, such as entering an environment that feels off or interacting with someone who makes you feel uncomfortable. On the other hand, the anxious chatter and panic induced by anxiety are different, usually loud and frantic, making it difficult to hear the gentle voice of intuition. Remember, nurturing your capacity to recognize and trust your intuition can empower you to make wise decisions, even when faced with anxiety. Trust in your inner wisdom and allow it to guide you towards choices that align with your well-being and safety.

Throughout this book, my primary goal has been to EMPOWER and encourage you to give top priority to your mental health and build emotional stability from within, enabling you to handle external changes with less reactivity.

Finding your emotional balance involves a mix of important elements. Giving priority to getting enough restful sleep is a key factor, as it significantly impacts how you feel. Alongside this, feeding your mind and gut with wholesome foods, dealing with negative emotions that linger and impact you, and facing your fears instead of avoiding or stuffing them all chip in to create a sense of emotional balance. Keep in mind that by actively embracing these practices, you're moving forward in looking after your emotional well-being and working toward greater stability in your life.

The preceding four chapters have provided you with the necessary tools to build emotional stability through the practice of self-care. If you find yourself feeling more anxious, take a moment to determine whether you have been nourishing your body with healthy food and taking care of your gut health. Evaluate the quality of your sleep and reflect on any potential factors that may have disrupted it, as restless nights can contribute to increased irritability and reactivity during the day.

To aid in improving your sleep, consider utilizing devices such as the Oura ring, Fitbit, or your smartwatch to monitor the quality of your sleep. If you frequently snore or experience frequent awakenings during the night, it may be beneficial to consider getting tested for sleep apnea.

Another beneficial practice is to incorporate regular journaling and engage in self-reflection to address troubling thoughts and emotions. By expressing your thoughts and feelings on paper, you can gain clarity and perspective. Additionally, consider utilizing techniques such as tapping or practicing QiGong to help diffuse the emotional intensity associated with these thoughts and emotions. These practices can provide a sense of release and promote emotional well-being.

Lastly, make sure that you stay consistent with taking your supplements and vitamins to provide your body with the necessary nutrients for proper functioning. By incorporating these daily check-ins into your routine, you can effectively maintain control over your anxiety and create emotional stability. Remember, by paying attention to these factors and making necessary adjustments, you can enhance your emotional well-being.

Setting S.M.A.R.T Goals

To keep up your progress in managing anxiety, it's necessary to set goals. As you create these goals, shift your focus towards the outcomes you want to achieve, rather than getting caught up in the obstacles that might pop up. Think of it like how martial arts students prepare to break a board – they concentrate on the space below the board, not how hard or thick the board is. By fixing your attention on the positive results you're aiming for, you can keep a strong mindset and overcome any hurdles that come your way. Remember, the strength of goal-setting lies in visualizing success and taking determined steps towards it, regardless of any challenges that might come your way.

It's not about being better than others,
but being better than you used to be
~Dr. Wayne Dyer

Learn how to create SMART goals—goals that are **Specific, Measurable, Achievable, Realistic,** and **Timely**—so you can continue improving in important aspects of your life, both short and long term.

Knowing your "why" is crucial for reaching your goals. For example, if you're trying to lose weight because you want to fit into a certain size, it might not be as powerful as if you're doing it for a major health benefit. By setting SMART goals and understanding the deeper motivations driving them, you'll be more motivated to succeed in your pursuits and continue your progress toward a more satisfying life. When you're outlining a goal to manage anxiety over the long term, start by identifying the specific actions necessary and the changes required to lessen your anxiety and enhance your overall well-being.

Begin with a clear vision of the outcome you're aiming for, but then dive deeper into the exact details of the steps needed to achieve that goal.

For example, in order for a goal to be *specific*, you must define the details of the goal by focusing on the who, what, where, and why:

- Who will be involved in reaching this goal?
- What exactly will be addressed or accomplished?
- Where will the goal take place?
- Why are you setting this goal? What makes it important, and what resources or limits are involved?

Imagine you were given a magical wand, capable of instantly bringing your desired outcomes to life. Picture waking up to discover yourself as the most remarkable version imaginable and visualize how this transformation would reshape your life. Take note of the substantial changes required to make this goal a reality. Use the insights from this exercise to refine and define your goal.

It's important that your goal is ***measurable***, enabling you to *track your progress* and determine when you've achieved it. By having a vivid, clear image of what you want to achieve, it becomes easier to recognize the steps needed to get there.

Let's use an example to explain this idea. Imagine you're currently experiencing around five panic attacks every week, and your objective is to bring that number down to 0-1 panic attacks per week. This specific goal gives you a clear idea of what the end goal is and helps you focus on what needs to be done to achieve it. You can now get clear about what exercises you need to include, what lifestyle changes you need to make, and what emotional clearing needs to take place so you can achieve your goal of 0-1 panic attacks a week,

By setting this *specific goal* that you can *measure*, you're able to monitor your progress and gradually work towards decreasing the frequency of panic attacks. It provides you with a concrete target to aim for and offers a distinct sign of success when you achieve the goal of having 0-1 panic attacks per week. This clear direction empowers you to take the required actions and implement strategies to manage and ultimately reduce the occurrence of panic attacks.

Another example to consider is weight loss. If you record your weight before setting the goal and then weekly check in to measure total inches or fat lost, you can observe a clear pattern emerging over a few weeks.

When you're setting goals, aim for a level of clarity and specificity that lets you see changes as time goes on. This method helps you keep a close eye on your progress and stay aligned with your overall goal of managing anxiety and boosting your mental and physical well-being. Having goals you can measure allows you to chart your progress, make any needed tweaks, and celebrate the milestones you achieve.

Clarity and measurable aspects create a strong base for staying motivated and keeping your attention fixed on your path toward a life that's richer and freer from anxiety.

Let's revisit the baseline you established in chapter 2, which represents your anxiety level when you began reading this book. Take a moment to reflect:

- Have you noticed any changes in your anxiety since then?
- Have you made the necessary lifestyle adjustments?
- Are you experiencing a decrease in the frequency of anxiety attacks or a reduction in overall anxiety levels?
- Did you complete the exercises as instructed?

Consider visually tracking your progress through a chart or other means. If you haven't seen significant progress, take a moment to reflect on the possible reasons why. It's important to evaluate your commitment to the process and identify any areas where you may need to make adjustments or seek additional support. Remember, progress takes time and effort, so be patient and persistent in your journey towards managing anxiety and improving your well-being.

The next step is really important because setting goals that are too ambitious or unrealistic can lead to feelings of defeat and the urge to quit. For instance, if you're not ready to take action toward a particular goal, you won't achieve the results you want or find success. It's important to make sure your goals are both sensible and attainable, since this will keep your motivation high and improve your chances of succeeding.

Setting goals that are *achievable & realistic* better equips you to stay focused and make steady progress in managing anxiety. Equally important is to consider whether a goal is practical and lines up with what you truly want to accomplish. Setting goals that matter to you and match your ambitions can ignite a sense of purpose and determination that propels you toward success.

For instance, if money isn't a big driving force for you, setting a goal of making a million dollars might not spark the motivation needed to get you going. Similarly, if you're someone who tends to avoid putting in the hard work and leans toward taking it easy, aiming for a million dollars might not be something you can realistically reach. It's important to make sure your goals line up with your personal values, what keeps you motivated, and your work style to ensure they're both meaningful and doable. When you set goals that really connect with your genuine dreams and match up with what you *can* do, you boost the chances of staying motivated and seeing real progress toward the outcomes you're after.

The last piece of a SMART goal involves putting a *time limit* on it. Having a target date or deadline can really boost your chances of achieving the goal by giving you focus and motivation. Think of it like running on a track – if you don't know where the finish line is, you can easily lose momentum and direction. That's why it's necessary to set doable timeframes for your goals. This creates a sense of urgency and responsibility that can push you ahead and make sure you're on the right path to reaching your goals. Remember, putting clear time limits on your goals is a key part of maximizing your shot at success.

Breaking down your goals into specific timeframes, whether it's six months, six weeks, or even daily, can be a real help in staying motivated and focused. Also, mixing up both short-term and long-term goals is a smart way to keep your motivation high and your path clear.

Personally, every year, either around my birthday or before the new year, I jot down some goals for the next six months, a year, or even five to ten years ahead. I like to organize my goals into five different areas, and then I jot down specific steps for each one. Here's how I do it:

- Spirituality
- Health
- Relationships
- Career
- Finances
- Personal Growth

For each category, I come up with 3-5 actions that will guide me toward my goals. Take "Health" for example; I'll break it down into groups like diet and nutrition, supplements, exercise, meditation, and my target weight, among other things.

While having time limits on goals can be useful, remember that not every goal will be achieved within the planned time. Some might need more time, stretching even to a few years, but what matters is sticking to it and keeping your focus until the goals are achieved. The main point is to keep consistently working on your goals, adjusting timelines if needed, and staying committed to the journey of moving forward and growing.

Dive in and start your journey towards accomplishing your goals by taking those first steps. The trick to moving ahead is to really pay attention to the feedback you get as you go, since your progress is always changing and growing. Reach out to others for their input, valuing what they think and what they can share, but also look within yourself. Stop and think if what you're doing lines up with both your short-term and long-term goals. This self-check lets you make sure your efforts match your desired outcomes, so you can make any needed changes and stay on course. By actively seeking input from others and checking in with yourself, you give yourself the power to make well-informed choices and navigate the path toward success.

Tune in closely to your body, because it's like the compass guiding you to your dreams. Feeling relaxed and joyful shows you're on the right track toward fulfilling your true purpose. But when exhaustion, tension, pain, unhappiness, or anger take over, that's a sign you need to adjust your course. Take a pause, listen, and understand the messages your body is sending you – your feelings and emotions are acting as your guide. Pay attention and ask yourself: *are you really picking up on what your body's saying?* By building a strong connection with your body and being open to its messages, you can make wise choices and navigate toward a life that's more aligned and fulfilling.

Alongside taking action, *persistence* becomes your biggest ally in reaching your goals. It's all about keeping up with your routines, staying strong in the face of challenges, and sticking to your objectives without wavering. As mentioned earlier, the urge to give up might show up, tempting you to go back to that comfort zone that used to fuel your anxiety. But your success really depends on your determination to keep going, keep pushing, and keep moving toward your goals. Settling for anything less shouldn't be an option. The mastery over anxiety is waiting for you at the end of this journey, and you have what it takes to achieve it. Stay steady, keep moving ahead, and embrace the life-changing strength of persistence.

Keep a List...

When anxiety seems to take over your days, consciously redirect yourself toward what brings you joy and makes you happy. It's through your choices that you open up a path for positive change.

To keep your motivation up and your spirit lifted while managing anxiety, make a list of things or activities that lift your mood and put that list where you can easily see it. This list can be a helpful reminder when you feel stuck or when anxiety creeps back in. Use it as a tool to calm anxiety and remember the steps you can take when it shows up. It becomes a valuable resource to guide you toward healthy actions, especially when your mind is overwhelmed and it's tough to figure out what to do next. By turning to this list, you're taking charge of addressing anxiety and putting your well-being first.

When anxiety starts to sneak in, pause and ask yourself, *"What can I do right now to make myself feel better?"* Write down the things that you think will improve your mood. Remember, there's no right or wrong answer – your list is all about what you personally *need.* Put down anything that you find helpful for easing your struggle with anxiety. Whether it's techniques you've learned from earlier chapters or other enjoyable and calming activities, this list is a comforting reminder that you hold the power to feel better and that the anxious feeling won't last long. Feel free to make your list your own, based on what clicks with you, and let it guide you toward finding comfort and relief when anxiety shows up.

When you're feeling happy and calm, take a moment to jot down all the things that boost your mood and bring you comfort, whether they're big or small. This collection of ideas will be a valuable guide for you during anxious moments and help you keep a positive perspective as you work on managing anxiety.

I've witnessed one of my patients finding immense relief by making a list of activities he enjoys in his everyday life, like reading, doing yoga, and cooking while spending time with his family. These reminders become a strong tool for him when he's caught up in negative thoughts. Adopt the habit of jotting down the things that make you happy and provide comfort, and let this list be a source of inspiration and support when times get tough.

You can personalize your list by adding activities you love, like petting your cat, listening to music, taking a soothing Epsom salt bath, meditating, practicing Tapping, journaling, dancing, or practicing QiGong. You can even add in strategies from this book that have worked for you, making them easy to come back to when you need them.

Keep your list simple and centered on activities that are easy to do, because when anxiety hits, complicated or time-consuming plans might not be doable. Make sure the things on your list don't demand too much time but can still give your mood a boost. After you've made the list, keep it where you can easily find it.

Your mind handles countless choices each day, so having a ready-made list of activities that make you feel good is much better than trying to come up with ideas when you're feeling anxious and stressed. With this handy resource, you can effortlessly turn to activities that bring you comfort and lift your spirits, giving you a useful tool for navigating through anxious moments.

Also, making a "feel good list" does more than just list activities – it reinforces positive ways to handle anxiety and moves you away from your old negative patterns. While you're putting this list together, put actions that match the kind of life you're working toward at the top.

Avoid numbing behaviors that could slow you down, like getting drunk, smoking, overeating junk food, or spending endless time on social media. Keep in mind that regularly practicing these positive ways of dealing with anxiety helps you build up good habits. Set aside some time to write down all the positive activities that come to mind – anything that boosts your well-being in a healthy and uplifting way. Use this chance to create a collection of activities that's all yours, bringing you happiness, calm, and a sense of accomplishment.

Put your list somewhere you'll see it often, like the fridge, bathroom mirror, or a whiteboard in your room.

Keep your focus on getting better at managing your anxiety and giving your mental well-being top priority. With time, these changes will turn into automatic, healthy habits – kind of like brushing your teeth or washing your face. Embrace the journey toward a life that's more balanced and satisfying, knowing you've got the tools and resources to get through tough moments and build up your sense of well-being.

Create Structure To Your Day

Living a structured life is of utmost importance when it comes to enhancing your mental health. Structure provides a sense of stability, predictability, and purpose, which are essential for maintaining emotional well-being. Establishing daily routines and sticking to a schedule can significantly reduce your feelings of anxiety and stress, as it eliminates uncertainty and chaos from your daily life.

A structured approach allows you to set clear goals and priorities, promoting a sense of accomplishment and control over your actions. It also supports building healthy habits, such as regular exercise, adequate sleep, and balanced nutrition, which are vital for mental and physical well-being.

By including structure into your life, you can build discipline, improve your time management skills, and create a stronger sense of self, ultimately leading to improved overall mental health and a greater capacity to cope with life's challenges.

Creating structure in your day can significantly improve productivity, focus, and overall mental well-being.

Here are some practical steps to help you establish a structured daily routine:

- **Set Clear Goals:** Start by identifying your priorities and setting achievable SMART goals for the day. Break down large tasks into smaller, manageable steps to make them less daunting.
- **Create a Daily Schedule:** Develop a daily schedule that allocates specific time slots for different activities, including work or study, personal time, exercise, meals, and relaxation. Stick to this schedule consistently to build a routine.
- **Wake Up Early:** Begin your day with enough time to spare by waking up early. Early mornings often provide a quiet and peaceful environment, allowing you to focus on important tasks without distractions.
- **Prioritize Tasks:** Arrange your tasks based on their importance and deadlines. Tackle the most critical tasks during your peak energy hours, which are usually in the morning for many people.

- **Time Blocking:** Implement the practice of time blocking, where you allocate specific time intervals for different activities. For instance, dedicate an hour for emails, two hours for work projects, and 30 minutes for exercise.
- **Include Breaks:** Integrate short breaks into your schedule to recharge and avoid burnout. Use these breaks to stretch, take a walk, or engage in a quick mindfulness exercise to refresh your mind.
- **Limit Distractions:** Identify potential distractions and minimize their impact. Turn off social media notifications and create a designated workspace that promotes focus and productivity.
- **Maintain Consistency:** Stick to your daily routine consistently to establish a habit. Consistency is key to making structure a natural part of your life.
- **Review and Adjust:** At the end of each day, review your accomplishments and reflect on areas for improvement. Make necessary adjustments to your schedule to optimize productivity and well-being.
- **Allow Flexibility:** While structure is important, it's important to allow some flexibility in your day to adapt to unexpected events or changing priorities. Embrace the adaptability of your routine without abandoning the overall structure.

By incorporating these strategies into your daily life, you can create a structured routine that enhances your mental health, boosts productivity, and brings a sense of accomplishment and satisfaction to your days.

Health "Snacks" For Better Mental Health

The introduction to the idea of "health snacks" came to my attention through an interview on Marie Forleo's Marie TV show featuring Dr. Rangan Chatterjee. As the popular BBC Breakfast doctor and bestselling author of "Feel Better in 5", Dr. Chatterjee emphasized the simplicity of achieving optimal health. He shared that by incorporating "health snacks" into our daily routines, we can make significant strides in improving our well-being. Just as we nourish our bodies with nutritious snacks, taking a few minutes each day to indulge in mental health activities can have a profound impact on our emotional state and overall outlook on life.

Whether it's practicing mindfulness meditation, deep breathing exercises, gentle stretching, or journaling, these short but meaningful breaks provide a much-needed opportunity to reset and recharge amidst the busyness of our daily life.

This concept highlights the power of small, manageable actions, which can have a profound impact on our overall health and happiness. By embracing these brief yet powerful practices, we can nurture our mental health and lead a more balanced and fulfilling life.

Mindfulness meditation allows us to be present in the moment, promoting a sense of calm while reducing stress. Deep breathing exercises are simple yet effective tools in promoting relaxation, as they activate the body's relaxation response. Gentle stretching helps release tension in the body, alleviating physical and emotional stress. Journaling allows us to express our thoughts and feelings, providing clarity and insight into our emotions.

Taking three to five minutes out of our busy day to incorporate these health snacks into our daily routine ensures that we prioritize our mental health and well-being.

Even just five minutes of dedicated time each day can make a significant difference, helping us build resilience, improve focus, and promote a more positive mindset.

By giving ourselves the gift of these healthy mental breaks, we can better navigate life's challenges and embrace a more balanced and fulfilling existence.

Remember, taking care of our minds is just as important as taking care of our bodies, and these health snacks are a powerful way to nourish our mental and emotional selves.

No More Zero Days!

Embracing the concept of "no zero days" is a powerful commitment to prioritizing your mental health every single day. It involves recognizing that even small, incremental steps towards self-care and well-being can have a profound impact on our lives.

By adopting this mindset, you vow not to let *a day go by* without doing something, no matter how small, to nurture your mental health. It might involve practicing mindfulness for a few minutes, engaging in physical activity, seeking support from loved ones, journaling, or pursuing a hobby that brings you joy.

Make a promise to yourself to move forward each day in different areas of your life, pushing you closer to your goals. If your goal is to be physically fit, commit to doing some form of exercise daily – it could be aerobics, lifting weights, taking walks, or even just stretching – even if it's just for 5 minutes a day.

Begin by setting five clear actions that you can track every day, regardless of the situation. Personally, my daily routine centers around journaling, taking my morning walk, praying, staying hydrated, and doing regular stretches. Think about the progress you could achieve with these five actions pushing you toward your important goals – you might even surprise yourself!

As a new year starts, take the opportunity to replace four negative habits with positive ones. In just five years, that's twenty new healthy habits shaping a life free from anxiety. These changes, no matter how small, add up to significant transformation. This total commitment to better mental and physical health will promote a more well-rounded and satisfying life. As time passes, these daily efforts will also build resilience, reinforce healthy coping strategies, and equip you to face challenges with a clearer and healthier mindset. By embracing the idea of "no zero days," you acknowledge the importance of your well-being and embrace the powerful impact of consistent self-care in building a happier and more resilient version of yourself.

Feel Empowered In Your Relationships

If you are dealing with anxiety, relationships can often increase symptoms of anxiety if you lack an understanding of how it affects you, how to establish healthy boundaries, and how to communicate effectively.

In order to feel more stable in relationships, it is very important to surround yourself with people who are *consistent, reliable,* and *dependable.* Being in a relationship with someone who engages in mind games, breaks promises, and lacks consistency can lead to increased stress and anxiety within the relationship.

In addition to choosing a consistent and reliable partner, it is also important to learn how to communicate effectively and establish healthy boundaries. These skills are necessary for building good relationships and taking care of yourself. When you improve your communication skills, it can reduce stress, boost your confidence, and make your connections with others more joyful and fulfilling.

To feel more confident in your relationships and in control of your anxiety, it's important to develop a sense of empowerment inside your relationships. Here are some important communication skills that can significantly improve your existing relationships. Learning the art of effective communication and setting healthy boundaries doesn't just empower you, it also changes the way you handle tough conversations. Armed with these necessary skills, you'll become *less reactive* and more in control when facing difficult discussions. However, if you don't set clear boundaries or improve your communication, you might start feeling resentful over time, which can make conflicts even worse.

For most of us, having strong communication skills isn't something that comes naturally. However, just like learning to talk or walk, effective communication is a skill that can be developed over time. Learning effective communication skills will naturally increase your sense of control in your relationships.

During my upbringing, I never had the chance to learn these important communication skills. As a result, I struggled with managing interactions and conflicts with others. I often took their words and actions personally, which created more problems for me. To make matters worse, even small arguments would escalate into major conflicts because I lacked the tools to navigate and resolve disagreements gracefully.

Many of us have grown up with feedback being presented in one of two ways: through shame or blame. These experiences may have influenced our perception of criticism and how we react to it. Unfortunately, this often means that we haven't learned how to give or receive productive and respectful feedback, which is a very important skill.

Learning how to provide constructive feedback is empowering. It allows us to communicate effectively, encouraging growth, understanding, and trust in our relationships. By adopting this skill, we can change our perspective on feedback, turning it into a positive tool that builds personal development and strengthens our connections with others. It's never too late to learn and improve.

In the world of communication, both giving and receiving feedback are skills that can be developed over time. To make our interactions healthier, we not only need to get better at offering constructive feedback but also at taking it in gracefully, no matter how it's given. When we get better at giving helpful feedback, we help others improve and grow.

And being open to getting feedback is just as important. Letting go of the need to control its delivery allows us to focus on the lessons we can learn from it. This two-way approach creates an atmosphere of understanding, kindness, and ongoing progress for ourselves and the people around us.

Sometimes, when our loved ones give us feedback, it can make us defensive – that's totally normal. It might stir up our worries and insecurities, making us feel uneasy. But what if we looked at feedback in a different light? What if we practiced listening carefully and taking it in without overreacting and giving their feedback too much importance? At those times, using positive self-talk can be a great trick. By telling ourselves things like "I can handle this feedback calmly and learn from it" or "I'm strong enough to get through this," we build up inner strength and bravery.

Think back to a time when you received feedback and felt defensive. Did you cross your arms? Were you ready to argue your point? Did you start feeling anxious, frustrated, and overwhelmed? If this sounds familiar, it's important to develop a way to comfort yourself and be open to the useful message in the feedback. Changing how you approach feedback by wanting to learn and understand can make a big difference.

When you're feeling overwhelmed, it's okay to say you need to talk later when you're calmer. You could simply say, "*I can only process so much right now. Can we talk about this when I'm feeling more composed?*" This shows you're taking care of yourself and sets the stage for a more productive conversation at a later time. Remember, it's totally fine to set your limits and express your feelings during these times. Saying, "*I need a break*" or explaining how someone's words or actions are affecting your ability to listen shows that you're aware of your needs and that you're practicing healthy communication.

When we take on this mindful approach, we're setting the stage for meaningful conversation, empathy, and personal growth. When we respect our emotional limits while still being open to feedback, we're making room for conversations that bring us closer and create stronger bonds with the people in our lives. By choosing to embrace feedback with kindness and understanding, we're building a safe place for our own personal growth.

Instead of getting defensive, we're choosing to learn from what we go through and create deeper connections with the people we care about. As we go down this path of learning together, we're making our relationships stronger and opening the door for growth, both individually and together.

Healthy communication also involves *how* we communicate. Switching from aggressive communication to a more assertive style is a life-changing journey that improves relationships and empowers you in many ways. Aggressive communication, often driven by strong emotions, leads to misunderstandings, hurt feelings, and strained connections. Unlike the aggressive style of communication, choosing assertive communication means confidently and clearly expressing your thoughts and feelings while being considerate of others. Assertive communication is not just about the words you use; it's also about how you convey them and your intentions behind them.

Adopting assertive communication not only prevents conflicts and improves understanding but also boosts your self-confidence and sense of control. It involves open conversations where your needs and boundaries matter, and you actively listen to others. Shifting from passive, passive-aggressive, or aggressive communication to assertive communication takes time and effort. Many of us didn't learn assertive communication at home; instead, more aggressive

281

approaches might have been the norm, leading to passive reactions. Learning how to confidently communicate your needs without fear and anxiety is a skill that can be easily mastered.

Before we dive in, let's get familiar with the four communication styles. Later, I'll share two skills that will help you handle any situation with confidence.

There are four basic communication styles: passive, aggressive, passive-aggressive, and assertive. Knowing these styles can help you recognize them when others use them. While assertive communication is the most effective, you'll often come across the other three.

People using the *passive* style of communication seem indifferent and tend to avoid directly expressing their feelings or needs. This can lead to misunderstandings, anger, and resentment. Passive communicators struggle with eye contact, display poor body language, and have difficulty saying no.

Here's an example of passive communication:

You're invited to a social gathering that you really don't want to attend. Instead of directly expressing your feelings, you decide to attend the event but show up late and leave early without explaining why. You might avoid making eye contact, not contribute much to conversations, and give off an overall vibe of disinterest. Your friends might notice your behavior and wonder why you seemed distant, but you haven't communicated your true feelings or needs clearly. This passive approach could lead to misunderstandings and potentially damage your relationships.

Passive-aggressive communication is a blend of passive and aggressive traits. It's an unhealthy way to express anger or resentment. Instead of directly addressing the person they're

282

upset with, they will communicate their feelings indirectly through grumbling, body language, silent treatment, or spreading rumors.

Here are some examples of the passive-aggressive style:

You have a roommate who frequently leaves dirty dishes in the sink, despite agreeing to take turns doing the dishes. Instead of addressing the issue directly, you decide to use passive-aggressive communication. You might start slamming dishes around while you're washing them, sighing loudly, and making comments like, "Wow, it's amazing how some people just can't clean up after themselves." You're not openly confronting the problem but rather expressing your frustration indirectly through your actions and comments. This passive-aggressive approach can lead to tension, misunderstandings, and a lack of resolution in the situation.

Aggressive communicators tend to be loud, demanding, and controlling, often blaming, intimidating, criticizing, and attacking others.

The best way to communicate and build strong relationships is through *assertive communication*. When you're being assertive, you can share your needs, desires, thoughts, and emotions while also considering the needs of others. Assertive communicators aim for **win-win** situations and show consideration for others' feelings while honoring their own. They often use "I" statements when expressing concerns, such as "I feel frustrated when you showed up late for the meeting." I will discuss "I" statements in more detail shortly.

Assertive communicators take responsibility for their feelings and behaviors without blaming others. To become more assertive, it's important to use "I" statements, make eye contact, and learn to say no confidently. Express your needs with self-confidence, since assertive communication can also help you set healthy boundaries. Learning assertive communication will empower you to navigate various situations with greater comfort and enhance your relationships.

Shifting from ineffective communication styles to being assertive might take some practice, but it's a really important skill for having good interactions. As you put in the time and effort, you'll get better at expressing yourself and building stronger connections with others.

Now that we've covered the differences between the 4 types of communication styles, let's dive into two useful techniques that can support you in reaching your goals while also supporting your relationships.

The first strategy is known as the **Sandwich Method,** also referred to as the *Sandwich Technique.*

The Sandwich Method is a powerful communication strategy that can transform your relationships, and it's surprisingly simple yet highly effective. Though it might require a bit of practice before it becomes effortless for you, the results are worth it.

Before diving into the sandwich method, it's important to make sure you are in a positive and receptive mental state. If you find yourself overwhelmed by anger to the point where coming up with a single positive statement feels impossible, it's best to hold off on implementing the sandwich method.

The sandwich method depends on constructive feedback, and for it to work well, you need to approach the conversation with a clear and composed mind. Taking a pause to breathe, reflect, and regain your emotional balance will make your conversation more productive and compassionate. So, whenever your emotions are intense, take the time you need to get into a positive mindset before using the sandwich method for effective communication.

Think of using the Sandwich Method for giving constructive feedback as building a sandwich.

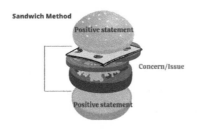

- **Step 1:** Start with the base of the sandwich, which involves saying something positive, either about the person or the situation.
- **Step 2:** Add what you need to say, whether it's a concern or a frustration, but do so constructively and respectfully.
- **Step 3:** End the communication with another positive statement.

This technique provides a creative approach to addressing difficult issues, while ensuring that others can genuinely hear your message without feeling attacked or becoming defensive. The Sandwich Method encourages understanding and supports open, constructive conversations, making it a valuable tool for enhancing your interactions with others.

Here are some examples using the Sandwich Method:
- **Example 1** - Talking to a Coworker:
  "*Hey, I really appreciate you helping me with this project. You've done an excellent job clarifying most of the details. I do have some concerns about the direction we're taking, and*

I suggest we try it this way instead. I know we make a great team, and I'm confident we can achieve success together."

- **Example 2** - Speaking with Your Mother-in-Law:
  "Linda, I want you to know how much I appreciate you watching the kids; they absolutely love spending time with you. I've noticed they've been getting used to eating processed foods lately, and I would like them to stick to the healthy foods I pack for them. They adore you and will listen to your guidance, so if you could encourage them to eat healthier, it would mean a lot to me. Thank you so much for your understanding."

Using the Sandwich Method allows you to address concerns and communicate your needs in a positive and respectful manner, making it easier for others to receive your message without feeling defensive.

This last example combines the Sandwich Method with the "I" Statement Method.

"I" statements, also known as "I" messages, are a communication style that centers around the feelings or beliefs of the speaker, rather than focusing on the person they are addressing.

For instance, a person might say to their partner, "I feel abandoned and worried when you consistently come home late without calling," instead of using a demanding tone like, "Why are you never home on time?" Using "I" statements empowers the speaker to express themselves assertively without making accusations, which can often lead to defensiveness in the listener.

Using an "I" statement helps you become aware of a problem and *take responsibility for your own thoughts and feelings*, rather than unfairly placing blame on someone else.

When used correctly, "I" statements can enable positive communication in your relationships and even strengthen them. Initially, using "I" statements might feel awkward and unnatural, but with regular practice, you will become fluent, and it will feel more natural. This strategy is so easy and effective that even children can learn how to use "I" statements successfully. Embracing "I" statements can significantly improve your communication and contribute to healthier and more harmonious relationships.

Begin your assertive communication using the following templates:

I feel _____ because _____.

(Example: I feel overwhelmed because I have too many tasks to complete)

When _____ happens, _____.

(Example: When you raise your voice, I feel intimidated)

What I need is _____.

(Example: What I need is some quiet time to collect my thoughts)

I feel	because	When	happens	What I need is
overwhelmed	I have too many tasks to complete	you raise your voice	I feel intimidated	some quiet time to collect my thoughts
frustrated	my ideas are not being considered	you interrupt	I feel disregarded	more clarity about the situation
anxious	I'm uncertain about the outcome	you criticize	I feel demotivated	reassurance and support
disappointed	my expectations weren't met	you cancel plans	I feel let down	open communication and understanding

287

Moving Forward

In the last five chapters, you've learned useful tips and strategies to gain long-term control over your anxiety. Real empowerment against anxiety requires a well-rounded approach that tackles your symptoms from different angles, helping you take charge of your life. Just concentrating on breathing or changing your diet isn't enough. It's a combination of adopting a healthier lifestyle, eating a healthy and balanced diet, getting good quality sleep, having a self-care routine, and practicing grounding that builds a strong inner calm, able to withstand external pressures.

Make your mental health a daily priority, striving for a balanced lifestyle that enhances both your mental and physical well-being. Should you ever find yourself struggling with anxiety, revisit the pages of this book and use the strategies that quickly restore your sense of *calm within*.

While setbacks may occur, use those moments to tune into your needs. Ask yourself if you need rest? Do you need to eat something nutritious? Listen carefully to the signals your body sends about its immediate needs. Practice this mindfulness daily until you're deeply connected with your own needs.

Achieving long-term control might not occur with just one attempt at these exercises. You may find it necessary to revisit the same emotions multiple times until they are fully processed and cleared out of your system. Feel free to use tapping and journaling as often as needed to release and clear any stuck emotions. There's no limit to how often you can use these techniques, so use them as many times as necessary to promote emotional healing and well-being. Persistence and continued effort are important for lasting transformation.

For this process to be effective, it's important to stay committed and continue applying the strategies that have proven helpful in managing your anxiety. Even if you forget or start feeling better to the point where you think you no longer need these techniques, remember to revisit the book and review the interventions as a reminder.

If your symptoms don't show improvement, consider seeking 1:1 therapy to address your specific challenges more directly. Investing in your mental health and taking the necessary time to heal will not only benefit you but will also create the cycle of healing for future generations.

To feel more at peace and calm in your day, shift your focus towards engaging in enjoyable activities, being more social with a healthy group of friends and family, exercising regularly, prioritizing self-care, maintaining a structured daily routine, setting achievable SMART goals, and creating support groups by involving friends or family to hold you accountable.

You have the power to TRANSFORM your anxiety and achieve long-term control over it, but it will require commitment and continuous practice of the skills you've learned in this book. Remember it's not about having an anxiety free, perfect life. It's about listening to the message your body is sending and learning from your experiences....the good and the bad.

If I could wish for my life to be perfect, it would be tempting, but I would have to decline, for life would no longer teach me anything
~Allyson Jones

Learn from your anxiety and use your imaginary tool belt with all the proven techniques whenever you need them.

Keep practicing these skills regularly so you can tackle anxiety whenever it shows up. Stay determined to keep anxiety in check and keep your mental well-being a top priority. By staying dedicated and determined, you can tackle any tough situation that comes your way and enjoy a more empowered and balanced life.

Wishing you a future filled with calm confidence and success!

Dr. Sekandari

**For more information about the comprehensive on demand virtual courses on creating long term control of Anxiety, OCD, and Fear, please visit transforminganxiety.com/resources*

About Dr. Nafisa Sekandari

Dr. Nafisa Sekandari, a Licensed Clinical Psychologist, specializing in anxiety-based disorders is licensed in California and Arizona and has a private practice in Phoenix, Arizona. She's currently an award-winning author, international keynote speaker, and podcast host.

Drawing upon her intimate understanding of anxiety through personal and familial experiences, coupled with over 15 years of dedicated work and extensive training with hundreds of patients, Dr. Sekandari unveils a transformative solution for anxiety-based disorders.

Introducing the simple yet powerful 3 step AIM program, she empowers individuals to achieve long-term anxiety control without relying on medication or extensive therapy sessions. This holistic and integrative approach to anxiety promises to promote lasting mental and physical well-being for anyone facing the challenges of anxiety.

To learn more visit transforminganxiety.com
Follow Dr. Sekandari on social media: Facebook @dr.sekandari | Instagram @dr_nafisa_sekandari | Youtube @ DrNafisaSekandari

Calm Within

Sources and References

To access the questionnaire, please visit
https://www.transforminganxiety.com/family-history

To enroll in the 21 day meditation challenge, please visit
transforminganxiety.com/meditate

To learn how to tap and use it to manage your anxiety, visit:
https://www.transforminganxiety.com/tap

Learn more about QiGong check out my youtube channel
https://www.youtube.com/@DrNafisaSekandari

1. Prevalence of Anxiety Disorder Among Adolescents, National Institute of Mental Health.
   nimh.nih.gov/health/statistics/any-anxiety-disorder
2. "Change Your Brain, Change Your Life", Daniel Amen, November 3, 2015
3. U.S. Leads in the Worldwide Anxiety Epidemic, Psychology Today. April 26, 2019.
   psychologytoday.com
4. Worldwide Impact of Anxiety Disorders, The Recovery Village. May 26, 2022. therecoveryvillage.com
5. "The Choice" by Eva Eger. September 4, 2018.
6. "The Biology of Belief" by Bruce Lipton. October 11, 2016.
7. Diagnostic and Statistical Manual of Mental Disorders. March 16, 2022.
8. "Why We Sleep: Unlocking the Power of Sleep and Dreams" by Matthew Walker. June 19, 2018.
9. "The Meaning of Anxiety" by Rollo May. May 4, 2015.
10. Elizabeth Gilbert's Facebook page.
    facebook.com/GilbertLiz

11. Centers for Disease Control and Prevention. cdc.gov
12. "The Hidden Messages in Water" by Dr. Emoto. September 20, 2005.
13. Tapping For Weight Loss, Tapping Solution.com.
14. Food for Thought: A Randomised Controlled Trial of Emotional Freedom Techniques and Cognitive Behavioural Therapy in the Treatment of Food Cravings. pubmed.ncbi.nlm.nih.gov
15. Clinical EFT (Emotional Freedom Techniques) Improves Multiple Physiological Markers of Health. ncbi.nlm.nih.gov

CREATE LONGTERM CONTROL OF YOUR ANXIETY WITHOUT MEDICATION!

Learn more by visiting transforminganxiety.com

Printed in the USA
CPSIA information can be obtained
at www.ICGtesting.com
LVHW041954171023
761387LV00004B/13

CALM
WITHIN

In this inspirational book, you will embark on a transformative journey towards conquering anxiety naturally, without relying on medication. The easy-to-follow 3-Step AIM program will equip you with valuable resources and strategies to regain control over your thoughts,emotions, and overall well-being. Dr. Nafisa Sekandari, a renowned expert in anxiety management, has curated this comprehensive guide based on years of research, personal expertise, and a proven track record of successful transformations. Drawing from her profound understanding of anxiety, Dr. Sekandari compassionately introduces you to a holistic approach that goes beyond mere symptom control.

Introducing the simple yet powerful 3 step AIM program, Dr. Sekandari will empower you to achieve long-term anxiety control without relying on medication or extensive therapy sessions. This holistic and integrative approach to anxiety management promises to foster enduring mental and physical well-being for anyone facing the challenges of anxiety.

Dr. Nafisa Sekandari, a Licensed Clinical Psychologist, specializing in anxiety-based disorders is licensed in California and Arizona and has a private practice in Phoenix. She's currently an award-winning author, international keynote speaker, and podcast host.

Drawing upon her intimate understanding of anxiety through personal and familial experiences, coupled with over 15 years of dedicated work and extensive training with hundreds of patients, Dr. Nafisa Sekandari unveils this transformative solution for anxiety-based disorders.
http://transforminganxiety.com/

ISBN 978-0-9909016-2
5 1 8
9 780990 901624